M

THE
BRIDE'S
HANDBOOK

THE
BRIDE'S
HANDBOOK

A Spiritual and Practical Guide for Planning Your Wedding

AMY J. TOL

Revell
Grand Rapids, Michigan

Published by Fleming H. Revell
a division of Baker Publishing Group
P.O. Box 6287, Grand Rapids, MI 49516-6287

Printed in the United States of America

Library of Congress Cataloging-in-Publication Data
Tol, Amy J.
    The bride's handbook : a spiritual and practical guide for planning your wedding / Amy J. Tol.
       p.   cm.
   ISBN 0-8007-5933-8 (pbk.)
    1. Marriage—Religious aspects—Christianity—Meditations. 2. Weddings—Planning. I. Title.
BV835.T64 2005
395.2′2—dc22   2004022809

To Brian,
my best friend and husband.

Thanks for being
the best groom a woman could ever have.

CONTENTS

INTRODUCTION

I dreamed of my wedding day from the time I was a little girl. Even before my Mr. Right came along, I had visions of flowers and lace in my head. So you can imagine my delight when I finally did accept a marriage proposal. Finally I was in a position to put those girlhood fantasies into reality!

As I look back on those engagement days now, I smile at many fond memories. There were so many precious moments—from the first time I saw my wedding dress to the surprise bridal shower my sister threw on my behalf. My family and friends came around me and made my engagement a very special time in my life.

Amid the good times, though, there were also times when wedding plans seemed overwhelming. My moments of dreaminess were often disrupted by a hectic schedule. I was finishing up my senior year of college, looking for a job, and trying to plan for my future home. Needless to say, my days were long, and my energy level sometimes ran short.

Somewhere in the middle of all the activity, I lost some of my excitement for God. I'm ashamed to admit it, but I faced a constant struggle to keep my priorities straight. Sometimes I succeeded. Often I did not. Bible study, prayer, devotional reading—they often got set on the back burner while wedding plans dominated my attention.

It wasn't until after my days as a bride that I found this special Bible verse: "As a bridegroom rejoices over his bride, so will your God rejoice over you" (Isa. 62:5). What a perfect verse for the bride-to-be! It's a beautiful wedding picture that speaks to the heart, helping us to see how much we're cherished by our heavenly Groom.

I wish I'd found that verse while I was engaged. Perhaps it would've helped me to pause and appreciate God's love for me. And maybe it would have motivated me to spend as much time building my spiritual life as I spent planning my wedding. I can only imagine how special it would've been to reflect on living as God's bride during my days as a real-life bride. And that's why I decided to write this book. My hope is that this unique wedding planner will make your own engagement a more meaningful experience.

Your days as a bride are precious. I hope you enjoy every one of them! You're experiencing anticipation and hope. You're busy planning and building a future. You have friends and family members encouraging you along the way. Have you ever considered how much your spiritual life mirrors these bridal experiences? That's probably why the Bible contains so many images of a bride. And that's why your engagement presents a unique opportunity to think about the character of your God, your faith, and your heart.

So dive right in! Soak up the wedding ideas. Ponder the spiritual reflections I've mixed in along the way. And as you do, I pray that Isaiah's image will live in your heart: "As a bridegroom rejoices over his bride, so will your God rejoice over you."

HOW TO USE THIS BOOK

I've packed this planner with ideas and inspirations to make you a beautiful bride. As you read, you'll notice that each chapter contains two main parts—planning tools and spiritual reflections.

Planning Tools

In the middle of each chapter, you'll find practical tools to guide you through the maze of wedding plans. Start by skimming through the table of contents and getting a feel for all the elements you'll need to plan for your wedding. Then, as you begin to plan specific details, read through the corresponding chapters more thoroughly.

Throughout the planning section, you'll find the following helps.

Planning Checklist—At the beginning of each chapter, you'll see a checklist providing an overview of the wedding tasks that are covered in that section. The checklist includes ideal time frames for each wedding task. This list was created with the average engagement (which usually lasts about one year) in mind, so if you're on a shorter timetable, you'll need to adjust those time frames accordingly.

Wedding Notes—You'll also find several worksheet areas, providing space for you to track important information about various wedding vendors and plans. Be sure to fill these in as you plan so that you can have a handy reference for later use.

Sidebars—To help you create fresh ideas for your special day, various sidebar articles are sprinkled throughout each planning section. Check them out for interesting wedding information and effective cost-cutting methods.

Spiritual Reflections

At the beginning and end of each chapter, you'll find spiritual reflections about various virtues of a godly bride. I encourage you to use these reflections as a springboard for personal devotion time. Since there are forty-eight reflections in all, you can read through one a day for a seven-week look at the virtues. Or for a slower pace, read through one or two reflections each week and follow up with related Bible passages during the rest of the week.

You'll also find sidebars mixed in with the spiritual reflections. Each sidebar gives a fictional account of a biblical story, with the Scripture references provided at the end so you can dig deeper into God's Word on your own.

Bible Brides—Women aren't mentioned frequently in the Bible, but when they are, their stories usually have a lot to say. "Bible Brides" sidebars give a brief synopsis of one bride's story—and how her faithful character can still speak to us today.

Love Story from God—God loves to tell stories. The Bible is stuffed full of them. So as you strive to weave the virtues into your own love story, these sidebars will give you encouragement and inspiration from the stories of God.

As you delve into the spiritual reflections of this book, I recommend that you keep a journal of your thoughts and prayers. At a time when many women forget about their spiritual lives, journaling can keep you in touch with your heart throughout the engagement. Take a few minutes each night to write about your wedding plans and engagement experiences. Someday, you'll really enjoy being able to look back at the thoughts and feelings you experienced as a bride.

1

. . . .

THE
ENGAGEMENT

*S*o . . . how did he propose?" It's a question we've all asked at some point—sometimes looking for news of a recent engagement, and sometimes just hoping for a glimpse of family history. I loved hearing my own mother's engagement story—how Dad offered a simple proposal, and then his friends "celebrated" the engagement by locking him in a huge crate, driving him to the middle of town, and calling my mom to release him.

Now that you've received your own proposal, you're probably eager to share the news with family and friends. Or maybe you're still pinching yourself to make sure it's all for real! Whatever your feelings, now's the time to get your engagement plans off to a great start. And while you're enjoying your love story, you also have a special opportunity to reflect on the God of love—and the transforming proposal he offers to us all.

Bride of Love

God demonstrates his own love for us in this: While we were still sinners, Christ died for us.—Romans 5:8

Above all, love each other deeply, because love covers over a multitude of sins.—1 Peter 4:8

For the LORD your God has arrived to live among you. . . . He will rejoice over you with great gladness. With his love, he will calm all your fears.—Zephaniah 3:17 NLT

A Good Love Story

Love stories—we love hearing them, especially those romantic proposal stories. There's something about the way a couple falls in love; it captures our interest and our hearts.

But love doesn't fit a simple formula; that's probably why it makes for so many good stories. Couples usually go through unpredictable twists and turns in the relationship. One moment everything's a dream, and the next, we're pulling our hair out, trying to decide if he's really "the one." No, romance isn't all roses and candlelight. It's a delightfully confusing path, with tangled feelings and hopeful hearts all jumbled up along the way.

In the end, though, that path leads to a beautiful place. When we've finally fallen in love, we feel comfortable—like our hearts have found a home. We can relax and be our quirky selves when we're with the one we love. In fact, sometimes we feel like a *better* self, just because they care. And with a simple proposal, this love we've "fallen into" suddenly becomes our support—a firm foundation for the days ahead. We can breathe a sigh of relief now. This love story is going to turn out all right.

We're not the only ones thinking about romance, though. God enjoys a good love story too. But just like our physical romances, spiritual love stories don't fit a nice formula. They follow that delightfully confusing path of hopes, dreams, frustrations, and fear. Sometimes we feel close to God, like our hearts have finally found a spiritual home. Then doubt makes an appearance. Something happens to shake our faith. Or maybe nothing happens at all and our feelings for God just seem to dwindle away. We feel torn and confused. Is God "the One"? Can we really trust him with our hearts?

As if everyday life circumstances aren't enough to shake our love story, there's another complication too: other lovers compete for our hearts. Yes, we love God. But other things tug at us: career success, the perfect home, popularity with friends. These attractions make things complicated. We'd prefer to keep control of these dreams rather than take our chances with God's love.

So, instead of falling in love with God, we sometimes push him away. Fear grabs on to our shirt collars, pulling us back with strangling thoughts. God might be too reckless. He may give us more than we can handle. Or he may not give us what we want. So we hold tightly to the job that gives money but not fulfillment. We cling to the friendship that pulls us down. And in thousands of similar ways, we push God away, leaving our spiritual love stories on rocky ground.

Despite all these complications, there's hope for this love story. God's a pretty amazing suitor. He hasn't given up quite yet.

Just consider these words whispered lovingly in our ears through God's Word: "I will make you my wife forever, showing you righteousness and justice, unfailing love and compassion. I will be faithful to you and make you mine" (Hos. 2:19–20 NLT). Sounds like a proposal, doesn't it? A proposal from God's heart to ours. And a proposal that could cut through our doubts and take this love story to a whole new level.

This proposal theme isn't just a random thought in Hosea, however. In his culture's engagement practices, Jesus also saw an amazing picture of our spiritual lives. In his day, grooms paid a "bride price" to their bride's father, then poured a glass of wine and presented it to the woman. As he offered it to her, he said, "In offering this cup, I vow that I am willing to give my life for you." If she drank it, the bride agreed to surrender her life for the groom in return.

Sound familiar to you? When Jesus offered a cup of wine to his disciples at the Last Supper, it was no coincidence that he used the gesture of a marriage proposal.* He was pointing to the deep love relationship God wants to have with us. Ever since Eden, God has been yearning to stroll by our sides again, holding our hands gently in his grasp. And all these years later, he's still pursuing our hearts.

In our society today, God is often discussed as though he were an impersonal boss barking random orders from heaven. But that's not the image we see in his Word. God's no stranger—he's a passionate lover, willing to do anything for you.

* This interpretation of Jesus's Last Supper actions comes from Ray Vander Laan's *Echoes of His Presence* (Colorado Springs, CO: Focus on the Family Publishing, 1996), chapter 2.

In his Lord's Supper gesture, he spoke of this love in a remarkable way: "This is my blood of the covenant, which is poured out for many for the forgiveness of sins" (Matt. 26:28). God knew our bride price would cost him his life. And he chose to pursue us anyway.

That's some love story, isn't it? God is a pretty amazing lover. He's just waiting for us to figure out that he's the One.

Consider God's proposal today. He's asking a simple but life-changing question: "Will you trust me in good times and bad? Will you give up your other lovers and put your life in my hands? *Will you be my bride?*"

Maybe you accepted his proposal long ago but it's time to recommit. Or maybe you're experiencing the truth of his personal proposal for the first time. Either way, God is waiting for an answer—with hope and a sparkle in his eye. The ending of this love story is up to you. Will you accept God's proposal or break his heart?

The Most Important Ingredient

It tasted awful.

My brother had decided to make Kool-Aid, a great way to quench summer-afternoon thirst. Out came the pitcher, the stirring spoon, and a brightly colored packet of Kool-Aid. Emptying the drink mix into the pitcher, he added water and patiently stirred the liquid until the mix had dissolved. It seemed simple enough—until we tasted it. Eyes watering from the bitter flavor, we quickly realized that he'd forgotten to add the sugar. And without that main ingredient, the Kool-Aid tasted horrible!

As a younger sister, I mercilessly teased my brother about that mishap. But I've made my share of mistakes in the kitchen too. I still have to double-check my recipes to make sure I'm not missing anything as I cook. And the more complex the recipe, the more paranoid I am that I'll leave something out!

Of course, there's nothing more complex than life. It's the most complicated recipe of all, with thousands of sights, smells, feelings, and sensations mixed together. Looking out at the world, with all its variety and color, a lot of people have asked the question, "What's the main ingredient? What makes life work?"

When it comes right down to it, anyone can instinctively answer that question. The main ingredient to life? It's love.

Without love, the world becomes a pretty dark place. The horror and hatred of September 11 gave a taste of life with all the love drained away. And it was a bitter taste indeed. Without love, all the other stuff just doesn't seem to matter. Money, relationships, fame, adventure—for hundreds of years, people have found that even with all these things, their lives feel empty without love. It's the key ingredient bringing sweetness to life.

As a bride, you have this wonderful ingredient in your life. You have the love of your fiancé—a love felt in the depths of your heart. It's a wonderful, romantic love, one that should be celebrated in the months ahead. But is romantic love enough? Can the love between man and woman hold the world together? Can it even hold a personal life together? What about all the challenges and heartaches that romantic love just can't prevent?

Truth is, there's a love even greater than that of man and woman. A love so great that all other kinds of love stand as a reflection of it: the love of God—or rather, the love that *is* God. He's the key ingredient. Without him, you miss the one thing that holds everything together.

Sure, you can try to become a bride of solid character without God. You can work on patience, trust, and kindness. You can try to maintain those romantic feelings for your guy. You can develop your faith and strive to be the most joyful personality in the room. But without love—without God—you'll never really pull it off. Without him, all those other pieces won't "taste" quite right. Deep down, you'll know that all your own efforts aren't enough.

The writer of 1 Corinthians put it like this: "If I speak in the tongues of men and of angels, but have not love, I am only a resounding gong or a clanging cymbal. If I have . . . faith that can move mountains, but have not love, I am nothing" (13:1–2). He went on to write one of the most famous sections of the Bible, the love chapter. Read through it sometime. You'll notice that love is the key ingredient for everything—patience, kindness, and all the other traits that make for a beautiful bride.

So during this engagement period, you have a choice to make. You can focus solely on the love of your fiancé and leave God on a back burner, or you can make God the key ingredient that permeates all of your life. A lot of brides choose the former. And though they enjoy a gorgeous wedding and have fun spending time with their groom, they miss out on the chance to experience the deepest love of all. They miss the opportunity to watch God's love filter into their character. And they miss seeing love deepen and enrich their relationship with their fiancé.

Don't make their mistakes. Instead, choose

BIBLE BRIDE

She wasn't the ideal Jewish bride. No pristine past. No innocent and submissive heart. No, Gomer was a woman of the night—a prostitute who understood all too well the ways of the world.

And then came Hosea, the strange prophet who'd taken her as his bride. Gomer had been confused by his offer. Why in the world would a man of God want her to be his wife? Why would he choose her to be the mother of his children? But Gomer had married him. After all, she had nothing to lose.

For a while, things had looked good. Gomer and Hosea had children, and it looked like she'd managed to turn her sordid life around. It didn't last long, though. Gomer walked out on her husband and children. Once again, she became a woman of the night. And she didn't expect any man of God to show up on her doorstep this time.

But he did! Hosea—the man she'd humiliated and spurned—came to buy her back out of her sinful life. And when she turned questioning eyes to him, he quietly explained, "It's what God wants for us. And just as he is faithful to his people, I will be faithful to you, no matter how many times you turn your back on me."

Years later, when people reminisced about Gomer's life, they saw in it a picture of God's love for his sinful people. As the story was told again and again, Hosea's words to Gomer became an echo of God's words to every believer: "I will betroth you to me forever . . . in love and compassion" (Hos. 2:19).

Check out the incredible story of Gomer in the book of Hosea.

love. Let God pour into every area of your life, from wedding plans to relationships and personal goals. Ask him right now to become the most important ingredient in your life. And then get ready for an amazing engagement—because with God in the center, life never tasted so sweet.

Your Engagement Plans

PLANNING CHECKLIST

BEFORE OR SOON AFTER ENGAGEMENT

- [ ] Select an engagement ring.
- [ ] Announce your engagement to family and friends (preferably immediately after you become engaged).
- [ ] If desired, send engagement announcements to acquaintances after the wedding date is set.

SIX TO TWELVE MONTHS BEFORE

- [ ] Arrange for engagement photos to be taken.

THREE TO TWELVE MONTHS BEFORE

- [ ] Place an engagement announcement in the local newspaper.

THREE TO SIX MONTHS BEFORE

- [ ] Order your wedding rings.

The Proposal

For many brides, the proposal happens so un-expectedly that they hardly believe it is real. Yet it's a defining moment—one you'll want to share with future generations. Take a few minutes to record the following information and get your proposal story in writing. Years from now, you'll treasure every word.

My Proposal

Where and when did he propose? _____

_____

_____

_____

_____

What were you doing at the time? _____

_____

_____

_____

What were you wearing? _____

_____

_____

Was anyone else there? How did they react?

_____

_____

_____

Did he have a ring? If so, where was it hidden? _____

_____

What did he say? _____

_____

_____

_____

What was your first response? _____

_____

What did you talk about after you said yes?

_____

_____

Did anyone know about the proposal ahead of time? Who? _____

_____

Who was the first person you told about your engagement? _____

How did they respond? _____

_____

_____

When did you tell your family? _____

_____

_____

What did they say? _____

_____

_____

When did you tell his family? _____

_____

_____

What did they say? _____

_____

_____

_____

_____

Other special proposal memories: _____

_____

_____

Announcing Your Engagement

Most couples eagerly share their engagement news. Your parents should be the first to hear about it, and if possible, it's best to tell them in person. You'll also want to tell close friends and extended family about your engagement soon after it occurs. You don't want to cause hurt feelings by letting them hear the news secondhand. Fill in the following "Who to Tell" list to ensure no one is left out, and note when you call or visit each person on the list.

WHO TO TELL

Bride's parents _____

Groom's parents _____

Bride's siblings _____

_____

_____

Groom's siblings _____

_____

Bride's grandparents _____

_____

Groom's grandparents _____

_____

Bride's aunts and uncles _____

_____

Groom's aunts and uncles _____

_____

Other relatives _____

_____

_____

Close friends _____

_____

_____

Formal Announcements

You may want to send formal engagement announcements to additional relatives and friends. Traditionally, engagement announcements are sent by the bride's parents and include the names of the bride and groom, as well as the date of their upcoming wedding. Today, many couples choose to forgo formal announcements and simply announce their engagement in local newspapers. Couples who want inexpensive announcements can use a computer to create their own rather than ordering from a printer.

ENGAGEMENT ANNOUNCEMENTS

Name of Printer: _____

_____

Contact information: _____

_____

_____

Number of copies: _____

Cost: _____

Delivery date: _____

Newspaper Announcement

After spreading the news to family, friends, and other acquaintances, most couples announce their wedding publicly in a local newspaper. Generally, engagement announcements appear three or four months before the wedding date, but an announcement can appear earlier or later if desired. Consider an announcement in more than one newspaper, especially if you and your fiancé's family live in different towns.

After you select the newspapers, contact them to discuss their procedure for submitting engagement announcements. Most papers will provide you with a form requesting the following information about the bride and groom: names, parents' names, schools attended, current jobs, and the wedding date and location. Smaller papers may request additional information or require that you write an announcement yourself.

NEWSPAPER ANNOUNCEMENT

Name, newspaper(s): _____

_____

_____

Date when announcement will appear: ____

_____

Fee: _____

Required information: _____

_____

_____

Engagement Photographs

A photograph of the bride and groom usu-ally appears with the newspaper announcement. Some couples submit a snapshot taken with their own camera, but others have formal engagement pictures taken by a photographer. Photographers often include engagement pictures as part of their wedding package, so ask about this when you are considering your photography options. Plan to have your pictures taken several weeks before you want the announcement to appear so that they'll be ready on time. Also, consider ordering extra copies for your family and friends.

DID YOU KNOW?

The average engagement lasts 13 months.

The average size of a diamond engagement ring is .75 carats.

Pope Nicholas I decreed in AD 860 that grooms should give a ring of gold to their bride as a symbol of financial sacrifice.

The tradition of wearing an engagement ring on the fourth finger of the left hand was based on the Greeks' belief that the vein from that finger ran directly to the heart.

Christian tradition places added significance on the ring finger because it is the weakest finger (fourth) on the weakest hand (left), reminding bride and groom that they must rely on God for the strength to have a godly marriage.

ENGAGEMENT PICTURES

Name and phone of photographer: _____

_____

Date and time pictures will be taken: _____

_____

Date when proofs will be ready: _____

Number of copies needed: _____

Cost: _____

Whether you choose to send formal an-nouncements, submit a newspaper announce-ment, or simply call your family and friends, enjoy spreading the news of your engagement. You have started an exciting new chapter of your life, and your loved ones will want to know all about it.

The Engagement Ring

Traditionally, jewelers suggest that the groom spend two months' salary on the ring. But many couples will choose to spend more or less, de-pending on their financial situation. Those with limited incomes can save money by purchasing a simple ring and adding or resetting the stones at a later date. Whatever the cost, the engagement ring is an important investment—a piece of jew-elry that will be with you for a lifetime.

Today, many women select their own ring or provide their fiancé with suggestions on the styles and gems they prefer. With basic knowledge about stones and settings, the bride and groom can shop wisely and find a ring that fits both their taste and their budget.

The Four Cs of Diamond Stones

Diamonds come with a high price tag, so it's helpful to remember the four Cs as you shop for this expensive investment. Learning about each of the elements will ensure that you get the best quality for the price you pay.

- Cut—The cut of a diamond creates a pattern of surfaces that reflect light off of each other. Generally considered the most important of the four Cs, the cut creates the sparkle and play of colors in the stone. Diamond cuts are categorized into four classes: Ideal Cut, Well Cut, Average Cut, and Below Average Cut.
- Color—Although diamonds appear colorless, they may have a hint of color. Diamonds are rated for color on a scale from D to Z, with Ds (the most expensive) being colorless and Zs having a yellow tint that is visible to the naked eye. The best buys are generally in the I to J range, with a rating of "near colorless."
- Clarity—Clarity refers to the number of flaws found in a stone. And diamonds are ranked based on the size and position of their flaws: FL/IF (flawless/internally flawless), VVS (very very slightly included), VS (very slightly included), SI (slightly included), and I (included/imperfect). Flawless stones are rare and therefore quite expensive. Stones in the SI to VVS range are more

affordable, and their flaws are not noticeable to the naked eye.

- Carat—The carat indicates the weight of the diamond. There are five carats to a gram.

Stone Shapes and Settings

Stones come in a variety of shapes, including round, marquis, oval, pear, and square. While round cuts are the most popular today, you may prefer another style. Ask your jeweler to show you several stone shapes. Then try them on your finger before you make a final decision, because what looks good in the jeweler's case may not look quite right on your finger.

The most common settings used in engagement rings are tiffany (a single diamond set high above the band) and illusion (smaller stones surrounding a large stone). But you may prefer a different style. Ask your jeweler for examples of other settings and choose one that suits your tastes. Consider your habits as well; brides who work heavily with their hands may not want a high stone setting that can get caught against other objects.

Other Options

Rather than purchasing a brand-new ring, some brides wear a family heirloom or antique. If the original ring setting doesn't suit her style, the old diamond can be placed in a new setting. Another beautiful alternative, colorful stones may be used instead of diamonds. Gemstones are less expensive than diamonds, and they can be used to symbolize the bride's birth date or other special qualities.

CARING FOR YOUR RING

As you gaze at your shiny new ring, you may have a hard time imagining that it can get dirty, chipped, or scratched. But if you want your ring to stay brilliant until your fiftieth wedding anniversary, you'll have to take good care of it. Use the following tips to keep your ring clean and safe from damage.

Clean your ring routinely in a mixture of water and ammonia or a jewelry cleaning solution from the store. Use a toothbrush to gently scrub the stone and the setting, then rinse with warm water.

Don't wear your ring while performing heavy work. Be especially careful when working with your hands. If your ring frequently knocks against other objects, the stone may get chipped or lost, and the setting may be loosened. Some brides who regularly perform heavy work purchase a simple wedding band to wear in place of their diamond ring during work hours.

When not wearing your ring, store it in a box lined with soft material.

Visit your jeweler once a year for a professional cleaning and setting check to make sure the stone is secure.

As you shop for rings, make sure you take the time to find a reputable jeweler. Ask family and friends for recommendations, and have your ring appraised before purchasing it. Appraisers will provide you with a detailed description of the stone quality, ensuring that your ring is worth the price being charged.

ENGAGEMENT RING

Name and number of jeweler: _____

_____

Ring description (stone, shape, setting): ____

_____

Inscription: _____

Finger size: _____

With This Ring . . . .

Whether you purchase wedding bands with the engagement ring or order them later in the engagement, you'll want to consider what wedding band will complement your engagement ring and what ring will suit your groom's unique style. Although wedding bands may be purchased in matching pairs for the bride and groom, it's not necessary to match the rings. Many couples prefer to order different styles that match each of their personal tastes. As you shop, use the same discretion you showed when finding a reputable jeweler for the engagement ring. You don't want any surprises or mistakes when it comes to the rings you'll be exchanging on your special day!

Garnet	January	symbolizes constancy
Amethyst	February	symbolizes sincerity
Aquamarine	March	symbolizes courage
Diamond	April	symbolizes purity
Emerald	May	symbolizes success
Pearl	June	symbolizes health
Ruby	July	symbolizes love
Peridot	August	symbolizes happiness
Sapphire	September	symbolizes wisdom

Opal	October	symbolizes hope
Topaz	November	symbolizes fidelity
Turquoise	December	symbolizes harmony

Wedding Rings

HIS

Jeweler: _____

Phone number: _____

Band style: _____

Finger size: _____

Inscription: _____

Cost: _____

HERS

Jeweler: _____

Phone number: _____

Band style: _____

Finger size: _____

Inscription: _____

Cost: _____

INSCRIPTION INSPIRATION

Need some ideas for the perfect wedding ring inscription? Read the suggestions below for some ideas and inspiration. The list is not exhaustive, so do some thinking and create a special inscription all your own!

Beloved

God for Me Provided Thee

Love Never Fails

Always Faithful

Forever

Heart to Heart, Never to Part

Never to Part

To Have and To Hold

My Beloved

Faith, Hope, and Love

I Am My Beloved's and My Beloved Is Mine

You can also inscribe a Bible verse reference on your wedding band (for example, "Song of Songs 6:3"). This is especially meaningful if you have a verse that has been significant to you as a couple.

Bride of Transformation

Therefore, if anyone is in Christ, he is a new creation; the old has gone, the new has come!—2 Corinthians 5:17

All of us have had that veil removed so that we can be mirrors that brightly reflect the glory of the Lord. And as the Spirit of the Lord works within us, we become more and more like him and reflect his glory even more.—2 Corinthians 3:18 NLT

Things Are Gonna Change

Ever watched the TV show *Trading Spaces*? In each episode, two sets of neighbors swap homes and redecorate a room in each other's house. Throw in a time limit, a strict budget, and interior designers with zany ideas, and you have one entertaining show. At the end of each episode, homeowners nervously wait to see their renovated rooms. Whether they respond with delighted cheers or cries of horror, one thing's for sure: their old room is history.

Trading Spaces may feature some radical transformations, but real life brings even bigger ones at times. Changing from "single" to "married" is one of the biggest. And if you haven't felt it already, it's sure to come—the feeling that things will never be the same. A twinge of sadness may come when Mom tears up about you leaving home. Or anticipation might surge when you think about settling in with your future husband.

It's natural to feel this sadness and joy, anticipation and hesitancy, all rolled into one. As you make the transition to married life, there'll be dozens of practical changes: living in a new place, changing your driver's license, creating joint financial accounts. In fact, the whole engagement process begins with a pretty major change: people notice the ring on your finger, and you're already someone different—a "fiancée" instead of "the girlfriend." You've changed, and as you start planning for a lifetime together, the changes just keep coming. Fortunately, most brides welcome these changes with a smile. After all, the changes are ushering you into wedded bliss.

It's too bad we don't always carry this positive attitude into our spiritual lives. When it comes to being God's bride, we often resist change. Sure, we talk about loving God—we go to church and read the occasional devotional. But when push comes to shove, our faith doesn't really make any difference in our lives. We often choose to stay in our comfort zone, ignoring the changes God calls us to.

Today, we're bombarded by messages of materialism and individualism. And yet for all our talk of "being an individual," most of us still feel pressured to conform. It's easier to just keep our faith private instead of challenging the values around us. And sometimes it's just plain tempting to give in to those worldly values instead of practicing what we claim to believe. So when outsiders look at us, they see people living just like everyone else—not brides carrying the glow of engagement to our Groom.

I don't know about you, but there are areas

LOVE STORY FROM GOD

Rahab waited anxiously, peering through her window as the Israelites marched around her city, Jericho. This was the seventh day of their strange activities, and they seemed to be marching and shouting longer than they had on the other days. Maybe this is the day, Rahab thought. Maybe today Jericho will fall and I'll finally leave my old life behind.

Rahab's "old life" had been one of emptiness, loneliness, and pain. She learned early how to handle men. And she'd sold her body to them so many times she'd lost track of her encounters. Her heart had grown cold toward Jericho—with its men so willing to use her and its women so quick to judge.

That's why the spies had so intrigued her. "We're Israelites," they'd told her. And immediately she'd remembered all the stories she'd heard about Israel and her God—the kind of God who worked miracles and cared about his people more deeply than any of Jericho's gods ever had. The kind of God she'd been searching for her whole life.

Rahab had hidden the spies, saving their lives when the city officials came looking for them. And then she'd asked them to save her, to spare her life when they finally came to destroy Jericho.

Now, as Rahab watched the Israelites and reflected on the events of the past few days, she realized that she wasn't the only one who'd been searching for something: Israel's God had been searching for her too. And that realization gave her a feeling she hadn't experienced in a long, long time—hope for a better tomorrow with this new and wonderful God.

Check out Rahab's whole story in Joshua 2 and Joshua 6:22–25.

of my life that I don't *want* to change. I remember God calling me to a particular volunteer position. I was scared because the job would put me way out of my comfort zone. So I resisted. For months, I ignored God's calling. I didn't trust that he could make it work.

Maybe you've had similar experiences—challenges you've ignored because you're afraid to try something new, or bad habits you haven't dropped because you're afraid to let go. We all struggle with the changes God calls us to make. Often, we prefer to be comfortable and take the quiet road through life.

But that's not the sort of life God calls us to. "Don't copy the behavior and customs of this world, but let God *transform* you into a new person" (Rom. 12:2 NLT, emphasis added). Our faith and our love for God should make a difference in our lives. In fact, they should make such a transformation that we seem like a "new" person—someone who stands out from the world.

And here's a little secret our world doesn't understand: making changes for God may make us uncomfortable, but it's always worth the effort. I eventually took that volunteer job God had been challenging me with—scared to death but knowing this was God's call. And guess what? It turned out to be one of the biggest blessings in my life.

That's the way spiritual change unfolds. We may feel hesitant, excited, hopeful, and scared, all at the same time. But when we jump in and allow God to make changes, we always come out stronger—and more blessed—on the other side.

Take stock of your life today. People can see the ring on your finger and ask about your fiancé, but can they see that you're God's bride too? Has your faith made any difference in your life? And is God calling you to make any changes in your personal

life? Such questions may bring tough answers, because in unique ways, God is always calling us to change. Yet there's comfort in those questions too. Because even though things are gonna change, with God, it's always for the better.

Works in Progress

When workers started building the Brooklyn Bridge, it was January of 1870. By the time the bridge was opened, more than twelve years had passed. Beethoven played around with various ideas for nearly a decade before he finally completed his famous Fifth Symphony. And the beautiful paintings above the Sistine Chapel? They took Michelangelo more than four years to paint. Sometimes, beautiful things just take time.

Weddings are like that. When it comes to planning a wedding, nearly everything is a work in progress. One detail follows another, right up until the last day.

So just imagine what would happen if you were forced to hold your wedding six months before the scheduled date. That's what happened to Elisa. When her fiancé received an unexpected job transfer, they decided to move the wedding up. With just two weeks to finish planning, Elisa felt panicked. The bridesmaids' dresses hadn't arrived at the bridal shop, the wedding musicians didn't have any music, and myriad other details were still up in the air. Elisa finally asked her fiancé if they could just elope. "There's no way for me to get everything done, and I don't want our guests to come for a half-finished wedding."

Like Elisa, you'd probably hate to hold your wedding while it was still "in progress" too. It takes time to finish a good thing. And when it comes to our spiritual lives, the same rule applies. We're all works in progress—brides busily planning for the day when we'll see our heavenly Groom. And that progress takes time.

In this book, we'll explore many ideas about developing God's character in our lives. Yet as much as we need to take those ideas to heart, we also need to remember that we're works in progress. The traits we'll be studying—things like loyalty, kindness, and patience—don't come naturally. In fact, our natural instincts often push us toward darker tendencies.

And that's why "transformation" plays such a key role in the lives of God's brides. For those of us who've given our lives to God, we start experiencing new instincts—the instincts of God's Spirit—prompting us toward good things. The Bible describes this experience as a casting off of the old self and a putting on of the new. We're being transformed from sinners to saints. From women who struggle with worry, fear, and sin to women with God's character in our hearts.

How I wish that this transformation happened overnight! But that's not how it works. Every day, our old ugly self still flares up. Yet God promises us that the new woman is there too, slowly emerging by his grace. "God, who began the good work within you, will continue his work until it is finally finished" (Phil. 1:6 NLT). God is not going to give up on us until his "good work" is done.

As you read on about all the other traits of God's brides, remember that transformation plays a part. God expects to see progress in our lives, not perfection. Frankly, as long as we live on this earth, we're going to struggle with sin. And with all the stress in her life, a bride usually has an especially hard time letting the new woman of grace and kindness shine through.

But don't lose hope! You may feel like it's impossible at times, that you might as well give up on being transformed until after the wedding stress dies down. That's just one of Satan's many lies, though. God doesn't lose hope for us, ever. He hates our sin, yes. But he doesn't hate us. And he hates how sin messes up our lives. But he doesn't give up on us.

Hopefully, you're excited about the wedding day—and the transformation from "Miss" to "Mrs." But just as that transformation will take a lot of time and planning, your spiritual transformation will take time and work as well. Thankfully, you're not working alone. If you'll give him the chance, God will do some amazing work of his own.

So don't give up when things look down. Just remember, you're a work in progress, a bride transforming from sinner to saint. In the end, that's one transformation worth working for!

2

. . . .

THE GROOM

As your engagement begins, you're probably feeling a surge of excitement about the upcoming wedding. It's sure to be a memorable day, and you'll want to jump right in to those wedding plans! But before you get bogged down with all those nuptial details, why not give some attention to something even more important—the man you love?

With new stresses and changes, engagement tests even the strongest of relationships. But these challenges aren't all bad—in fact, they're a great training ground for marriage. Through the ups and downs of engagement, you and your groom can build trust in each other and in God—something that will be a good foundation for your marriage. And when you add true-blue loyalty to your relationship, you'll find it easier to focus on the man—and the God—you love, no matter how hectic wedding plans become.

Bride of Loyalty

Let love and faithfulness never leave you;
bind them around your neck,
write them on the tablet of your heart.—Proverbs 3:3

A friend is always loyal.—Proverbs 17:17 NLT

Loyalty makes a person attractive. And it is better to be poor
than dishonest.—Proverbs 19:22 NLT

Mr. Right

I used to spend a great deal of time dreaming about "Mr. Right." I thought about the qualities I wanted in a man and how wonderful it would be when I finally found him. I dreamed about the ways he would romance me, and I longed for the day when he'd ask me to marry him.

But like many young women, I wondered if Mr. Right would ever show up. I saw beautiful sunsets and worried that I'd never have someone to share them with. I took walks with no guy to hold my hand. And I spent many a night with tears on my pillow, feeling very alone. I promised myself if I ever did find the love of my life, I'd never forget what a blessing he is.

Today I enjoy the love of a wonderful man. He's a constant friend amid all of life's changes. But guess what? I've forgotten my promise. I've gotten so used to his love and loyalty that I take it for granted. I forget that he doesn't have to be there—he could've chosen someone else. And I could still be alone.

How about you? Did you endure lonely moments before you met your groom? Do you ever find yourself taking him for granted, now that he's yours? Even during our most hectic days, we should strive to treat our grooms like the special guys they are. We should give them more compliments than criticisms. And instead of making subtle jokes about them when we're with others, we should be their biggest cheerleaders. By affirming them in these ways—instead of taking them for granted—we not only acknowledge their loyalty, we also show our loyalty to them.

Of course, loyalty doesn't come naturally for most of us. We're usually tempted to do what's best for ourselves, even when it may not be best for our guys. So if we really want to get a handle on this loyalty thing, we'll need some help. And I know of a great place to find it.

It's been a while since I spent those lonely nights crying in my pillow, but I still remember the valuable truth I learned during those heartaches: while I was waiting for a husband, I already had the perfect person in love with me. Through all my ups and downs, God was already the "someone" who was staying by my side. He was my Mr. Right, faithfully waiting to capture my attention.

God reveals his loyalty to all of us in one way or another. For me, it was the pain of failed romance that made me recognize his faithfulness. Maybe it was something different for you—a car crash, a broken family, a lost job. Through it all, your God was there to lean on, to listen, and to comfort. And sometimes, he was the only one who stuck around to help you bear the pain.

God is the groom who loves so deeply that

LOVE STORY FROM GOD

Jesus was talking about his death again.

And Peter hated the thought of it. He didn't want to lose Jesus, the man who'd taught him so much. *Don't let him die*, he silently prayed. *Please, dear God, don't let him die.* Jesus's words broke into Peter's thoughts: "In my Father's house are many rooms . . . I am going there to prepare a place for you . . . I will come back and take you to be with me."

He's leaving us. It was a thought Peter didn't want to believe. Yet Jesus's words also stirred a beautiful memory. Preparing a room in his Father's house—it was a word picture that reminded him of the wedding traditions of Galilee, where he'd grown up.

In Galilee, grooms often went home to prepare a room in their father's house after their engagement had been sealed. When the room was complete, they'd return to the bride's village, announcing the wedding with a blow of the horn. The bride didn't know when the groom would return, so her focus went to wedding preparations. She'd busily organize her bridesmaids and belongings, wanting to be ready on the big day.

Jesus is our groom, Peter realized. And as he thought of the many brides he'd watched, faithfully waiting for their grooms, he felt a new prayer surging in his heart. God, keep me loyal when he's gone. Don't let my attention wander. And when he comes back and it's time for that heavenly wedding to begin, he prayed, I want to be ready.

We don't know if Peter really connected Jesus's words to the wedding customs of his day, but given his cultural context, it's probable that he did.* Check out John 14:2–4 to read Jesus's words for yourself. Then read Revelation 19:7 to see that same image describing his return.

* See Ray Vander Laan's *Echoes of His Presence* (Colorado Springs, CO: Focus on the Family Publishing, 1996), chapter 2, for a closer look at this connection.

he actually gave his life to save his bride. He's so incredibly loyal that he would take on the fire of hell just so that he could be with her. Words alone can't really describe the loyalty of this heavenly groom. The image of nail marks and a cross only begins to tell the story of his love.

With such an awesome God, you'd think his brides could never contain their excitement about him. You'd think they would spend every day marveling at his loyalty and his love. But do we?

I'm ashamed to confess it, but just as I sometimes take my earthly groom for granted, I sometimes take my heavenly Groom for granted too. I've been given his unswerving loyalty, but I often forget about him. And when I do, all my other loyalties falter too. I stray from the people and causes I believe in.

Sound familiar to you? I think we all struggle with loyalty to God. But we're not stuck in the mud. God's always there to help us change. He's truly our Mr. Right. And with our eyes on him, we can weave loyalty into the fabric of our hearts.

So try this simple assignment today: take a few moments to think about God's loyalty. Think of Bible stories, family history, and your own personal life. You'll probably feel overwhelmed when you focus your heart on God's faithfulness in all of these areas. But you'll also find a wonderful thing happening to you, because as you look at your spiritual Mr. Right, you'll find the inspiration to make loyalty a part of your character too.

Weed and Seed

Janet started out by writing letters to Edward every day. He'd left to fight in WWII, just a few months before their wedding. And in the first months, she missed him terribly and prayed for his safe return.

But as time passed by, she found it difficult to stay faithful. Guys she worked with showed interest in her. She ignored them at first, but soon she started returning their flirtations, telling herself it was all in good fun. Then she started sharing lunch with Ron. She intended to keep it as a friendly relationship but found herself falling in love.

Janet continued to write to Edward, keeping the relationship intact just in case things didn't work out with Ron. Of course, Edward was heartbroken when he returned home to find Janet and Ron together. And Ron was surprised to discover that Janet had never broken things off with her old guy. In the end, they both decided she wasn't worth the time.

I don't think any bride wants to turn into a Janet. On her wedding day, a bride wants friends and family to think of her as someone who has always been faithful. But Janet's mistakes are easy to make. She started with good intentions but let things slip. Step by little step she walked away from her man.

Most of us aren't tempted to run after another guy, as Janet was. But there are countless other ways we allow little weeds of disloyalty to creep into our relationships. Maybe we hide a decision from our groom when we know he'd disapprove. Or instead of being constant with our support, we use our groom's weaknesses against him when we're mad. Disloyalty crops up in other areas too. We gossip about a close friend or stand silent when someone ridicules our beliefs. We keep the money to ourselves rather than giving it to the organization that has asked for our support. In such little ways, we betray the people we love and the causes we believe in.

Even our relationship with God gets affected by these weeds. Though we try to justify "little" sins, they're really little betrayals of God. And sometimes Satan pushes brides away from God simply by filling their lives with too many other things to do. Instead of dreaming about God, we dream up our own plans. And we find ourselves being attracted to other gods—things like comfort and cash, popularity and pleasure. We may even play the same game as Janet, trying to be loyal to these gods while we also claim loyalty to God.

But we can't play that game for long. As Jesus said in Matthew 6:24, "No one can serve two masters." When we grow loyal to idols in our culture, we end up cheating on our spiritual groom. And we allow the ugly weeds of disloyalty to take root in our hearts.

As a young girl, I knew all about ugly weeds. My parents used to pay me a quarter to pull up a bucket of dandelions out of our yard. I real-ize now that I could've asked for better wages. But I guess I got a more valuable benefit from the job, because I learned an important lesson: you have to pull weeds out as soon as you can. Otherwise, you just end up with bigger and uglier weeds.

I hope you're savoring each moment as a bride. But in the midst of your dreams and plans, don't forget to do some weeding. It's not always a pleas-ant task, but without it, you run the risk of be-coming a Janet—a bride who betrays her love. So take some time to examine your loyalties. Are there any weeds growing there—any thoughts or behaviors that need to be plucked out before they spread?

In the end, weeding out disloyalty will leave you with fertile ground in which virtue can grow. And each time you cut out a disloyal thought or word, you'll actually plant the seeds for something spectacular: a loyal bride.

Your Groom

Great Expectations

Bride and groom each carry a unique set of expectations into marriage. They come from different families, so they have different ideas about the role of husbands and wives and the way things should be done in a house. An acquaintance of mine once said the most frequently used expression in his first month of marriage was, "My mom didn't do it like that!"

Many couples make a mistake by assuming they have the same expectations about married life. After the wedding, when they're settling into their new life, they realize they have different ideas after all. Some young married couples become deeply disappointed in marriage because it's not everything they expected it to be.

You can avoid this disillusionment if you discuss your expectations together *before* the wedding day. Having different ideas doesn't doom a marriage relationship. In fact, when you take the time to discuss important issues before the wedding, you're laying a strong foundation for a healthy marriage. As you discover your differences and make compromises, you'll develop a new set of expectations that fit you both.

The Hot Topics

Many issues surface during a lifetime of marriage, so it's impossible to discuss every single one before you begin your life together. But couples will find it helpful to discuss the following topics as they shape their marriage expectations.

Religion

What are your religious beliefs? How important is religion to you? How important is it that your spouse shares your religious beliefs? Are you part of a particular church or denomination? Do you want to stay at that church/denomination or seek a new one? What religion would you like to teach your children?

Money

What is your view on finances? Are you a spender or a saver? Do you place a priority on long-term investment or on enjoying the pres-

PLANNING CHECKLIST

THREE TO SIX MONTHS BEFORE WEDDING

- [ ] Arrange for premarital counseling sessions or seminar.

THROUGHOUT ENGAGEMENT

- [ ] Set aside regular "date nights" with fiancé that will not be spent on wedding plans.

ent? How do you feel about debt? What types of items are you willing to splurge on (vacations, household items, recreational activities, nothing, etc.)? What are your financial goals?

Sex

Do you have any apprehensions about sex? Does either of you have a sexual history? (If so, talk about it and pursue further counseling if needed.) How frequent do you expect sex to be in your marriage? Will you use contraceptives, and if so, what kind are you comfortable with? When do you want to start a family? How many children would you like to have?

Family History

What kind of marriage relationship did your parents demonstrate? What aspects of their marriage do you want to strive for in your own? Were there any bad behavior patterns in your home that you want to avoid? Does your family history make you feel well equipped to start a marriage of your

own? Or has it made you feel uncertain about how to achieve a healthy marriage?

Communication

What is your style of communication? Are you straightforward or shy? Are you comfortable expressing your feelings? How does someone know if you're upset? How will you resolve disagreements with your spouse? Do you have a hard time admitting when you're wrong or do you take more blame than you should? Are you prone to angry outbursts or do you bury resentment and let it fester? Are you a good listener?

Needs

What are your major needs from the relationship? Will your fiancé realistically be able to fulfill all of these needs all the time? If you could choose only three of those needs to have met, what would they be? What things make you feel loved and cared for? What makes your fiancé feel loved and cared for?

Lifestyle

What kind of lifestyle do you envision? Do you like to go to lots of events and social gatherings or do you prefer to spend quiet time at home? What activities would you like to participate in? What standard of living do you want to attain? How much time do you like to spend alone? How much time do you like to spend together?

Roles

What is a husband's role? What is a wife's role? Will one of you be the primary breadwinner or will you both work? Should there be equal division of housework? Who will handle fix-it and home-maintenance jobs? Who will be responsible for children if they arrive?

Expectations

On a separate piece of paper, write down your expectations for marriage in each of the areas listed above. Ask your fiancé to do the same and then compare your answers. Where are your expectations the same? Where are they different? After discussing and compromising where needed, create a new list of expectations and goals you can reach together.

Groom Gripes

While brides have traditionally planned the wedding, many of today's grooms would like to have a say in the wedding plans. They feel sidelined when their bride plans every detail without ever asking for their opinion. On the other hand, some grooms prefer to leave planning to their bride. It's torture for them to sit through endless outings about invitations, bridesmaids' dresses, and reception halls.

So how can you plan your dream wedding without getting on your guy's nerves?

Don't assume that you know how your fiancé feels about the issue. Instead, have an honest conversation about his involvement as soon as your wedding plans begin. Give him a chance to explain what wedding details he'd like to be involved with and explain your own expectations as well. If your guy's the type who expresses little interest in wedding details, you'll probably have a happier engagement if you back off and take care of matters yourself. But if he does want to be involved with wedding plans, make an effort to include him as you plan for the big day.

No matter what, remember that the wedding and the marriage are two different things. Even if your guy doesn't seem as excited about the wedding as you are, you can bet he's still excited about your future together.

The Man You Love

There are many practical ways to strengthen your relationship and prepare for marriage. One of the best is to simply spend time with each other. Try to set aside special times that will not be spent on wedding plans. Instead, focus on learning more about your fiancé. Ask him about his hopes, dreams, interests, and fears. Try to figure out his greatest needs and how you can fulfill them. You may be surprised at what you will learn.

A Good Book

Reading a book with your fiancé provides another great way to learn more about marriage. There are lots of good resources about marriage that give healthy advice about how to handle conflict, how to stay in love despite hard times, and how to compromise when you have different expectations. If you have special concerns about certain aspects of married life—finances, sex, communication, etc.—find a book devoted to that particular topic and explore it together.

Reading Assignment

Books my fiancé and I want to read together:

_____

_____

A Wise Counselor

Couples who want to build a healthy marriage should start with premarital counseling. Counselors guide discussions about the various hot topics of marriage. They will help you create healthy communication patterns and identify problematic behaviors that should be checked. Most counseling takes place during a series of short sessions, but there are also engagement seminars and retreats that provide a more intense experience during a short time.

Many pastors require counseling before they will marry a couple, and they often provide the counseling themselves. Other churches may provide an older married couple to mentor and counsel you during your engagement. Even if your church doesn't require counseling, you should consider it. Ask your pastor, family, and friends to recommend a counselor or investigate seminars that you can attend together. Your future marriage is worth the time.

PREMARITAL COUNSELING

Name of counselor: _____

_____

Phone number: _____

Dates and times of counseling sessions: _____

_____

_____

_____

Location of counseling sessions: _____

_____

Cost: _____

DID YOU KNOW?

Hundreds of years ago, Germanic grooms would sometimes steal a bride from a neighboring village if there were no pleasing women in their own village.

The tradition of a bride standing to the groom's left began when grooms feared that the bride's family would try to take her back. This position left the groom's right hand free to grab his sword and defend his bride.

Why is it "bad luck" for the groom to see his bride on the wedding day? Long ago, marriages were often arranged without the groom ever seeing his future bride. On occasion, if a groom saw his bride before the wedding day—and didn't like what he saw—he would back out of the wedding!

Time for Each Other—and God

If you haven't already started reading the Bible and praying together, your engagement is a great time to start. By making God a part of your relationship today, you'll create a good foundation for your upcoming marriage. Here are a few ideas to get you going.

Read each other's favorite Bible verses/chapters and talk about what they mean to you.

Read a book of the Bible that you're both curious about, discussing it as you go.

Use a devotional book. Many bookstores offer devotional books written especially for couples.

Every time you say good-bye, say a prayer to thank God for your time together.

Set aside a half hour each week to talk about each other's prayer requests and pray for each other.

Bride of Trust

Those who know your name will trust in you,
for you, Lord, have never forsaken those who seek you.
—Psalm 9:10

Trust in the Lord with all your heart
and lean not on your own understanding.—Proverbs 3:5

Can all your worries add a single moment to your life? Of course
not! And if worry can't do little things like that, what's the use of
worrying over bigger things?—Luke 12:25–26 NLT

Bridge Building

As a young girl, I went on many vacations with my family. We spent memorable days hiking through the caves, mountains, and canyons of the West. I just loved drinking in the sights and sounds of those new places.

But occasionally our adventures brought us to places I feared. I remember one hike along a canyon wall. A waterfall ran off the cliff into a turbulent river below. And our trail crossed the river by way of an old, weather-beaten suspension bridge. I gripped the chain in fear as I walked along that swaying bridge, praying I'd make it to the other side.

Trust is a lot like that suspension bridge, isn't it? It's a tenuous line that we stretch out to others, praying that it will be safe. Trust connects us, but it sometimes lets us down. When storms come, those suspension bridges can break.

But trust also grows over time. What starts out as a flimsy bridge of rope and planks can develop

BIBLE BRIDE

Sometimes, her heart just ached. Ruth was a widow, scared about the future, saddened about the loss of her past. And just at the time when she most longed for the comforts of home, her mother-in-law, Naomi, had decided to move to a different land.

Loyalty. Trust. They were words she often thought about lately—words she'd felt challenged to live out in her life. In loyalty, she'd decided to follow Naomi to Israel instead of abandoning her. And in trust, she'd never turned back, even though every step took them farther from Ruth's homeland.

Now her loyalty was being tested again. Ruth had been struggling to adjust to this foreign land, trying to fit in with the people here. And tonight, Naomi had given the strangest instructions—asking Ruth to sneak into a man's home and sleep at his feet, of all things! Some women might have just walked out at such a crazy suggestion.

But Ruth trusted Naomi—and the God Naomi believed in. And now she was walking the path to Boaz's house. *I wonder how this is all going to turn out?* Ruth asked in her mind. But even as she did, she felt a familiar sense of calm. Somehow, she just knew this plan was going to turn out right.

Though Ruth's actions probably received little attention at the time, she was an extraordinary bride in God's eyes, eventually becoming an heir to Israel's greatest kings. Read her entire story of trust and loyalty in the book of Ruth.

into a stronger bridge supported with cables and concrete. As a friend proves their trust, we gain more and more confidence to use that kind of bridge.

And then there's marriage—which requires a huge amount of trust. Planning a future with your fiancé is much like building a house right in the middle of the bridge. You have to have a lot of trust in each other to start moving your prized possessions out there.

If we look around our culture, though, it seems as if marriage bridges need better reinforcement these days. The statistics say newly married couples have only a 50 percent chance of staying married. They make marriage sound like a night at the casino—just something to take your chances at. It's hard to trust in the "foreverness" of marriage with statistics like these. That's why many couples don't bother trying to build on their bridge. They sign a prenuptial agreement—sometimes on paper, sometimes in their mind—and keep their valuables to themselves. They prefer stable ground to the uncertainties of the bridge.

And is that such a bad idea? Whether the bridge of trust is strong or weak, it inevitably faces storms. After all, life throws curveballs. Emotional earthquakes rumble, causing marriages to collapse. You might as well be prepared, right?

But what if there's a better way to handle life's storms? What if you can build right in the middle of your bridge and stay standing even when earthquakes shake you up? Take heart, dear brides. The better way exists.

Just think in triangles. Sure, a simple line from one side of the chasm to the other will do the job, but triangles will make a bridge stronger. It's one of the engineer's golden rules: use triangles to make structures strong. And that's the secret for marriage too. It takes a triangle to keep trust strong. As the writer of Ecclesiastes put it, "A cord of three strands is not quickly broken" (4:12).

Even in the most perfect relationship, earthquakes can happen. Maybe you've even experienced a few tiny rumbles with your groom during all the wedding plans. Sometimes the earthquakes shake enough to damage the bridge and put cracks in our trust. And that's exactly why so many marriages fall apart. Too many cracks eventually break the bridge.

To withstand these rumbles, you need to make God that third point in your marriage. When both bride and groom build a line of trust to God, they create a firm triangle—something to keep their bridge strong. But it can't be a one-person effort. If your groom doesn't have faith in God, one side of your triangle will be broken. Your bridge may fall apart in the storms.

When both bride and groom have trust in God, though, their marriage becomes stable and secure. Even when the earthquakes temporarily shake their trust in each other, God is always that third point holding them together while they fix the damage. So go ahead. Shrug off those dour statistics and expect the best. Build your life right there in the middle of your bridge.

When you build a marriage with triangles, you can trust that it will survive a lifetime.

Swimming with Dad

Have you ever watched a young child swimming with her dad? She may not even know *how* to swim. But with Dad around, she becomes a daredevil. Jumping into the waves, she bobs her head underwater and lets Daddy toss her in the air. All the while, she smiles confidently, knowing her father won't let her drown. She trusts—completely. And then she has the time of her life.

Why is it so much easier to have that kind of trust when we're little kids? What makes us grow up and, with doubt in our eyes, ask our heavenly Father to leave us on our own two feet?

Frankly, I think we grow too smart for our own good. We're taught to quit reading fairy tales and start using our heads. We experience heartaches and avoid future disappointments by keeping expectations low. And somewhere along the way, we learn that if God doesn't seem to deliver on his promises fast enough, we'd better find a way to help ourselves.

We call this sophistication. I think it's really a loss of trust.

Sure, we've been taught to "trust and obey, for there's no other way." Sounds simple enough. But sometimes trust comes hard. Sometimes we just don't understand what our heavenly Groom is up to.

Proverbs 3 says to "trust in the LORD with all your *heart* and lean not on your own understanding" (v. 5, emphasis added). Too often, though, we approach trust from our heads. We consider all the things we've learned. We create beautiful, logical plans based on all this knowledge. And then we say, "God, I trust these plans to you."

But is that trust? That's equivalent to telling your groom that you trust him to make your financial plans and then ignoring him while you run ahead and make plans of your own.

Real trust isn't found in your head; it's beyond logic. It gives in to the plans of your Groom, even when they don't make sense to you. It has great expectations, even when your mind tempts you to worry and doubt. And as Proverbs points out, real trust requires *all* your heart. You can't go halfway when it comes to trust. You either believe in God, or you don't. You either follow when he calls, or you stay put.

Children understand this—they naturally trust with their hearts. After all, they don't have too much "understanding" to distract them yet! So they're content to follow someone else's lead, and they have an adventure doing it. No wonder Jesus once told his followers to become like children in their faith (see Mark 10:14)!

Most adults, on the other hand, let their minds get in the way. That's what happened to the Israelites when they reached the land of Canaan. They trusted God's plans to enter the Promised Land—until their spies reported that giants lived there. That's when their minds flew into high gear and they started doubting God's plan. And because they lost their trust, they lost their opportunity to experience God's blessing. That generation never stepped foot in the land they had traveled so far to see.

Of course, the Israelites aren't the only ones guilty of letting their minds override trust. We all worry instead of trusting, often settling for our low expectations rather than God's amazing plans. We miss the exhilaration and adventure of riding the waves with our Father.

But we don't have to miss everything. Imagine what might happen if we gave our hearts to our Groom, trusting him with all those worries we've harbored in our minds. Instead of forging ahead on our own, what if we just left things in God's capable hands and followed his lead? Instead of worrying about drowning, what if we trusted God to help us swim?

I think the results would be astounding. Because with real trust in God, we get to dive in to a rich life. And as we play in the waves, we'll experience all the wildness and joy of living in love.

So what are you waiting for? Jump in. It's time to swim with your Dad.

3

· · · · · · · · · · · · · · · · · ·

THE BUDGET

Most brides don't dream of budgets when they envision the perfect wedding. Budgets aren't glamorous. The guests won't admire them. And sometimes, they seem to squeeze your dreams out of the wedding. To avoid stressful money blunders, however, you'll want to create a budget before you purchase any wedding services and supplies. With a smart budget in place, you'll find it's possible to translate your wedding dreams into reality—at a price you can afford.

Of course, your budget will be useless unless you have the self-control to follow it. And the same could be said of your life. No matter how good your intentions are, you won't be able to develop healthy habits and relationships unless you learn to show some restraint. Yet even the self-controlled bride sometimes needs to let go—and that's when she's showing grace. Grace shines the brightest when it's given with no restraints. So as you examine all those budget numbers, take some time to examine your life as well. Are the qualities of self-control and grace adding up in your life?

Bride of Self-Control

Those who control their tongue will have a long life; a quick retort can ruin everything.—Proverbs 13:3 NLT

Do not wear yourself out to get rich;
have the wisdom to show restraint.—Proverbs 23:4

Therefore be clear minded and self-controlled so that you can pray.—1 Peter 4:7

Counting the Costs

Julia stared at her father, dumbfounded by what he'd just told her. "What do you mean there's no more money for the wedding?" she cried. "Dad, I haven't even ordered my wedding dress yet!"

Julia's dad pointed to the pile of receipts on his desk. "Honey, you spent three times as much as we had agreed to on that photographer you wanted. You ordered all those expensive candles for wedding favors. And I have to set aside enough to feed the four hundred guests you want. I'm sorry, but your mom and I just can't afford to pay for anything else. Maybe you could borrow your sister's dress from last year."

Julia started to get angry, but then she saw the look on her dad's face. She could tell he was just as disappointed as she was. And he *had* offered a very generous amount to put toward wedding expenses. She just hadn't realized how quickly all the money was being spent.

When it comes to wedding plans, it's important to count the costs, isn't it? Unless you keep track of your expenses, you risk running out of money like Julia did. And then you may find yourself with only half the wedding you were hoping for. That's what always happens when we forget to count the costs—we miss out on something. And it's not just wedding budgets that are affected. Ignoring the costs creates problems in other areas of life too.

Consider Jack. In a moment of thoughtless anger, he hit his girlfriend. And now she's long gone. Or think about Melanie. She got drunk at a party one night and ended up pregnant, not even remembering who the father was. And then there's Rachel. All she did was tell a "harmless" joke about her friend's private family problems. Now her friend keeps her at an emotional distance. They all forgot to count the costs. They all got caught up in the moment and lost self-control. And now they're all haunted by what could've been.

I wish I could say that I'm always a shining example of self-control myself. But I'm not. I've said unkind words behind someone's back. I've bought the shoes that I didn't need. I've watched television programs that fill our culture with trashy values. And I've felt regret.

Have you ever been there, done that?

Proverbs 25:28 says, "Like a city whose walls are broken down is a man who lacks self-control." Those words really ring true, don't they? All it takes is a few poorly chosen words or actions, and suddenly our character starts to crumble like city walls. Sometimes we even wonder how we could've done something so stupid—we feel like some foreign power just invaded the "city" of our mind.

BIBLE BRIDE

It had been another long day. She waited until the other women finished their daily walk to the well before she walked there herself. She preferred to draw water alone, away from the disapproving stares and verbal jabs of the other women. She already knew how they felt about her lifestyle—she didn't need to hear it from them again.

I don't need their snide remarks to remind me how sinful I am, she thought to herself that day. *I already know that God's done with me.* She'd been with five different guys, and now she was fooling around with another man—yet another guy who would probably use her and move on to settle down with a "nice" girl.

Approaching the well, the Samaritan woman noticed a man sitting there—he looked like a Jew. Sighing, she wondered if she should turn around. The last thing she felt like doing was putting up with the degrading attitude that most Jews hurled at Samaritans. But she really needed some water, so she kept going.

"Will you give me a drink?" the man asked her. She froze. A respectable Jewish man was talking to her? For the next several minutes, the Samaritan woman conversed with this Jewish rabbi. But they shared no small talk. This man asked her questions that probed deep into her heart, awakening her thirst for a better life. And by the end of their conversation, she was certain of two things: this man was the Messiah—God in the flesh—and he hadn't given up on her!

The Samaritan woman probably hadn't experienced much grace or self-control before she encountered Jesus that day. But the Son of God didn't care about social stigma or her shady past. He just talked with her, offering her a drink of salvation that could change her life.

Read the Samaritan woman's story in John 4 and see how God can bring grace to the most out-of-control lives.

Truth is, foreign powers do try to invade our minds and hearts. "[The devil] prowls around like a roaring lion" (1 Peter 5:8). And I'm sure he loves to find people without self-control. Those people are easy targets for his temptations. And his underlying goal? To pull you away from your Groom. He'd love to put you in Julia's shoes—indulging so much that you miss out on the wedding feast of heaven.

That's why we need to fortify our hearts from enemy attack. We need to count the costs.

Thinking before we speak. Praying before we act. Always asking that vital question: will this bring me closer to or farther away from God? When we guard our hearts in this way, we won't miss out on God's amazing plans for our lives. Instead, we'll gain self-control and make it harder for Satan to attack.

But most important, with self-control guarding our minds and hearts, we'll stay safe in the arms of the Groom we love. And no amount of tugging on Satan's part will be able to pull us away.

Fighting the Spending Bug

I remember some days when the spending bug bit me hard. I'd lost a job. I didn't know what to do with my life. I was confused. And in the midst of my frustration, I heard the promises of materialism: "You know, Amy, you'll at least feel better about yourself if you can look nice in some trendy new clothes." And so off I went, buying clothes with abandon—until the guilt settled in.

Then I started looking at the receipts, wishing I'd had a little more self-control. Even with all my new purchases, the doubts and questions still nagged. Only now, on top of it all, I felt bad about overspending too.

Sound familiar to you? In American culture, it's hard to avoid the materialism bug. Most of us have probably been infected at some time or another. It can take on different symptoms—overeating, overspending, overworking—but in almost every case, materialism has a way of breaking down our self-control. And bit by bit, it tries to take over our lives.

Sometimes people shrug off the issue of materialism. Maybe you've heard them say, "There's nothing wrong with wanting some nice things." And on one level, they're right. God's brides don't have to live in filth and rags, wondering where their next meal will come from. I think God genuinely enjoys the unique homes and lifestyles we create with his blessing. I even think he enjoys the beautiful plans we incorporate into our weddings. After all, he's a creator too.

But there's a big difference between *enjoying* God's material blessings and *putting our faith in* those materials. At its core, materialism beckons us to do the latter. We're tempted to chase after certain things, friends, and "looks"—not as a way of enjoying God's blessings, but as a way of finding fulfillment away from him. Materialism breaks through our self-control, urging us to cheat on God by pursuing worldly things.

And when it comes to weddings, materialism can be especially vicious, pushing a bride to replace her excitement about marriage with an insatiable drive for the best wedding around. Her priorities get twisted. And suddenly she's getting more worried about the kind of vegetables being served at the reception than about the health of her love relationship!

Materialism distorts our hearts, making us long for things we don't really need and neglect the things we already have. It's a vicious sickness. And maybe that's why the Bible is filled with warnings about the disease.

Consider Proverbs 23:5: "Cast but a glance at riches, and they are gone, for they will surely sprout wings and fly off to the sky like an eagle." What a picture the writer gives! I envision a stockbroker standing at the New York Stock Exchange during the 1929 crash. The day before, he'd been gobbling up good buys and accumulating tremendous wealth. And the next day, the market crashed. Now he's rubbing his throbbing head, wondering how his money could just "fly off" in a day.

Solomon—the man who had it all—also warned about materialism: "Whoever loves money never has money enough; whoever loves wealth is never satisfied" (Eccles. 5:10). Isn't that exactly what happens when people put their faith in material things? They put all their hope in having the "right" house, the "right" clothes, the "right" hobbies—and then they wake up one morning to realize they still haven't found the peace and self-confidence they crave. Emotionally and spiritually, they still feel like paupers.

That's the brutal side of materialism. It pushes us to spend money without restraint, but we also end up spending ourselves. It promises to heal us of all our self-doubts and fears—and then it makes us sick with insecurity and jealousy. So whether materialism just tempts us a little or whether it has sucked us into a whirlpool, we need to fight this brutal disease.

We need a vaccine—a simple formula to fight the spending bug. And here's one that works: just remind yourself that you can't take it with you.

When you start feeling jealous about your friend's new car, remember, you can't take it with you. And when you're tempted to buy those wedding favors with the money you were going to tithe, remember, you can't take it with you. Those six little words have a way of changing your outlook. Suddenly, the promises of materialism look empty—and the promises of your Groom grow more dear.

And what promises God has given us! "But their trust should be in the living God, who richly gives us all we need for our enjoyment" (1 Tim. 6:17 NLT). God will give us what we need, and he wants us to really enjoy it. But we'll miss out on that joy when we trust in the things rather than the Giver. As Hebrews 13:5 challenges us, we can "be content with what [we] have"—thanking God for the blessings we've been given.

So when it comes to "things," God's brides shouldn't worry or lose control. We don't need to chase after riches—our Groom can handle the finances.

Planning Your Budget

Getting Started

Start your wedding budget with a realistic picture of how much money you can spend. Shortly after your engagement begins, you and your fiancé should discuss your financial situation and decide

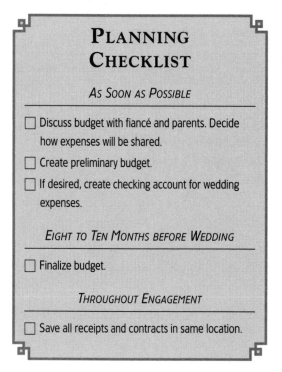

PLANNING CHECKLIST

As Soon as Possible

- ☐ Discuss budget with fiancé and parents. Decide how expenses will be shared.
- ☐ Create preliminary budget.
- ☐ If desired, create checking account for wedding expenses.

Eight to Ten Months before Wedding

- ☐ Finalize budget.

Throughout Engagement

- ☐ Save all receipts and contracts in same location.

on an overall budget amount. As you make this decision, be sure to consider the trade-offs between your wedding and your future plans. For example, a smaller wedding budget could allow for a down payment on a new home. Or a shorter honeymoon could allow more splurging on the wedding itself.

Since parents usually contribute to wedding costs, you'll need to include them in the budgeting process. Arrange meetings with both sets of parents to discuss the budget and decide who will pay for various wedding needs. While wedding expenses have traditionally been covered by the bride's parents, many families agree to split the costs evenly today. Bride and groom may also wish to alleviate the financial burden on their parents by paying for some or all of the wedding costs themselves.

As you discuss the preliminary budget with your parents and future in-laws, approach the issue with a spirit of compromise. Hurt feelings and ruffled feathers can be avoided if you're willing to make adjustments to your own ideas. Once you've determined how much each party will contribute to wedding costs, you'll know your overall budget amount.

Who Pays for What?

When planning a wedding, many people ask "Who pays for what?" The answer to that question is never set in stone, and the division of costs varies dramatically from one wedding to the next. But the following charts can help by listing who has traditionally covered which expenses.

Our Wedding Budget Amount

Bride's family: _____

Groom's family: _____

Bride and groom contribution: _____

Other contributions: _____

Total budget: _____

Creating the Budget

Your budget should include a detailed breakdown of wedding costs. The Wedding Budget Worksheet provides several broad wedding categories (Ceremony Fees, Flowers, Music, etc.) and lists various items within each. You may wish to add additional items to each category or eliminate some of those listed, based on your specific wedding needs. Once you've completed the list of wedding expenses, discuss each item with your fiancé and fill in the priority level with a number between one (high) and three (low).

Start the Estimated Costs column by entering an amount in your Safety Fund category. This amount, reserved for unexpected expenses, should equal 3 to 5 percent of your total budget. Next, fill in the estimated cost for fixed fees, such as the officiant's fee, postage for invitations, and site

PARENTS—DO THEY GET A SAY IF THEY PAY?

Bride and groom are full of ideas for their own wedding. But inevitably, some of their inspiration won't fit the wedding picture their parents had in mind. When parents insist on having it their way, the couple often feels like their special day has turned into their parents' pet project. So how much say should the parents have?

Understandably, parents share your excitement about the upcoming wedding. And if they're also providing wedding funds, they should have a vote in how the money is spent. Try to compromise—especially on matters you don't have strong preferences about. If his dad really wants candles at the ceremony, why not go ahead and order a few, even if you weren't planning on them? If a few small changes can prevent a lot of hurt feelings, it's worth the sacrifice.

Of course, the parents' vote shouldn't be the only vote. After all, the wedding is for the bride and groom. So whenever possible, the couple's wishes should be incorporated as long as they will not offend family members or ruin the budget.

If you're concerned about conflicts arising over particular issues, consider paying for those services or supplies yourselves. For example, if you anticipate arguments about your wedding dress, pay for the dress yourself. You can still invite family to shop with you and provide opinions. But when it's time to pay the deposit and order the dress, you can make the final decision alone.

rentals. Then fill in the expected costs for other items, beginning with your high priority items and working your way through to the low priority items. As you work, be sure that your total costs are within the budget amount you agreed upon earlier. If you need budget adjustments, start by cutting expenses on your lowest priority items. This will leave the bulk of your budget to cover the expenses that you consider most important.

Expenses of Bride

groom's wedding ring
groom's wedding gift
gifts for her attendants
gift for her parents
bridesmaids' luncheon

Expenses of Groom

bride's wedding ring
bride's wedding gift
gifts for his attendants
gift for his parents
marriage license
officiant's fee
bride's bouquet
honeymoon
bachelor dinner

Expenses of Bride's Family

reception expenses
rental and decoration of wedding site
bride's wedding attire
wedding stationery

floral decorations for ceremony
    and reception
bridesmaids' flowers
videography and photography
musicians
transportation of bridal party to reception
bridesmaids' lodging

Expenses of Groom's Family

groom's attire
ties and gloves for groom's attendants (if not
    part of rental package)
corsages for mothers and grandmothers
boutonnieres for fathers, grandfathers, and
    men in wedding party
rehearsal dinner
groomsmen's/ushers' lodging
shipment of wedding gifts to bride and
    groom's home, if necessary

Expenses of Attendants

wedding attire and accessories (purchase or
    rental)
travel expenses
bridal shower gift
cost of hosting bridal shower and bachelor or
    bachelorette party
wedding gift for couple

Expenses of Guests

travel expenses
hotel accommodations
wedding gift for couple

Wedding Budget Worksheet

Budgeted Items	Priority Level	Estimated Cost	Actual Cost
Safety Fund (3–5 percent of budget)			
Ceremony Fees			
Site Fee			
Officiant's Fee			
Decorations			
Other			
Flowers			
Ceremony Flowers			
Bridal Bouquet			
Bridal Attendants' Flowers			
Corsages			
Boutonnieres			
Candles			
Reception Flowers			
Equipment Rentals (candelabras, kneeling bench, aisle runner, etc.)			
Other			
Attendants			
Accommodations			
Bridesmaids' Luncheon			
Bachelor Dinner			
Other			
Music			
Organist/Pianist Fee			
Vocalists			
Reception Music			
Other			

Budgeted Items	Priority Level	Estimated Cost	Actual Cost
Photography			
Engagement Photographs			
Wedding Photography			
Videography			
Other			
Stationery			
Engagement Announcements			
Invitations and Enclosures			
Thank-You Notes			
Postage			
Programs			
Other			
Wedding Attire			
Bridal Gown			
Headpiece and Veil			
Undergarments			
Shoes			
Accessories (jewelry, garter, etc.)			
Groom's Attire			
Bride's Rings			
Groom's Ring			
Beauty Treatments (hair, makeup, etc.)			
Other			
Transportation			
Transportation for Bridal Party			
Parking Attendants			
Trips Home for Planning (if you live away)			
Other			
Reception			
Site Rental			

Budgeted Items	Priority Level	Estimated Cost	Actual Cost
Setup Fees			
Decorations			
Food/Beverage Expenses			
Gratuities and Tax			
Wedding Cake			
Wedding Favors for Guests			
Equipment Rentals (linens, dinnerware, tables, etc.)			
Other			
Gifts			
Gifts for Bride's Attendants			
Gifts for Groom's Attendants			
Gifts for Parents			
Bride's Gift for Groom			
Groom's Gift for Bride			
Other			
Legal Issues			
Marriage License			
Physicals/Blood Test Fees			
Wedding Insurance			
Other			
Miscellaneous Fees			
Wedding Consultant Fees			
Unity Candle			
Guest Book			
Ring Bearer's Pillow			
Janitorial Service			
Welcome Baskets for Out-of-Towners			
Rehearsal Dinner			
Other			

Estimating Expenses

To create realistic estimates, you'll want to request price quotes from various wedding service providers. As you fill in the estimated costs on your budget worksheet, select amounts that fall midway between the higher and lower quotes you've received. As a starting point for estimating how much should be spent on each category, the following percentage estimates may be useful.

Reception fees 45–60%

Wedding attire 10–15%

Photography 7–10%

Flowers 5–10%

Rings 5–10%

Music 4–8%

Stationery 3–5%

Gifts 3–5%

Miscellaneous fees 3–5%

Ceremony fees 1–3%

Transportation fees 1–3%

Signing Contracts

As you shop for wedding supplies, expect to sign contracts with each service provider. Before you sign, however, be sure to read through the entire document. Many contracts contain hidden costs, such as setup fees, cleanup fees, overtime costs, and equipment rentals. Most contracts also require a 10–50 percent deposit. Be sure that the contract suits your needs and budget, and don't be afraid to ask questions. It's better to discover potential problems now, rather than on the wedding day. And don't forget about gratuities and taxes—ask your supplier if they've been included in the contract as well.

SAVING PENNIES FOR THE BIG DAY

Is your budget looking a little cramped? Would you like to add a few more elegant touches but can't find a way to pay for them? Here are a few ideas to help you and your groom save up for those wedding and honeymoon expenses:

Eat brown bag lunches instead of going out. If you each cut out just two lunches a week, you could save twenty to thirty dollars a week.

Host a garage sale. Ask friends and family if they have old items they'd be willing to donate.

Go on "cheap" dates. Rent movies instead of going to the theater. Pack a picnic instead of eating at a restaurant.

Instead of spending money on birthday presents for family, friends, and each other, offer services such as washing a car, doing laundry, or giving a back rub.

If you can, join a carpool to save on gas money.

Wedding Insurance— Who Needs It?

Most weddings cost thousands of dollars, making them a significant investment for those who pay the bill. That's why several insurers now offer coverage for weddings. In the event that a wedding must be canceled or postponed, wedding insurers can reimburse nonrecoverable costs. Insurance may also cover other problems such as lost deposits when a wedding supplier goes out of business, replacement costs for lost or stolen bridal attire, and damaged wedding gifts or photography. The specific coverage and cost vary, but regardless of what policy you choose, check with the Better Business Bureau to ensure that your insurance provider has a legitimate enterprise.

Many families will take their chances without insurance. But you may want to look at wedding insurance more closely if you face the following situations.

The health of immediate family members could force your wedding to be canceled or postponed.

The bride or groom serves in the armed forces and could be deployed, forcing the wedding to be canceled or postponed.

Your wedding is being held in a location where weather conditions could cause cancellation or postponement.

Tracking Expenses

Once you've started paying for wedding supplies, you can track your expenses in the Actual Cost section of your budget worksheet. If expenses in one category become too high, you'll need to adjust your budget by taking money from your safety fund or reducing the estimated cost of items that haven't been purchased.

COST-CUTTERS*

Having the wedding of your dreams doesn't have to break the bank. Consider the following tips to economize on wedding plans:

Start Your Planning Early—Often, the more affordable service providers are booked early. (Everybody else wants to save money too!) Shop early and leave yourself plenty of time to search for affordable wedding packages.

Cut the Guest List—The reception accounts for about half of your total cost. Cutting the number of people you need to accommodate will be the easiest way to reduce expenses.

Do It Yourself—Perform wedding duties (such as assembling wedding favors or decorating the church) yourself instead of paying someone else to do it for you.

Borrow Supplies—When possible, borrow supplies— table linens, jewelry, decorations, etc.—rather than purchasing or renting them.

Ask Around—Ask your friends and family if they know of any people who provide discount wedding services. Many people offer wedding services out of their home at more affordable prices than you can find in a store. But before you use *any* provider, be sure to check their references and ensure the quality of their work.

*Look for more Cost-Cutter boxes throughout this planner for additional ways to save.

You may want to consider opening a separate checking account for your wedding funds. Using one account will make it much easier to track expenses. Also, be sure to save all contracts and receipts in case you need to recheck an agreement or deposit amount. You can staple them to your planner or keep them in a separate file that travels with your planner.

Bride of Grace

If you, O LORD, kept a record of sins, O Lord, who could stand? But with you there is forgiveness.—Psalm 130:3–4

Be kind and compassionate to one another, forgiving each other, just as in Christ God forgave you.—Ephesians 4:32

The Budget of Grace

SF, blonde, blue eyes, who enjoys sporting events, cooking, and animals seeks SM, tall and dark, who likes sports, adventure, and good times. Must be employed, romantic, and willing to have kids.

Even if you never bothered with the personals, I'll bet you had a mental checklist of traits you were looking for in a man. Maybe your list was quite detailed, with some traits labeled "negotiable," others "nonnegotiable." Or maybe your only requirement was "romantic chemistry must explode."

Can you imagine, though, if your groom suddenly decided to create a checklist for *you*, his soon-to-be bride? Imagine him writing a list, like the sort you find in the personal ads, to make

sure that you measured up to his expectations. "Does she give me back rubs?" Check. "Does she remember my birthday?" Check. "Does she keep her house clean and try to look good herself?" Check. Check.

I have a feeling that if your guy wrote this checklist, he'd be getting a punch in the arm—or worse! No one wants to feel like a rent-a-bride. We don't want to *earn* our groom's love through roast beef sandwiches, weeded flower beds, or a nice pair of legs. We just want to be loved for who we are—on good days and bad.

Though checklists seem to work in the personal ads—narrowing the field and weeding out the people who won't work—they just don't work well in real-life romantic relationships. When it comes to marriage, who wants to live with someone who's measuring his or her performance on a daily basis?

Funny thing is, sometimes that's just how we view God. We think of our spiritual life as if it were a personal ad: "Awesome, all-powerful God seeks someone who will pray every day, attend regular church services, and volunteer to help the needy at least two times a week." So we do those things and try to be "better" Christians. But deep down, we still worry that it's not enough—that we won't measure up to God.

When that feeling starts haunting me, I usually start looking for something else to do. Hmm . . . the church nursery needs volunteers? Sign me up. The food drive wants donations? Here's my money. Surely those are on God's checklist. They should move me up a notch or two in his eyes, right? But trying to earn God's love usually leaves me feeling tired and frustrated—and still feeling like I should do more.

Truth is, I *can't* do enough. None of us can. Paul once wrote, "There is no one righteous, not even one" (Rom. 3:10–11). That seems pretty clear. We can't be "right" people on our own, no matter how hard we try. So why keep running around trying to earn the "righteous" badge on that heavenly Girl Scout scarf?

After all, God's budget is pretty simple. There's a column that lists all our faults and sins, diseases of the heart. And it's got some ugly red words listed in the "Total" column: "The wages of sin is death" (Rom. 6:23). Then there's a column for payments. And there, written in the red blood of Jesus, are the words "paid in full."

That's all there is to it. And all our accomplishments, volunteer efforts, service projects—they don't even show up in the budget. God doesn't need them to pay our debt. Jesus already paid the price for our sin. The bottom line: we don't get what we deserve. Instead of death, we get grace—and we get the kind of life we can't possibly earn on our own.

That's hard to swallow in this self-improvement world. The magazines tell us to make ourselves prettier, thinner, wealthier, more outgoing. After we've read all the articles and followed their self-help programs, then we'll be admired by those around us, or so we're told. So we switch to the checklist mentality of life—trying to be self-sufficient, and wearing ourselves out in the process.

But God doesn't have a self-help checklist for us. He's not waiting for us to make ourselves "more" before we can be his bride. Instead, he woos us with his grace, offering to save us despite our mess-ups. Offering his love on good days and bad.

If you've been running the rat race lately, trying to earn a "righteous" mark on God's checklist, stop for a minute and listen to these words: "Come to me, all you who are weary and burdened, and I will give you rest" (Matt. 11:28). God's not expecting you to earn righteousness on your own—that's a burden too heavy for you to bear.

Instead, just remember the budget of grace. You don't need to buy God's love or salvation— he already loves you for who you are.

Parable of an Unforgiving Woman

Anne felt horrible. She'd done the unthinkable—kissing her best friend's fiancé. But that wasn't really the worst of it. The kiss might have been forgivable if it'd been a fluke. But it wasn't.

Anne had been trying to attract Ethan's attention for weeks, conveniently "being there" whenever he needed a listening ear. She'd manipulated the conversations, trying to make him feel like he should end the engagement. And when he started to confess his feelings for her, she didn't do a thing to stop him as he moved in for a kiss.

After several weeks of this clandestine relationship, Ethan had broken off the engagement with Anne's friend Stephanie. Stephanie's hurt quickly turned into anger, and she made it clear that she'd never talk to Anne or Ethan again. Hoping for the best, Anne tried to believe it would all blow over.

Years later, though, Anne still hadn't heard from Stephanie. And even though she and Ethan had eventually broken up, she still felt bad about betraying her old friend. So when she bumped into Stephanie at a concert one night, she seized the opportunity, asking her to coffee the next day.

Stephanie agreed, and the following night both women had the chance to share what had been on their hearts for years. Anne apologized profusely, begging Stephanie to forgive her. "I know there's no way I could repay you for all the hurt I caused," she explained, "but I was really hoping you might give me another chance. I never did find another friend like you."

To her surprise, Stephanie smiled. "I forgave you for all that a long time ago," she said. "I just couldn't bring myself to talk to you about it because I thought you didn't care anymore."

Feeling relieved, Anne jumped up and gave Stephanie a hug.

Three weeks later, Anne found herself with a new problem.

Months ago, one of her favorite necklaces had gone missing. It hadn't really had sentimental value, but she'd worn it frequently enough. She searched the house from top to bottom, hoping it would show up. Annoyed when she couldn't find it, she finally just purchased a new necklace.

Now, with a weekend visit from her younger sister, Laci, the original necklace had resurfaced. Looking sheepish, Laci brought out the necklace and explained how she'd borrowed it during a past visit and forgotten to return it. "I'm sorry, sis." She looked troubled when she saw Anne's jaw tighten. "You weren't around that night or I would've asked to borrow it."

Anne was livid. She'd spent good money replacing that necklace, and now her sister breezed in as if it had been a little mistake? "Laci," she fumed, "that was my favorite necklace, and you just went off and *stole* it from me. Don't think you can just come here with a sad face and get away with it. You owe me fifty dollars for the cost of the new necklace I bought. And don't plan on staying here again until you've paid me every cent."

Wait a minute, you're thinking. *That's not how the story is supposed to go.* One moment, Anne finds restored friendship and forgiveness, even after stealing her best friend's fiancé. The next, she's throwing her sister out of the house because of a *necklace*?

Unfortunately, Anne's story sometimes gets echoed in our lives, doesn't it? Wedding stress gets the best of us, we have a bad day at work, or the checkbook bounces—and suddenly we lose sight of the important things. We forget God's amazing grace. And when someone crosses us, we're ready to make them pay.

Romans 12 says, "Do not repay anyone evil for evil . . . but overcome evil with good" (vv. 17, 21). Vengeance doesn't really help anyone. After all, we don't really cancel the evil by getting even; we just end up with two hurting hearts instead of one. But when we show grace—giving forgiveness, even when we have a right to make the offender pay—we cancel the evil with something very good, indeed.

And that's just what a truly graceful bride does. She's been captivated by God's grace, and she can't help but share it with others. She lives out the words of 1 Corinthians 15:10, which say "But by the grace of God I am what I am, and his grace to me was not without effect."

If you want to be a bride of grace yourself, don't worry about the smoothness of your words or the elegance of your walk. Real grace lives in the heart. And it shows itself by offering forgiveness and second chances. So take today's parable to heart, and let God's grace have a lasting effect on you.

(You can read the parable of the unforgiving debtor as Jesus originally shared it in Matthew 18:21–35.)

LOVE STORY FROM GOD

Saul was a hard man. He'd been "religious" his whole life, reading Scripture, studying under the best teachers, and eventually working himself into a position of religious influence himself. He was a devoted and zealous Jew. So when he saw a threat to his religion, he went to great lengths to fight it.

Ever since a man named Jesus walked the ground of Israel, thousands of Jews had become his followers. Saul watched this energetic Christian community grow, and his anger grew too. He persecuted Jerusalem's Christians with a passion, "breathing out murderous threats" against them (Acts 9:1).

Their vibrant faith gnawed at his heart—in part because he thought their beliefs were misguided, but mostly because he didn't feel the same fire in his own soul. So he pushed harder. He started traveling to Damascus, planning to imprison any Christians he might find there. And he was ready to taste more blood.

But God had other plans for Saul. No doubt the Christians had been begging God to do something about this guy for a while. After all, he was one of the greatest opponents to Jesus's followers, a man filled with such hate that he deserved a painful death and an eternal hell.

Yet God had something else up his sleeve. He didn't see Saul as just "that guy who persecutes Christians." Looking at Saul, God saw potential—a man who needed to experience grace, who could passionately share that grace with the world.

And so instead of killing the hard-hearted persecutor, God transformed Saul forever. Blinding him with a bright light, God led him to Ananias, a dedicated disciple of Jesus who shared the Good News with Saul. And as he accepted the message of salvation for the first time, he found a new passion—a passion for sharing Jesus Christ. So Saul, once the zealous persecutor of Christianity, became Paul, the passionate apostle who eventually gave his own life as a martyr for the Christian faith.

Check out Paul's conversion story in Acts 9 to see what happens when we look at people through the eyes of God's grace.

4

. . . .

THE BASICS

I *have so many ideas for my wedding,* you may be thinking, *but where do I start?* As you begin planning, avoid the temptation to start with your favorite details. It won't be helpful to buy those pretty Christmas wedding favors only to discover all the local reception halls are booked for the holidays. And planning an elaborate dinner reception may be fun, but what if your wedding officiant is only available for a morning ceremony?

To avoid such hassles, plan the basic details first. *When* will you get married? *Where* will the wedding be? *Who* will be there? And *what* kind of style or theme would you like to follow?

The basics of time, place, and style will lay the groundwork for a beautiful wedding. But they're also the cornerstones of spiritual life. So as you plan the when and where of your wedding, set aside some special times and places to build your devotion to God. And then reflect on your personal "style." As you do, you'll discover the disciplines to take your spiritual life to the next level.

Bride
of Devotion

Love the LORD your God with all your heart and with all your soul and with all your strength.—Deuteronomy 6:5

Now devote your heart and soul to seeking the LORD your God.—1 Chronicles 22:19

The Real Thing

It was the seedy side of town. Broken windows wore a shield of plywood protection, and trash littered the cracked pavement. Respectable people didn't come out here. Half of the nearby signs blinked "XXX" or boasted "Nude Showgirls."

Lindsey had obviously taken a wrong turn. Sighing, she hit the lock button on her Ford. She felt creepy as she noticed the men on the sidewalks staring at her. *I sure hope I recognize one of these street names*, she thought, looking for signs that might point her out of this bad neighborhood.

With relief, she noticed a church coming up on the right. The building looked old and dark, but maybe someone would be there—someone with directions to a better part of town. Grabbing her mace from the glove compartment, she parked by the door. It was comforting to see the brick cornerstone. Chiseled into it were the words "This building dedicated to the service of God. 1958."

Lindsey opened the door. Instead of a quiet sanctuary, she found a bar, some scattered tables, and half-clad women dancing on a stage. The mixed aromas of smoke and alcohol assaulted her senses. Turning quickly, she hurried out the door before anyone noticed her presence.

It wasn't until she turned out of the parking lot that she saw the unlit sign reading "Sexcapades Club: Come Inside to See Good Girls Gone Bad." *Whoa*, Lindsey thought. *I'll bet it's been a long time since anyone came here for a church service!*

Hopefully, you've never found yourself at a church turned strip club. I'm sure it would be an unsettling experience. But have you ever seen a person who's like that church? On the outside, they say they've devoted themselves to God. But what's inside suggests the opposite. When it comes to devotion, their lifestyle doesn't show the real thing.

We've all met these false advertisers. It's pretty easy to see through them. Sometimes we even get angry, wondering how they could claim to love God when their lives so clearly ignore him. *That's not devotion*, we think. And we're right: real devotion shows itself in the way we live, not in the words we say or the labels we wear.

If you're reading this book, you're probably someone who considers herself a devoted bride—to both God and your groom. It's the label you wear. Maybe you even sing praise songs about devotion to God, or you belt out love songs about your fiancé in the car. But do you have what you're advertising? Can others see real devotion when they look at *your* life?

As you plan your wedding, you'll start by making the major decisions: where and when you'll get married, what style you want to convey. Those big decisions impact all the little details you plan later on. And in the end, all your choices build a unique wedding that reflects who you are.

We also make a lot of choices in life. How will I spend my time? What style of life am I going to lead? The way we answer those questions impacts the many "little" choices we make each day. Will I go to church this morning or sleep in? Will I compete with my friend's lavish lifestyle or be content with what I have?

In the end, these choices create a lifestyle that says something about who we are and who we want to be. They cut past our lip service to God and reveal whether or not we're really devoted. And they answer the big questions: Are we devoted to our groom—or does our lifestyle center on ourselves? Are we devoted to God—or do we live as though he isn't really there?

Do some soul-searching and consider those questions today. It may hurt a little—you may discover that lifestyle changes need to be made. Or you may need to revisit some of the big decisions you've made. But it's always worth the effort to eliminate false advertising from our lives. And in the end you'll have something special to give to God and your groom—a devotion that's the real thing.

Finish with Those Chores

A young boy got caught trying to cut down his neighbor's flowers. "You evil boy!" the angry neighbor yelled at him. "You better stop acting like the devil or you'll live to regret it." The boy looked up with concern in his eyes. "But I ain't evil at all. I read my Bible every day just like Ma says, and it don't say nothin' about cutting flowers down."

How often do we carry around that little boy's attitude? We put our time in with devotions, reading our Bibles and saying our prayers. But we miss the point. We don't let God's words travel from our brain to our soul. We settle for a mediocre dose of spirituality when God wants to touch our hearts.

With such hurried lives, it's no wonder we have a hard time slowing down to catch our spiritual breath. Our schedules already overflow with things to do. Devotions feel like one more chore we have to get through before climbing into bed. But does it have to be this way? What if devotions weren't just another item on our task list? What if they were the place where we got *away* from our busy schedules?

It's possible, you know.

When I left for my honeymoon, I felt relieved. The whirlwind of wedding plans had finally ended, and suddenly I could breathe again. The next six days, I simply relaxed with my new husband under the warm Cancun sun. And we enjoyed every moment. After so many weeks of hurried activity, it felt good to be alone—just the two of us, devoting all our time to each other.

That's what our devotions should feel like. Have you ever noticed the core word of *devotions*? Devotions are our way to *devote* ourselves to our spiritual Groom. For a few minutes, we can leave the hustle and bustle of life behind us and simply bask in the warmth of God's love. And through that process, we gain renewed energy to stay devoted to him throughout the rest of our day.

So imagine how God feels when we treat devotions like a chore. He wants us to enjoy a quiet vacation from life's pressures, but we never get past the airport. He wants some time alone, just the two of us, but we come with distractions and busy schedules. And while we're keeping our eye on the clock and thinking about our next task, God's just wishing we could ponder life's deepest questions together while we wriggle our toes in the sand.

BIBLE BRIDE

At eighty-four years old, Anna had outlived most of her friends and family. Her husband had died long ago, just seven years after their marriage. And as a widow, Anna now devoted her time to God, spending day after day worshiping him at the temple.

When younger women came to the temple—along with their giggling children and protective husbands—they probably looked at Anna with pity. Maybe some never noticed the widow at all. She was just an old lady—with nothing better to do with her time than sit at the temple every day.

But God saw her as a beautiful bride. He adored her amazing discipline—Anna had faithfully fasted, prayed, and worshiped for years. And because of her devotion, Anna's heart had been open to the voice of God. She became a prophetess, sharing God's wisdom with those around her.

One day, this old bride enjoyed an incredible experience. Anna was just going about her routine at the temple when suddenly she saw a tiny baby in his mother's arms. Though Jesus was just a helpless infant at that time, Anna recognized him as the Messiah. And in front of everyone gathered there, she thanked God for letting a devoted old woman live to see the Son of God.

Read Anna's story in Luke 2:36–38 to see a bride of devotion in action.

God longs for true devotion from us. He wants some time with us, out of the busyness of our day. And he simply asks us to relax. To breathe. And to enjoy quiet moments with him. Maybe you'll talk to him in prayer, pouring out your deepest feelings or asking questions about his Word. Maybe you'll listen to his voice by reading the Bible. Maybe you'll journal, or sing, or just sit in silence while thinking about him.

Whatever it is that you do, don't miss the point of devotions. God is calling you to "come with me by yourself to a quiet place and get some rest" (Mark 6:31).

Jesus understood this. He lived a busy life, with twelve disciples following him everywhere and crowds flocking to hear his teaching. He probably put in some long days. And you might think that devotions would be the first thing he'd drop from his schedule. After all, he already spent most of his time teaching about God.

But the Gospels mention several times when Jesus spent quiet time with God. After feeding five thousand people in one day, "he went up on a mountainside to pray" (Mark 6:46). The night before selecting his disciples, "Jesus went out to a mountainside to pray, and spent the night praying to God" (Luke 6:12).

So often throughout his ministry, Jesus took the time to be with his Father. And it sounds like he had a special place—"a mountainside"—where he liked to spend that time.

We all need a mountainside for our devotional time with God—a place that reminds us how special it is to be with him. Many people offer suggestions for creating this special space. They'll give formulas for the best Bible-reading schedule or designate certain areas of prayer. Their ideas may be good, but don't box yourself into these plans if they make devotions feel like a chore. God made us all so wonderfully different. And he gives us freedom to explore and seek the devotional space that's uniquely ours.

So as you spend some time picking locations, style, and time for your wedding day, give some thought to a special place and time for your devotions too. Take an adventurous spirit to your "mountainside" and try new things. Ask God to fill your heart with a devotion to Bible reading and prayer. He'll help you find it.

Soon, you'll be finished with devotions that feel like chores. And instead, you'll have the chance to rest in the presence of your wonderful Groom.

Planning Your Basics

Setting the Date and Time

Try to have several wedding dates in mind as you start planning. After you've verified your officiant's availability and selected wedding locations, you can select the specific date and time that works best for you.

When it comes to choosing a season for your wedding, the sky's the limit. While summer and early fall months are wedding favorites, you can cre-

ate a lovely setting for your nuptials any time of the year. As you select a time frame for your wedding, consider the length of your engagement. Would you prefer a lengthy engagement period with time to complete other goals, or do you want to get married as soon as possible? Also, consider the schedules of your family members and guests. Are certain months more or less convenient for them?

Once you settle on a month for your wedding, you should think about a day of the week. Most weddings are held on weekends, taking advantage of the customary days off work. However, weekday weddings may also be desirable, particularly if your friends and family live nearby. Weekday weddings leave the weekend free for both you and your guests, and they usually result in lower prices and increased availability of wedding vendors.

With the date set, you're ready to pick the time. Generally, the later a wedding is held, the more formal it tends to be; but a tasteful and elegant wedding can be achieved at any time of day. Consider your budget as you set the time. If your wedding takes place around lunch or dinnertime, your guests will expect a full meal at the reception. A morning or midafternoon wedding, on the other hand, could be followed by brunch, hors

PLANNING CHECKLIST

As Soon as Possible

- ☐ Choose date and time for wedding ceremony and reception.
- ☐ Reserve locations for wedding ceremony and reception.
- ☐ Contact and reserve wedding officiant.
- ☐ Determine approximate size of your guest list.
- ☐ Discuss and select wedding style and theme.

d'oeuvres, or desserts—lighter food options that cost less. Think about your own personalities as you pick the time too. If you're an early riser who goes to bed early, for example, you may want to avoid an evening wedding that would continue late into the night.

WEDDING TIME

Date: _____

Time: _____

Selecting an Officiant

There won't be a wedding without someone to marry you! So early in your planning process, decide who you'd like to officiate your wedding—perhaps a pastor, family member, or friend. As soon as possible, call your officiant to verify their availability for the date and time of your wedding. Be sure to discuss the officiant's fee and travel needs so that you can budget accordingly. Also, arrange an appointment with your officiant to go over ceremony details before the big day. (See chapter 10 for ceremony planning information.)

WEDDING OFFICIANT

Name: _____

Phone: _____

Appointment date and time: _____

Fee: _____

Travel fees: _____

Date confirmed: _____

How Many Guests?

While there's no need to create an in-depth guest list during the early stages of your plans, you'll need to determine the approximate number of guests you plan to invite. To investigate ceremony and reception locations, you'll need to know how many guests need to be accommodated. And the size of your guest list may also impact the wedding style. Now is the time to decide whether you want an elaborate gala with hundreds of guests or an intimate gathering of close family and friends.

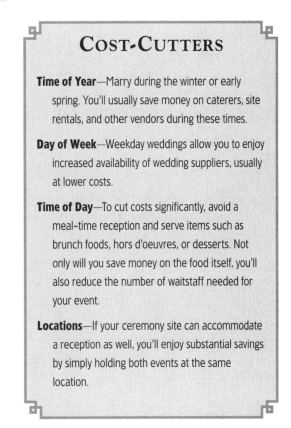

COST-CUTTERS

Time of Year—Marry during the winter or early spring. You'll usually save money on caterers, site rentals, and other vendors during these times.

Day of Week—Weekday weddings allow you to enjoy increased availability of wedding suppliers, usually at lower costs.

Time of Day—To cut costs significantly, avoid a meal-time reception and serve items such as brunch foods, hors d'oeuvres, or desserts. Not only will you save money on the food itself, you'll also reduce the number of waitstaff needed for your event.

Locations—If your ceremony site can accommodate a reception as well, you'll enjoy substantial savings by simply holding both events at the same location.

Guests

Approximate number of groom's parents' guests: _____

Approximate number of bride's parents' guests: _____

Approximate number of bride and groom's guests: _____

Total approximate size of guest list: _____

Choosing a Location

Ceremony

Whether you're planning to marry in a large cathedral, a quaint chapel, or a quiet garden, you'll want to reserve the location for your wedding day. If possible, try to reserve two or three dates while you coordinate your final decision with the availability of the wedding officiant and reception hall. Be sure to ask questions and take careful notes as you investigate ceremony locations.

What is the rental fee? _____

Do they provide any ceremony decorations? _____

Will you have the site for the whole day, or will you be required to leave by a specific time? _____

Are janitorial expenses included in the rental fee? _____

How Do I Tell People They're Not Invited?

Whether you've decided on an extravagant wedding with hundreds of guests or an intimate gathering of close family, your guest list will have its limits. Inevitably, there are some people you can't invite, leaving you with this dilemma: how do I explain my decision to the people who aren't invited?

When you're talking to an uninvited friend or acquaintance, be honest. Simply explain your desire to include the closest family and friends first and express your regrets that you didn't have room to invite her. You may feel awkward, but your honesty will go a long way toward minimizing hurt feelings.

If it's appropriate, consider a post-wedding party for co-workers, family, or friends who weren't invited to the wedding. That way, you can have the quiet ceremony and reception you desire, but you can still celebrate with those who want to share in your special day.

Can this location accommodate the size of your guest list? _____

Reception

In some areas, reception sites can be booked more than a year in advance. So before you finalize the wedding date, check site availability. Bear in mind that the style of your wedding should carry over to the reception style as well. And since your reception will account for a large part of your time and budget, you'll want to consider both cost and convenience. For example, some reception halls and hotels will require that you use their in-house caterer. This service may be more costly than outside providers, but the convenience may be worth the added cost.

When you reserve a location, allow approximately three to four hours for your reception. Avoid sites that would be too spacious or too cramped for the size of your guest list. And if you have many out-of-town guests, consider a hotel reception that would offer them convenience and discounted rooms. Be sure to ask questions and take careful notes as you call various reception sites.

What is the rental fee? _____

Do they provide any decorations? _____

What time can you set up in the reception hall? What time do you need to leave? __ _____

Are janitorial expenses included in the rental fee? _____

Can this location comfortably accommodate the size of your guest list? _____

What reception packages are available? ___ _____ _____ _____ _____

Is an in-house caterer available? Are you required to use this service? _____ _____

Outdoor Locations

If you'd like to hold your ceremony and/or reception outside, you'll need to make some special accommodations. Check out the expected weather conditions for your wedding date. While an outdoor wedding can be beautiful and memorable, it's not a good option if you're planning to get married during cold or rainy months. Regardless of the expected weather conditions, you should create a backup plan in case of inclement weather. Rent a tent or reserve an alternative indoor location for your festivities.

In most outdoor locations, you'll also need to rent and assemble extra items such as dance floors, portable restrooms, tables, chairs, and lighting. Check with the site coordinator to ensure that your seating is safely distanced from sprinklers and power lines. Transforming an outdoor space into a dreamy wedding can be costly and stressful; budget your time and money accordingly.

CEREMONY LOCATION

Name: _____

Phone: _____

Fee: _____

Notes: _____ _____ _____ _____

Date confirmed: _____

Reception Location

Name: _____

Phone: _____

Fee: _____

Notes: _____

_____

_____

Date confirmed: _____

Wedding Style

Before you make final decisions on location, date, and guests, you and your fiancé need to decide what wedding style you prefer: formal, semiformal, or informal. Ideally, the style of your ceremony is carried over into the reception. The following lists, which provide the basic characteristics of each style, will help you determine your preferred style.

Formal Weddings

The ceremony usually takes place in a church, synagogue, large home, or garden.

The reception generally includes a seated, multicourse meal and music provided by a band or orchestra.

The bride wears a long gown with a chapel-length or cathedral-length train and veil.

The bridesmaids wear floor-length gowns made of formal fabrics.

The groom and his attendants wear formal attire.

LOCATIONS GALORE

Looking for a creative place to celebrate your special day? As you search for wedding locations, consider the following options:

Historic estate

Museum or art gallery

Park

Garden

College/university chapel

Boat/yacht

Ballroom

Barn

Rooftop

Vineyard

Country inn

Wedding attendants include five to ten bridesmaids, five to ten ushers, maid or matron of honor, best man, ring bearer, and flower girl.

Formal weddings usually include two hundred or more guests.

Invitations are engraved.

Semiformal Weddings

The ceremony usually takes place in a church, synagogue, home, garden, chapel, or hotel.

The reception generally includes a buffet and music provided by a small band or DJ.

The bride wears a long gown with short train and veil.

Bridesmaids wear long or tea-length gowns.

The groom and his attendants wear formal suits or tuxedos.

Wedding attendants include two to seven bridesmaids, two to seven ushers, a maid/matron of honor, and a best man.

Semiformal weddings usually have seventy-five to two hundred guests.

Invitations are engraved or thermographed (printed with slightly raised lettering).

Informal Weddings

The ceremony takes place at a chapel, garden, home, or other special location.

The reception takes place in a home or restaurant and includes a light meal or refreshments and music played through sound system or provided by single musician.

The bride wears a white or pastel gown, dress, or suit.

Bridesmaids wear gowns, dresses, or suits to complement the bride's attire.

The groom and his attendants wear suits.

Wedding attendants include a best man, a maid/matron of honor, and one or two additional bridesmaids and ushers.

Informal weddings usually have fewer than seventy-five guests.

Invitations are made verbally or written by hand.

FINDING YOUR STYLE

With so many options for wedding styles, locations, and themes, how can you choose the combination that's right for you? To get you started, circle four words from the list below that seem to best describe you and your fiancé. Then ask your fiancé to do the same. Ideally, the words you choose should also describe your wedding.

Traditional	Musical
Romantic	Spontaneous
Reserved	Sentimental
Creative	Laid back
Fun	Dramatic
Friendly	Thoughtful
Casual	Energetic
Elegant	Classic
Active	Clever
Simple	Whimsical
Refined	Extravagant
Fashionable	Artistic
Old-fashioned	Emotional
Eclectic	Formal
Quiet	Smart

Wedding Theme

Many of today's couples choose to design their wedding around a specific theme. While theme weddings can be both elegant and beautiful, a theme should never detract from the sacred nature of the ceremony—an event that unites you in marriage before God, family, and friends. Some whimsical or lighthearted themes may be better reserved for the reception only.

The following list provides a few examples of wedding themes.

Colors—Choose a favorite color as a subtle wedding theme. Dresses, floral arrangements, wedding stationery, and decorations can incorporate varying shades and hues of the theme color.

Destination—If you plan to marry at a dream destination—whether it is Europe, the Caribbean, or your old hometown—you may want to incorporate elements of the local culture as a wedding theme.

Hobbies/Special Interests—Do you love sports? Was your first date a visit to the art gallery? Your hobbies and interests can be used as a delightful wedding theme, particularly at the reception. The couple who loves golf, for example, may hold their reception at a local golf club and pass out golf balls as wedding favors.

Holidays—Weddings held on or around holidays, such as Christmas, Valentine's Day, or Thanksgiving, could incorporate holiday decorations and traditions.

Bible Passages—Many Bible passages paint pictures that provide lovely theme ideas. "A cord of three strands is not quickly broken" (Eccles. 4:12), for example, may be printed on your invitations and programs, read during your ceremony, and incor-

MILITARY WEDDINGS

Requirements—If you or your fiancé serves in the armed forces, you have the option of planning a military wedding. Requirements vary based on your branch and rank of service, so it's wise to discuss wedding details with your protocol officer.

Attire—Generally, the groom and groomsmen wear their uniforms, while nonmilitary groomsmen wear matching suits or tuxedos. Boutonnieres are not given to men in uniform; medals are worn instead. Military brides and bridesmaids may wear uniforms, although most prefer to wear gowns. Parents and guests are also invited to wear uniforms, and your invitations should note that "mess dress uniform is invited" (for formal weddings) or "class A/service dress uniform is invited" (for semiformal weddings).

Military Chapel—Though you are not required to do so, you may marry at a military chapel. If you choose this option, be sure to reserve the space several months in advance. Ask if they provide regulation decorations or if you need to provide your own.

Arch of Sabers—The arch of sabers, under which the bride and groom usually pass through as they leave the building, is perhaps the most well-known feature of the military wedding. Traditionally, swords are not unsheathed inside a religious sanctuary, though some couples today create the arch of sabers inside the church as they exit the sanctuary. Six to eight groomsmen and/or guests create the arch; only commissioned officers can participate.

Reception—Military elements can be incorporated at the reception. The band might include military music on its play list, flags may be displayed, or you might try cutting the cake using the groom's sword.

porated into your decorations by weaving decorative cording throughout your floral arrangements.

Culture—Some couples may wish to incorporate traditions, symbols, and colors from their ethnic background into a wedding theme.

Bride of Discipline

Physical exercise has some value, but spiritual exercise is much more important, for it promises a reward in both this life and the next.—1 Timothy 4:8 NLT

No discipline seems pleasant at the time, but painful. Later on, however, it produces a harvest of righteousness and peace for those who have been trained by it.—Hebrews 12:11

For God did not give us a spirit of timidity, but a spirit of power, of love and of self-discipline.—2 Timothy 1:7

Open to the Wind

Oh no, I thought as I started reading. *Here we go again. Another book that's going to make me feel rotten about my spiritual life.* I'd picked up a book about spiritual discipline after deciding it was time for me to get serious about my devotional life.

Hoping for a book with practical advice about developing discipline, I ended up with an instruction manual for becoming Mother Teresa. At least that's how I felt as I read it. Fasting, serving, prayer, solitude, evangelism—the list went on and on. And it made me feel like a spiritual midget. I was having a hard time with simple devotions. Now I was supposed to add all those other things too?

Needless to say, I never finished the book. And maybe you've grown discouraged with the spiritual disciplines too. It seems like the spiritual giants have set the bar a little too high, doesn't it? So maybe it's time to rethink the meaning of "spiritual disciplines."

Often, the disciplines feel like a checklist for godliness—if you just work hard enough and practice them all, then you'll earn the gold star labeled "perfect Christian." But where are all those gold stars? I don't know a single person who practices *every* spiritual discipline. Do you? And isn't it possible to practice these disciplines and still lack a real love for God?

No, a checklist approach to the disciplines doesn't work. Instead, I think we should look at spiritual disciplines as we do the equipment at the fitness center: we know our weak areas, and we choose our exercises accordingly. Need stronger muscles? Head to the weight room. Want to build some cardio endurance? Try out the treadmill.

When it comes to practicing the disciplines, we need to take an honest look at ourselves. What things cause us to waver in our faith? What character traits stand in the way of a deeper relationship with God? Once we've defined those weaknesses, we can choose a discipline that intentionally forces us to work on them.

Maybe one woman finds herself negatively influenced by her friends—she may need the discipline of solitude to focus on God's will and distance herself from her friends' persuasion. Maybe someone else struggles with finances—she may especially need the discipline of tithing.

When we think of spiritual disciplines this way, they become much more manageable—and meaningful. Instead of trying to tick off items from an overwhelming list, we use the disciplines that we need the most. And instead of practicing disciplines for their own sake, we practice

with a purpose—to improve our relationship with God.

Of course, disciplines will never be easy. They push against our natural instincts—and that can hurt, bad. At times you may wonder, is it really worth the effort? Does it really make a difference?

When that question confronts me, I just think of my neighbor's wind chime. When a soft breeze blows, I hear its pretty tinkling sound. It's as if God has shaped the wind just so I hear this unique tune. And when the next gust comes, he'll play a whole new song.

God wants to make music in our lives too. But sometimes we're too caught up in ourselves to notice. Our spiritual lives go on like a wind chime stuffed in a box—silent and still. But spiritual disciplines get us out of the box. They push us into a space where we're open to the Wind. It's our way of saying, "God, here I am. I'm trying to become more like you. Please, make music in my life." And when we open ourselves up like that, great things begin to happen. God's Wind blows through our hearts—and we're always better off for it.

So if you find yourself giving up on spiritual disciplines, don't! Without the discipline, you'll miss the opportunity to see God moving in your life. So hang that wind chime up by practicing a spiritual discipline. It may be a "traditional" discipline such as fasting, prayer, or worship. Or maybe it will be something unconventional such as putting your alarm clock in the living room so that you'll get up in time for devotions.

Whatever it is, keep at it. And when you hear those gentle chimes of God's Spirit in your life, you'll know it was worth any effort.

Staying in Shape

I have a popcorn problem. I really love the stuff. In fact, I recently told my husband I could switch to an all-popcorn diet and be perfectly content. But popcorn doesn't do good things to my figure—especially when it's dripping with butter and salt.

Since I can't seem to control my love for popcorn, I figure I should at least try to be disciplined about my exercise program. Usually I can tell how disciplined I've been by the way my clothes fit. During the times when my workouts slip to the bottom of my priority list, my jeans feel a bit too snug. But when I've been really faithful for a while, oh happy day—I can pull on that new dress without feeling like a whale!

Now that you've selected a date for your big day, maybe you've put yourself on a strict exercise program. If you have, you know that it takes a lot of discipline to stay in shape. You usually need to plan those workout times into your schedule way ahead of time. But all that effort will be worth it when you look and feel good while you're walking down that aisle!

Of course, workouts aren't just about the way we look. Exercise keeps us healthy. And without it, we're bound to have heart troubles.

Imagine for a moment that an anxious husband looks across the table at his wife, wondering what's going through her mind. She left him a month ago, just up and walked out of the home one morning without even a word of good-bye. And he'd begged her for weeks to meet with him, to explain what went wrong. "What did I do?" he asks, hoping he can undo the damage.

"It's not what you did," his wife explains. "It's what you didn't do. For three years, you've been working those crazy hours, hardly ever spending time at home. We stopped talking. We stopped making love. We stopped everything. Did you really think I'd stay in love with a man I hardly knew anymore?"

This imaginary couple demonstrates a not-at-all-imaginary love lesson: without regular exercise, love can get out of shape. And without the discipline of regular "love workouts," heart problems are bound to develop.

Of course, many engaged couples are so madly in love that they don't believe their love could ever fade. If that's where you are, enjoy the moment. But be prepared—life's pressures will eventually try to crowd out your time together. The commitments of work and family take a lot of your energy, not to mention all the other activities you're involved in. And if you don't make a commitment to "exercising" your love now, it's going to drop to the bottom of your schedule.

This idea may seem to dash your dreams of happily ever after. After all, it's not very romantic to talk about *working* on love. And it's depressing to think that most couples eventually lose the stars in their eyes. But I actually think love grows *more* romantic when we discipline ourselves to see it through the pressures of everyday life. Working on your love shows that you care enough to protect it. And it develops into the kind of love that keeps a couple together for fifty or more years.

So start now, and commit yourself to keeping your love in shape. When life gets hectic and crazy, you'll need discipline to stick to your love workouts—those special times that you devote only to each other. As you plan for your wedding, you may find that you have less time for your fiancé already. So pick a date and a time—not just for your wedding but also for some regular dates when you leave wedding stresses behind and just focus on your guy.

Think of it this way. Each of your dates has given you an opportunity to exercise your love. And they've gotten your love in such good shape that you want to get married. Now you want to stay in shape for a lifetime. So don't stop dating—not now or even after you're married. Keep going to movies together, hiking mountains together, or whatever it is that you love to share with each other. It'll take discipline, lots of it, because there will be countless "important" things that come up and try to disrupt your time.

But someday, when you're seventy-five and still holding hands, you'll be glad you made the effort to keep your love in shape.

LOVE STORY FROM GOD

They had been working long days. Stone by stone, they'd slowly rebuilt the Jerusalem wall that had been torn down years ago. Back then, the Jewish people had been dragged off into Babylonian captivity. But now the Persians were in charge of the area. And they'd allowed some Jews to return to their land and rebuild Jerusalem's walls.

The Jewish workers had a great leader in Nehemiah. He'd led the charge to rebuild the wall from the beginning, and his administrative gifts were invaluable to their construction efforts. But they also had their enemies. Some of their neighbors ridiculed their efforts. And when their sharp words didn't discourage the Jews from building, they threatened to physically attack.

But Nehemiah wouldn't back down, and neither would the faithful Jews who worked under his charge. Nehemiah told them, "Don't be afraid of them. Remember the Lord" (Neh. 4:14). He posted extra guards and gave every man a weapon. In fact, many of the workers could use only one hand to work: "Those who carried materials did their work with one hand and held a weapon in the other" (Neh. 4:17).

It had been a difficult way to build a wall. But they'd made it. Through prayer and constant vigilance, they'd kept the enemies away. And once their haughty neighbors realized that God had been the one behind the wall building, they backed down in a hurry. Now it was time to celebrate! The wall was finally done.

Read the whole wall-building story in the book of Nehemiah. And consider the parallels to your own life. Nehemiah and his men had to hold a sword in one hand while they built Jerusalem's walls with the other, all because of some enemies who wouldn't leave them alone. God's brides have a formidable enemy in Satan, and Satan will use a lot of different tactics to distract us from being disciplined. He'll ridicule us when we slip up. He'll try to fill our minds with worry. And he loves to use wedding plans against us, turning them into a distraction from our spiritual Groom.

Don't let Satan get away with it. Your quiet time with God is too valuable to postpone until after the wedding. So take up your sword—ask God to keep you focused and ask a friend to hold you accountable to your spiritual goals.

5

· · · · · · · · · · · · · · · · · · ·

THE PEOPLE

reating a guest list and choosing attendants: many brides dread these difficult decisions. After all, there are real people—and real feelings—involved. With careful planning, though, you'll make these decisions with wisdom and finesse. And after thoughtfully considering your options, you'll be able to tactfully explain your choices to others.

But if guest lists and attendant selections are difficult, working with all those people throughout the wedding plans can be nearly impossible. Everyone seems to have an opinion. Few seem to understand your own ideas. Even your dearest friends and family members sometimes step on your toes. Fortunately, there's a way to survive these clashes and conflicts. With patience and selflessness guiding your actions, you can handle all those people with grace.

Bride of Patience

Be still before the LORD and wait patiently for him.
—Psalm 37:7

People with good sense restrain their anger; they earn esteem by overlooking wrongs.—Proverbs 19:11 NLT

Finishing is better than starting. Patience is better than pride. Don't be quick-tempered, for anger is the friend of fools. —Ecclesiastes 7:8–9 NLT

Good Housekeeping

Home maintenance—it's not exactly a strong point for my husband and me. But we're learning, sometimes the hard way.

A few summers ago, we worked hard to fix up our lawn and flower beds. When fall came around, we rushed to rake up leaves, cut down plants, and mulch flower beds before winter came. I was already dreaming of the glorious flowers I'd plant the next spring. But amid all this activity, we made a crucial mistake. We accidentally left our hose and nozzle hooked up, with the water turned on.

I remember learning in grade school that water expands when it freezes. Why I didn't apply this knowledge to my water hose is anyone's guess. But the water did expand when it froze, causing the hose to burst sometime during the winter. When the spring thaw finally came, all that melting water started gushing out of the hose, down through the ground, and right into our basement.

What a mess it was! We groaned often as we dumped out water and started fixing the damage. Leaving the hose on was a little mistake—but it led to a big home maintenance problem.

It's easy to make maintenance mistakes in our relationships too. Life throws lots of different people in our pathway, and it's hard to put up with their faults and quirks at times. Sometimes we make little mistakes—and we end up with a big relationship mess.

Even with close friends and family, it's hard to show patience, especially when there's a wedding to plan. Maybe an attendant cancels her dress fitting because she's "busy." And your mom bought hideous decorations for the reception. And your fiancé forgot to make the hotel reservations you asked him about weeks ago. Each little frustration builds on the other, and your patience for people grows paper thin.

With that kind of stress, mistakes happen. You may get short-tempered, saying things you don't really mean and exploding over issues that aren't worth it. And your mouth becomes just like my hose—it's supposed to offer refreshing water, but instead it bursts out and causes a lot of damage.

So how do you avoid impatient mistakes? How can you put up with others' faults and opinions? "Be patient, bearing with one another in love" (Eph. 4:2). This simple verse reminds us that patience and love are linked. To "bear with" each other—even when we're getting on each other's nerves—requires love. And a patient person learns to look at others through the eyes of love—the eyes of God himself.

In Ephesians, we also see a glimpse of people from God's perspective: "You are . . . members of God's household, built on the foundation of the apostles and prophets, with Christ Jesus himself as the chief cornerstone. In him the whole building is joined together. . . . And in him you too are being built together to become a dwelling in which God lives by his Spirit" (2:19–22).

That's a powerful image! Each one of us fits a unique and necessary niche in God's house. And instead of viewing our differences as a frustration, he sees them as an asset. After all, the house wouldn't be much if it was all nails and no lumber, bricks, or doors. And despite all our differences, we still have one thing in common—Jesus, the cornerstone who holds it all together.

Problem is, impatience causes poor home maintenance. Our busy schedules leave us with no patience to care for the people God has placed in our path. So we forget to "fix up" by encouraging our friends. We don't "add on" by sharing the truth with the hurting people around us. And sometimes we even "do damage," throwing insults at each other because we aren't patient enough to sit down and work through a problem. And as our heavenly Groom watches all this, it breaks his heart. This isn't the house of his dreams.

Thankfully, though, it's never too late to fix up God's house. You can start today, showing patience to those around you, no matter how busy wedding plans may be. And as you see people through God's eyes—looking for their special niche in the house—you may just find yourself with more patience than you've ever had before.

And who knows? With a little more patience, we could maintain that dream house after all.

The Waiting Game

I remember those days before Christmas. Unlike the mischievous neighbor boys, I never dared to unwrap and peek at my presents before the big day, so I had no idea what was inside all those pretty wrapped boxes. Would I get that new toy I wanted? Would I unwrap the dollhouse I'd been nagging my parents about? As Christmas drew closer, I spent the nights squirming with anticipation, struggling to fall asleep.

Waiting doesn't get any easier as we grow older, does it? The things we wait for may change, but the anticipation doesn't. And sometimes the stress of wondering and worrying about the future can still give us sleepless nights. You lose a job, or a family member is diagnosed with cancer—so you ask God for help, and then you're left to wait.

As an engaged woman, you're also in the waiting game. You've already promised love and loyalty to your fiancé, but it hasn't been made official yet. You're not single anymore, but you're not married either. You're in between, waiting. And even though there's joy in this waiting, anticipation and worry still crop up. Will the ceremony go all right? What will married life be like? What challenges will the future bring?

Waiting is tough. It's the place where patience gets put to the test.

Jill learned the tough side of waiting. Her wedding got postponed when Paul, her fiancé, was deployed with his army unit just a month before the big day. He had a year of service left to complete, and they'd known deployment was a possibility, so they'd planned a short four-month engagement. Not wanting to push their already-rushed wedding plans even further, they agreed to wait until his return. So just when she'd thought the waiting was almost over, Jill suddenly found that a whole new waiting period had begun.

Paul's deployment lasted for nearly a year because of the uneasy circumstances in the Middle East. Jill was proud of her fiancé's service, but she couldn't help but question God's timing. "Why did world events have to heat up now,

just when we were supposed to be starting our new life together?"

As the months dragged on, Jill and Paul wrote dozens of letters to each other. Both of them wrote freely, often sharing thoughts and feelings they would've had difficulty voicing in person. In fact, their letters even caused some areas of disagreement about their future to surface—issues they hadn't even considered during the initial whirlwind engagement. As they "discussed" each other's feelings through letters, they were able to reach compromises without ever getting in a fight. And by the time Paul returned home, they'd gained a new appreciation for each other—and a deeper love that had been tested by time and distance.

So even in the waiting, God was still working, building a maturity and strength that Jill and Paul hadn't seen in their relationship before. And eventually, Jill and Paul got what they were waiting for: sixteen months after their original wedding date, they celebrated their wedding day with family and friends. The waiting was finally over. And they'd grown into a remarkable couple along the way.

Patience—that quiet trusting of God's timing—didn't come easily for Jill. And it doesn't come easily for most of us either. No matter what we wait for, whether it's a house, a job, a friend, or a miracle, it's easy to get frustrated with God's timing. He doesn't always answer our prayers with the speed we've come to expect in our fast-paced world. He often asks us to wait.

But we don't always listen to his request. Sometimes impatience surges through our veins, and we choose anxiety over trust. Instead of looking for God's handiwork in our hearts, we give up on him and grasp for dreams on our own. And in the end, we're more worried and frustrated than when we started.

But there's another way to wait. Solomon described a godly wife by saying, "She can laugh at the days to come" (Prov. 31:25). And when it comes to waiting, that's what we need to learn. God wants us to relax, even laugh, while we wait for the days ahead. Because no matter what may come—whether God gives us what we want or not—he'll always give us what we need.

Truth is, God does some of his best work while we wait. Somewhere in the middle of the prayers and the anticipation, God starts working on your heart. And you change. You gain new appreciation for some things. You start to worry less and trust more. You learn to let go and give it all to God.

And in the end, you discover this gem of truth about patient waiting: the kind of bride you become while you wait—that's just as important as the thing you're waiting for.

LOVE STORY FROM GOD

Hannah wiped tears from her eyes, trying to focus on her work as she drew water from the well. It was always tough when Peninnah came along—Peninnah with her biting comments and her brood of sons and daughters. It reminded Hannah about the thing she longed for most: a child of her own.

But it hadn't been part of God's plan, at least not yet. She had a wonderful husband who loved her and treated her well. And for that she was thankful. But she still felt sad. Month after month, no baby was conceived, and her heart broke with disappointment. It was hard to wait on God's timing.

So Hannah prayed, turning all her grief over to God. And then she waited. Prayer and waiting—that was her life. Yet God also sent her encouragement. Like the old priest Eli. He'd gotten angry with her a while ago, thinking she was drunk when he saw her praying silently at the temple. But once the misunderstanding was cleared, Eli had listened to her story and offered reassurance. "Go in peace," he'd said, "and may God give you what you've asked for."

Moments like that had always made her feel better, reminding her that God could be trusted—that he was right beside her while she waited. Remembering these things always calmed her heart, even when the tears of sadness flowed.

But today's tears were different. Standing at the well with Peninnah, Hannah was only half-listening to the underhanded jokes about her childlessness. Because Hannah had a secret. For now, just she and God were in on it, but soon the whole village would know. Hannah was finally going to have a baby. And for that, she cried tears of joy.

Read Hannah's story of patience and waiting in 1 Samuel 1:1–2:11.

Planning for Your Guests and Attendants

Making a Guest List

Traditionally, the bride's family and groom's family each select a third of the guests, with the couple's friends comprising the other third. Of course, this formula can vary depending on your particular circumstances. If the bride's family is much larger than the groom's, for example, they'll understandably invite a greater number of guests.

Give each of your families a target number when you ask them to create a list of people they'd like to invite. That way, they can eliminate or add names as needed. Hopefully, by the time they give their lists to you, the need for additional revision will be minimal.

Compromise should be the rule as you and your families negotiate the guest list. Though you may have some disagreements on whom to invite, a spirit of cooperation and mutual respect will ensure that the final list is livable for all.

Cutting Your List with the ABCs

If you find yourself with a longer list of guests than you can accommodate, you'll need to do some

cutting. Use the guest list ABCs to keep the process as simple and pain-free as possible.

First, separate your list into three categories. The A category includes all your must-have guests—immediate family and wedding participants. The B category includes extended family and close friends. And the C category lists additional friends and acquaintances whom you'd like to have present on your big day. You may want to break your C category into smaller groups as well, such as high school friends, neighbors, co-workers, etc.

As you start cutting the guest list, look at your C list first. Try to cut entire groups together, as this can reduce any hurt feelings. If you want to cut some co-workers, for example, it's best to cut them all and avoid the awkwardness of explaining why you invited only a few.

If you've cut your entire C list and still need to eliminate some names, you'll have to turn to your B list. Again, it's good to cut in groups. Perhaps you can cut all the children or invite

PLANNING CHECKLIST

SOON AFTER ENGAGEMENT

☐ Choose bridesmaids and groomsmen.

SIX TO NINE MONTHS BEFORE

☐ Create tentative guest list.

☐ Begin compiling names and addresses for your guest list.

☐ Find accommodations for out-of-town members of the bridal party.

☐ Finalize guest list so that invitations can be ordered.

THREE TO SIX MONTHS BEFORE

☐ Keep attendants informed about necessary fittings and alterations appointments.

ONE TO THREE MONTHS BEFORE

☐ Purchase gifts for attendants.

☐ Plan attendants' party, if you're having one.

TWO WEEKS TO ONE MONTH BEFORE

☐ Send attendants final wedding details, including advance notice of the rehearsal time.

WHAT ABOUT KIDS?

For a variety of reasons, some couples limit their wedding to adult guests. If you'd prefer to have no children at your reception, you'll want to spread the word to family and friends. Don't write "no children" on the invitations. Instead, use phone calls or written notes to explain your preferences.

If children will be present at your reception, you may want to plan some special activities to keep them occupied. Here are a few ideas:

Create goodie bags with candies, small toys, and activity books to be placed at each child's seat.

Give children paper and crayons and ask them to create a wedding card for the bride and groom.

Hang a piñata filled with candy or small toys.

Reserve a room where children can play or watch videos during the reception. Hire a babysitter to monitor the activities in the room.

Create large cut-outs of a bride and groom to hang on one wall. Then cut out various paper dresses, flowers, suits, jewelry, and shoes that can be fastened to the cut-outs with Velcro. Children can have fun creating outfits for the giant paper dolls.

Standby List

Once you've settled on the master guest list, you can place some of the cut names on a standby guest list. Invitations can be mailed to those on the standby list as you receive declines from the master list. Be discreet with your standby list. Make

only uncles and aunts instead of including all your cousins. Usually, it's especially difficult for families to agree on cuts from the B category, so be prepared for respectful negotiations.

sure you plan enough time for responses from your master list—at least five weeks—so that you can easily invite the standby guests.

Staying Organized

With your guest list finalized, you should start organizing the phone numbers and addresses of your guests. Buy an index card holder and a set of index cards. Create a card for each guest/couple, adding their contact information as you find it. After your invitations are sent, you can track responses and food selections on these cards as well. You'll also find them handy when it comes to writing thank-you notes for shower and wedding gifts.

Out-of-Town Guests

If you have out-of-town guests arriving for your wedding, you'll need to make special efforts to give them an enjoyable stay. Guests are expected to pay for their own travel and lodging expenses, but you can make their plans easier by sending them an area map and a list of nearby hotels.

For a large number of out-of-town guests, you may want to reserve a block of rooms at a nearby hotel. You'll probably be required to provide credit card information to reserve the rooms, but most hotels won't charge you, even if some rooms aren't filled. Be sure to ask about discounted room rates for your guests.

While it's not necessary, it's nice to provide some sort of dinner or activity for your out-of-town guests. Ask an in-town friend or relative to host an informal party at their home. Or perhaps you could reserve tickets for guests to attend a theater event or ballgame together the night before your wedding. Whatever you choose, make the activity optional. Some out-of-towners may prefer simply to rest up before the big day.

Sample Guest Index Card

Name: Andrea Smith and Guest

Address: 4763 Sun Valley Drive, North Beach, NC 47831

Phone: (431) 555-3686

Response: Will attend with guest, Nick Granger

Food Selections: 1 Beef, 1 Chicken

Special Notes: Nick has broken leg, using crutches. Seat them at
                        outside table so he won't have to weave between tables.

GUESTS OF THE GUESTS?

Should single guests always be invited to bring a guest?

In most cases, engaged and dating guests should be invited to bring their significant other to your wedding. It's also a nice gesture to invite unattached single guests to bring a date if they wish. However, when space and budget are limited, you may ask a group of friends or co-workers to come by themselves. Always keep your guests' comfort in mind. If a single guest won't know anyone else at your wedding, they should be invited to bring a guest.

What if one of your guests asks to bring a guest?

Sometimes, single guests take matters into their own hands by requesting to bring a date or adding a date's name to their reply card. Though the situation feels awkward, it's not impolite for you to turn down their request. Kindly inform them of your space and budget constrictions and reassure them that you'd still enjoy their presence at the wedding.

Selecting Attendants

Soon after your engagement, you should select attendants and invite them to stand up for you at the wedding. Of course, you'll first need to settle on the time and location so your attendants can verify their availability. But once you've determined who you'd like to stand up for you, have fun asking them. Write a card to explain why they're so special to you. Or perhaps you could buy them a flower and tell them you'd like them to carry a bouquet as an attendant at your wedding. You could even invite all your attendants out to lunch and ask them together. Whatever you choose, be creative and enjoy the special moment of friendship.

Generally, the more formal the wedding, the more attendants you should have, so consider the style of your wedding as you make attendant choices. To determine the number of ushers, couples traditionally choose one usher for every fifty guests. But you may also ask your groomsmen to serve as ushers if you wish. Just remember to leave the best man free so he can stay with the groom during those final moments before the ceremony begins.

Ask friends and family that are closest to you to stand up at your wedding. And if you have difficulty choosing between various people, consider whom you envision remaining close to during the years ahead. While you certainly aren't required to do so, asking the siblings of both bride and groom is a great way to strengthen family relationships.

Taking Care of Your Attendants

Once you've finalized your attendants, you should provide them with the names and contact information of the entire wedding party. If your attendants do not know each other, you might consider an informal pre-wedding party that allows them to be introduced before the big day. Throughout your engagement, it's also nice to keep attendants updated about wedding details that affect them. As you plan, keep in mind the following matters that should be shared with your attendants:

ROLLING OUT THE WELCOME WAGON

Wondering how to make your out-of-town guests feel at home? Here are a few ideas:

Ask some friends or family members to greet guests arriving by plane. For some added fun, have them wear a top hat and/or an old bridal veil, and have them hold a sign welcoming guests to your wedding.

Create welcome baskets for your guests. You could include snacks, candies, cookies, soaps, candles, golf tees, or a good book. You'll want to tuck in a note of thanks, along with directions to the wedding ceremony. Arrange for the hotel to hand out these baskets as your guests arrive.

Provide out-of-town guests with a guidebook or brochures about local attractions. If you live in a large city, include maps and information about the public transportation system.

Give out-of-town guests a small gift package with a few items that are unique to the city where you'll be getting married.

A list of their responsibilities (can be copied from the following pages)

Information about wedding day, including arrival time, dressing location, photography times, and transportation arrangements to the ceremony and reception

Out-of-town attendants will require special attention. Try to arrange fittings and parties to coincide with dates when they will already be in town. If it's not possible for them to visit before the wedding, you may need to arrange for their dress alterations and tux fittings to take place in their own town. While attendants usually pay for their own transportation to the wedding, the bride and groom customarily provide their lodging. Look for attendants' accommodations at least six months in advance, otherwise local hotels may be booked for other events. To keep expenses at bay, you may prefer to ask close friends or relatives to host your attendants.

Attendants' Responsibilities

Traditionally, attendants' responsibilities include these listed on the following pages. However, brides often adjust the traditional responsibilities to suit their personal desires. A few common exceptions include the following:

Some brides select both a maid and matron of honor, who then divide responsibilities.

A male friend/relative may serve as the bride's honor attendant or a female friend/rela-

Information about dresses, tuxes, fittings, and alterations

Arrangements for bridesmaids' hair and makeup

Notice of showers and/or parties they'll be invited to

Rehearsal date and time

tive may serve as the groom's attendant. Responsibilities are adjusted as needed.

Some brides invite a friend to be their personal assistant on the wedding day, giving her some of the responsibilities that would otherwise go to the maid of honor.

Many couples ask ushers to serve as groomsmen.

When attendants are unable to afford clothing and travel expenses, bride and groom may offer to pay for those items.

Maid or Matron of Honor

Is usually a close friend or sister of the bride

Helps the bride with pre-wedding plans as requested

Attends all pre-wedding events, including the rehearsal dinner

Makes alterations appointments and attends fittings, wearing the lingerie and shoes she'll use at the wedding

Pays for her own attire and travel expenses

Organizes bridesmaids' gift to bride

Helps bride dress on wedding day

Directly precedes bride and father during processional (unless a flower girl and ring bearer are participating)

Holds the groom's wedding ring

Arranges veil and train before and throughout ceremony

Holds bridal bouquet during ceremony

Witnesses and signs the marriage certificate

SPECIAL ROLES

Many couples would like to include special friends or relatives in their wedding but simply don't have enough budget or space to create a large wedding party. If you face this problem, consider these special roles they could be asked to fill:

Master and Mistress of Ceremonies (supervise attendants, coordinate details throughout wedding day, serve as hosts at reception)

Gift Table Attendants (supervise gift table, assure that all cards are taped to gifts)

Punch Bowl Attendants (pour coffee, punch, or tea at reception)

Ceremony Participants (readers, soloists, musicians, etc.)

Guest Book Attendant (stands by guest book and invites guests to sign)

Program Attendants (distribute programs to guests)

Reception Assistants (help decorate reception site, travel to site immediately after ceremony to make sure final details are attended to before guests arrive)

Keeps the bride on schedule throughout wedding day

Stands next to the groom in receiving line

Helps bride change into her going-away clothes

May offer toast to new couple at reception

Returns bride's gown to designated place after wedding

Bridesmaids

Are usually at least sixteen years old (younger girls may be included as junior bridesmaids)

Help the bride with pre-wedding errands as requested

Attend all pre-wedding events, including the rehearsal dinner

Make alteration appointments and attends fittings, wearing the lingerie and shoes they'll use at the wedding

Pay for their own attire and travel expenses

Contribute to bridesmaids' gift to bride

Arrive at beauty appointments and dressing location on time

Walk alone or with groomsmen during processional

May stand in the receiving line, if asked

Mingle with guests at reception

Best Man

Is usually the groom's most faithful friend or sibling

Makes appointments for fittings

Picks up his formal attire before the wedding, trying on clothing in store in case any size adjustments are needed

Pays for his own attire and travel expenses

Coordinates groomsmen/ushers' gift to groom

Hosts a bachelor party

Helps groom confirm honeymoon arrangements and may help him pack

Attends rehearsal and rehearsal dinner

Transports the groom to ceremony location; may drive bride and groom to reception

Presents the officiant with his fee

Holds marriage license until time for signing; witnesses and signs license

Enters ceremony with groom before processional or walks with maid of honor during processional

Holds the wedding ring during the ceremony

Proposes the first toast to new couple at reception

May serve as master of ceremonies at reception

Checks that all luggage is in honeymoon car and escorts bride and groom to their car after reception; may drive them to hotel or airport

Returns his and groom's rented apparel after wedding day

Groomsmen

Make their own appointments for fittings

Pick up formal attire before the wedding, trying on clothing in store in case any size adjustments are needed

Pay for their own attire and travel expenses

Attend rehearsal and rehearsal dinner

Contribute to groomsmen/ushers' gift to groom

Arrive at dressing location on time

Enter with bridesmaids during processional or enter with groom before processional

Escort bridesmaids during recessional

May stand in the receiving line, if asked

Mingle with guests at reception

Return rented apparel after wedding

Ushers

Make their own appointments for fittings

Pick up formal attire before the wedding, trying on clothing in store in case any size adjustments are needed

Pay for their own attire and travel expenses

Attend rehearsal and rehearsal dinner

Contribute to groomsmen/ushers' gift to groom

Review special seating arrangements with head usher before ceremony begins. Review order of seating (grandparents, groom's parents, and bride's mother last)

Greet guests as they arrive

Ask guests if they wish to be seated on the bride's side (left) or the groom's side (right)

Offer right arm to female guests, with her escort and/or family following behind

Accompany single men to their seats

When two female guests are seated together, take the right arm of the elder woman, with the younger one following behind

Hand programs to guests as they are seated

Put aisle runner in place before processional begins

After ceremony, check pews and dressing rooms for any belongings left behind

Direct guests to reception

Return rented apparel after wedding

Head Usher

Performs responsibilities of usher

Supervises ushers, assuring their arrival is on time and informing them of special seating arrangements or duties

Ensures that special guests (such as grandparents, mothers, musicians) receive cor-

---

COST-CUTTERS

Need to squeeze a few more pennies out of your budget?

Cut your guest list—Host an informal post-wedding party for all your friends at a much lower cost than inviting them all to the reception.

Select a smaller number of attendants—This will reduce your costs for attendants' gifts and lodging.

Lodge out-of-town attendants with family and friends—This could save you a bundle on lodging costs.

Make your own attendants' gifts instead of buying them—Believe it or not, a lot of items can be handmade without looking "cheap." Candles, soaps, fleece blankets, picture frames—visit your local craft store to buy supplies for these and other great gift ideas.

sages and boutonnieres as they arrive at ceremony

Sees that guests are seated in proper order (grandparents, groom's parents, and bride's mother last)

Escorts the mothers of bride and groom, both before and after ceremony

Ring Bearer and Flower Girl

Are between three and eight years of age

Attend alteration appointments and fittings as arranged by their parents

Clothing and accessories paid for by their family

Attend rehearsal (may attend rehearsal dinner as well, with parents)

Precede bride and her father during processional; follow bride and groom during recessional

Stand with bridal party or may be seated during ceremony

Wedding Attendants List

MAID OF HONOR

Name: _____

Address: _____

_____

Phone: _____

Your gift for her: _____

BRIDESMAID

Name: _____

Address: _____

_____

Phone: _____

Your gift for her: _____

BRIDESMAID

Name: _____

Address: _____

_____

Phone: _____

Your gift for her: _____

BRIDESMAID

Name: _____

Address: _____

_____

Phone: _____

Your gift for her: _____

BRIDESMAID

Name: _____

Address: _____

_____

Phone: _____

Your gift for her: _____

BRIDESMAID

Name: _____

Address: _____

_____

Phone: _____

Your gift for her: _____

FLOWER GIRL

Name: _____

Address: _____

_____

Phone: _____

Your gift for her: _____

BEST MAN

Name: _____

Address: _____

_____

Phone: _____

Your gift for him: _____

USHER/GROOMSMAN

Name: _____

Address: _____

_____

Phone: _____

Your gift for him: _____

USHER/GROOMSMAN

Name: _____

Address: _____

_____

Phone: _____

Your gift for him: _____

USHER/GROOMSMAN

Name: _____

Address: _____

_____

Phone: _____

Your gift for him: _____

USHER/GROOMSMAN

Name: _____

Address: _____

_____

Phone: _____

Your gift for him: _____

USHER/GROOMSMAN

Name: _____

Address: _____

_____

Phone: _____

Your gift for him: _____

RING BEARER

Name: _____

Address: _____

_____

Phone: _____

Your gift for him: _____

Bride of Selflessness

The Star of the Show

"It was horrible." Rachel was describing her experience as a bridesmaid at her cousin's wedding. "I drove six hours, paid for the expensive dress, and footed the bill for my hotel room because she never offered to pay. And then my cousin had the nerve to yell at me when she heard I had gone in with my family to buy her a wedding gift. She thought I should get her a *personal* gift since I was standing up in the wedding!"

Selfish—that's the best word to describe Rachel's cousin. And sadly, it's a word that describes many brides today. And no wonder. The multi-billion-dollar wedding industry revolves almost exclusively around the bride-to-be, encouraging her to splurge on herself. The bridal magazines overflow with articles urging the bride to pamper herself—because, after all, she's the star of the show.

In the middle of such wedding whirlwinds, should we be surprised when some brides start acting like divas?

Hopefully, your wedding plans haven't carried you off to diva land. But if you're like most brides, it's hard to avoid diva syndrome at times. After all, you receive all the presents at bridal showers. You get all the attention when you walk through the bridal shops. And you make the major decisions about your special day. With all that attention, it's tough to strike the balance between enjoying the moment and remembering that the world doesn't revolve around your wedding.

Truth is, the bridal magazines are right about something: brides really are stars. They're in a vital role as they plan the wedding. And they capture all the attention when they walk down the aisle. So when it comes to curbing selfishness, the question isn't whether or not it's right to be the star, but rather, what kind of star should God's brides be?

We've all heard stories about spoiled stars: they've gotten angry about being given the wrong kind of drinking water, they've thrown fits over the color of their hair, and they're always demanding more money. Though we listen to their music and watch their films, we roll our eyes at news of their latest gripe. And we feel sorry for the people who have to live in their self-centered world day after day.

But then we see stars we admire, not just because of their entertaining power but also because of the way they manage to keep a level head about it all.

While I was on vacation in South Carolina, some locals told me that Tom Hanks stayed in their town while working on a film. Apparently one day, as he was riding in his limousine, he saw a church wedding ahead. The young couple was getting ready to leave for the reception, piling into a small sedan. Seeing the sad state of their wedding transportation, Hanks asked his driver to stop at the church. He offered the young couple his congratulations and offered his own limo for their ride.

I don't know if this story is true or not, but the locals I talked with spoke affectionately about this movie star. And after hearing the story, I liked him better myself. It's always heartening to hear about stars who aren't so full of themselves—who remember that the world doesn't revolve around them. They don't complain all the time. Instead, they use their stardom to help other people out.

That's the kind of star God's bride should be—*selfless* rather than full of herself.

When writing to the Corinthians hundreds of years ago, Paul said, "Nobody should seek his own good, but the good of others" (1 Cor. 10:24). And that's the motto of a selfless bride. In a culture that breeds selfishness, she looks out for others first. She considers how her actions affect the people around her. And she's more interested in giving to others than in seeing what she can get from them.

But most important, the selfless bride remembers that she's not the only star in the show—her heavenly Groom actually plays the leading role. She embraces her supporting role with the words of 1 Corinthians: "Whatever you do, do it all for the glory of God" (10:31).

So as you enjoy the pampering, gifts, and attention that fall on the bride, have fun being a star. But take the time to consider the kind of celebrity you'll be. Demanding diva or selfless star—which one will describe you as the big day arrives?

Outside the Comfort Zone

I'd learned some amazing things during my senior-year trip to Israel, but it had been fourteen long days of hiking, sweating, and eating unfamiliar foods. By the time I boarded the plane for my return trip, my head was overloaded, my bags were overstuffed, and my body felt overtired. Throughout the twelve-hour flight back home, I dreamed of my quiet bedroom and the smell of my mom's roast beef dinner. I was ready for the comforts of home.

We all long for comfort, don't we? After difficult days, we love to sink into a bathtub and listen to quiet music. After a grueling task, we look forward to the soda we'll grab from the fridge. And at the end of an adventurous vacation, we can't wait to crawl into our own bed. Something deep within our hearts always searches for a place to rest.

Thoughtful brides recognize this need for comfort. They offer updates and information to put their attendants at ease. And they organize everything from welcome baskets to dinner parties to make their guests comfortable. When it comes to their wedding day, every bride hopes that her guests will feel right at home.

God wants us to feel at home too. And that's why he's always there to offer comfort when we need it. When a friend offers a hug during tragedy—those are God's arms giving comfort. Or when a card comes in the mail, offering encouragement during a difficult day—those are the comforting words of God. He whispers sweet comforts through soft breezes and quietly assures us with passages from his Word. We may not always see these comforts, but they're there just the same. Behind the scenes, God is always moving to provide for our needs.

BIBLE BRIDE

Priscilla always had her hands full. She and her husband, Aquila, made tents together, a job that occupied much of their time. And when they weren't making tents, they were busy with the church, doing whatever they could to minister to the Christians in Rome.

They'd been in Rome for a while now, and the local church met in their home. It meant lots of time preparing for the meetings and cleaning up after everyone went home, but Priscilla didn't mind. She loved helping others, and she didn't stop her ministry, even when it meant danger for herself.

And Priscilla understood danger. Years ago, her family's faith had put them on the emperor's blacklist and got them expelled from Rome. Moving on to Corinth, they eventually ran into the apostle Paul. Priscilla and Aquila opened their home to him, despite the risks. And he later wrote about their sacrifice, saying, "Greet Priscilla and Aquila, my fellow workers in Christ Jesus. They risked their lives for me" (Rom. 16:3). They'd gone on to minister in Ephesus for a time before finally returning to Rome and hosting a house church there.

It had been an interesting journey for Priscilla, often pushing her beyond the comfortable and familiar. At times, she'd been tempted to give up—to stay somewhere safe. But then she'd remember the salvation that God had given her. And that was a gift she just couldn't keep to herself, no matter what the sacrifice.

To read more about this selfless bride, check out her story in Acts 18 and see how she was described in Romans 16:3–5; 1 Corinthians 16:19; and 2 Timothy 4:19.

But this comfort shouldn't just be soaked up like a sponge. God offers us the hopes and comfort of salvation "so that we can comfort those in any trouble with the comfort we ourselves have received from God" (2 Cor. 1:4). God fills us up with blessing so that we can pour it out on others.

The devil has other ideas, though. Satan constantly tempts us to hoard God's blessings. He wants us to get *too* comfortable, to ignore God's call when we're asked to help a neighbor in need.

There was once a wealthy young woman who lived alone because her parents had died. She dabbled with the idea of taking in some orphans, using her wealth to send them to good schools and give them nice clothes. But she always squashed the idea in the end, fearing that some youthful orphan might rob her of her jewels and run away. Besides, she figured that children would be too disruptive to her elegant way of life. And so she lived comfortably—but she also lived with the nagging thought that she was hoarding all her comforts to herself.

To some extent, that young woman lives inside each of us. Don't we all fear what might happen if we reach out to someone else? Don't we all worry that our safe, comfortable lifestyles may be disrupted when we respond to God's call? After all, it's one thing to make a wedding guest feel comfortable—but it's another thing to walk over to that lonely stranger's house and offer some comfort. Or to share our faith with a friend. Or to volunteer with the local mission.

These things could make us uncomfortable. And like the wealthy young woman, sometimes we'd just as soon hoard our comforts to ourselves. But when we try to stay safe and comfortable, we end up missing out on one of the best comforts of all—knowing that we've given help and hope to someone in need.

So take a few moments today to consider someone who needs a helping hand. And then ask God to show you a plan. It may be risky. And it may take you out of your comfort zone. But if you don't show people God's comfort, who will? There's a world of spiritual orphans out there. Let's start making the welcome baskets.

6

. . . .

THE FLOWERS

Bouquets of roses, sprays of larkspur, vases bursting with hydrangeas—nothing says romance quite like flowers. Translating your floral fantasy into reality can be a bit of a challenge, though. It's not always easy to find a florist, choose flowers, and work out all the details. But planning ahead can help. Armed with the right questions and information, you'll be ready to create the floral design of your dreams.

Whether you prefer simple white tulips or a profusion of colorful lilies, there are two special flowers that should be included in every bride's bouquet. They're the blossoms of joy and peace—and if you'll take time to develop these special traits during your engagement, they'll keep blooming long after the wedding day passes.

Bride of Joy

Perfume and incense bring joy to the heart.—Proverbs 27:9

Shout for joy to the LORD, all the earth.—Psalm 100:1

Always be full of joy in the Lord. I say it again—rejoice!
—Philippians 4:4 NLT

Scents of Heaven

What does God smell like?

A silly question, maybe. But indulge me for a moment and imagine what it feels like to inhale God's fragrance. For me, he would smell like spring lilacs, sweet and full. Maybe you imagine God's scent as the delicate scent of a rose or the vibrant aroma of fresh-cut lilies. Breathing in the joy and grace that God has given us—it's a beautiful fragrance.

But some people don't share our enthusiasm.

Take Andrea, for example. She's getting married. She's pregnant. And she's sick of the disdainful glances she receives every time she walks into her church. Andrea made an embar-

rassing but heartfelt apology in front of the whole church, something church leaders pushed her to do. And instead of forgiveness and understanding from the congregation, she's received only snide comments and smirks. Now, some people say she shouldn't be allowed to marry in the church. And her pastor just told her he won't marry two people who've been brought together by sin.

To Andrea, God doesn't smell like flowers. In fact, lately he's smelling so bad that she's ready to walk away for good.

Why is it that the beautiful aroma of God so often gets distorted by his followers? He fills his people with such great joy, hoping they'll share it with the world. But instead, they hoard it, practice hypocrisy, and give off a stench that turns people like Andrea away from God.

Hopefully our actions don't smell as bad as those of Andrea's church. In fact, hopefully we can bring joy into the lives of those around us, creating an inviting aroma. It may be giving simple words of encouragement to a friend. Or maybe it's giving a couple hours a month to serve food at the local homeless shelter. In countless little ways, we can bring joy to the people God has placed on our path. And what a wonderful smell that is!

In 2 Corinthians God tells us that "through us [he] spreads everywhere the fragrance of the knowledge of him. For we are to God the aroma of Christ among those who are being saved and those who are perishing" (2:14–15). That's a pretty amazing concept—instead of filtering his joy directly into people's lives, God uses us to give off the "smell" of his love.

So we're left with some thought-provoking questions: What kind of aroma do we create? Do our words and actions bring joy to those around us? Or do we selfishly hoard God's joy until it spoils and creates a stench? As God's representatives to the world, do our lives smell like fragrant flowers? Or do we have hypocrisy and apathy that make God smell like rubbish?

Ephesians 5:1–2 says, "Be imitators of God . . . and live a life of love, just as Christ loved us and gave himself up for us as a fragrant offering and sacrifice to God." What better way to make our Groom look good than by imitating his perfect love? Healing lepers, eating with social outcasts, taking time to play with little kids—Jesus brought joy to people because he loved them, even when it cost him to do so. And when we offer that sacrificial love, we give off God's sweet-smelling joy too.

Remember that line from the animated classic *Bambi?* The little skunk looks up with bright eyes and says to Bambi, "You can call me Flower if you want to." And as God's bride, I do the same thing. I'm not perfect. Sometimes I mess up. Sometimes my life kind of smells like a skunk. But when I make the effort to share God's joy with others, I'm transformed. I start smelling nice. You can call me Flower if you want to.

And you can call yourself a flower too. Offer God's love and joy to the people around you today. Let your life give off scent of heaven—one that attracts people to both you and your Groom. Then, when your big day finally arrives, people may appreciate the soft candlelight and creative floral arrangements. But when you walk down the aisle, they'll admire the sweetest-smelling blossom of all.

Winter Blooms

Winter is rough where I come from. By mid-January, the snow has usually piled up to more than a foot, and the temperatures have plummeted so far that I don't even want to listen to weather reports. But that's not the worst of it. By February and March, the white, fresh snow has become dirty and slushy. Snowfalls still come on occasion, but so does the sun, melting the snow just enough to show bits of ugly brown grass and bare tree branches. It's not a pretty scene.

Thank goodness for crocuses. I remember being startled when I first saw them blooming in my backyard. They were purple and yellow—and completely unexpected on a March day when patches of snow still covered the ground. They made me smile. Spring was finally on the way.

Joy is like that. It blooms even during the winters of life, making other people look twice. And it carries the promise of better days ahead.

In our world, though, people confuse joy with happiness. Happiness feels like the summer garden in full bloom, basking in the warm sun. But happiness can't take the winter winds. Like the summer flowers, it fades away as soon as the weather grows rough.

Problem is, we're living in winter. Our lives take place between the Garden of Eden and the gardens of heaven, where trees blossom year round (Rev. 22:2). We're not in the Garden anymore. And sin brings cold, stormy weather.

Of course, we still have glimpses of summer warmth in our lives. Weddings, proposals, bridal showers—those moments fill us with happiness, and we should cherish them. But happiness alone can't see us through, because life also holds so many "winter" moments. The car breaks down, a co-worker spills coffee on your favorite pants, you have a disagreement with your guy—and suddenly happiness crumbles away in the wintry reality of life. Faced with the inevitable bumps in life's road, happiness often gives way to tears.

So thank goodness for joy—that crocuslike blossom that blooms even during unhappy moments. Unlike happiness, joy sticks around, even on the tough days. It gives us hope for the future, even when things seem to be falling apart. Joy gives us a reason to smile during life between the gardens.

But only God can make joy blossom. He loves to bundle up a bouquet of it for his bride—and it's a blossom you can't find anywhere else. Sure, you can substitute gardens of happiness for a while when

LOVE STORY FROM GOD

He couldn't believe the feeling of joy. For a long time, his life had been nothing but violence, darkness, and pain. And then the Teacher came and changed everything. The moment he saw the pigs running into the lake, he knew he'd been set free. His demons were gone for good.

At first, the man had asked Jesus if he could travel with him. Not wanting to lose an ounce of his newfound joy, he'd wanted to stay right beside the man who'd given him new life. But the Teacher turned him down, urging him to stay and tell his family about what had happened.

It wasn't what he'd expected Jesus to say. And he was puzzled about it for a while. But as he watched his neighbors drive Jesus out of the village, a spark began to burn in his heart. These people didn't battle demons the same way he had. But they were still living in darkness. Turning to their pagan gods, they found scattered moments of happiness but no lasting joy.

Seeing the dullness in their eyes and hearts, the man just couldn't keep his joy to himself. So he started talking about it. All the time. To anyone he could find. He was one lone believer in Jesus. But his faith caught on. The people "were amazed" (Mark 5:20). And when Jesus later came back to the area, one man's joy had spread around—many believers greeted Jesus at the shore.

To read this story of a man who shared his joy, see Mark 5:1–20.

life is going your way. But what can you offer to a friend who's going through a tough time? What can you do when the sun goes behind the clouds and you feel the winter wind again?

God promises to stand by his bride—during sunny days and cold, dark days. And he's asked *you* to be his beloved. You've got a wedding feast in heaven to look forward to! And in the meantime, God is tugging you ever closer to his side. He'll laugh with you in the sunny moments, and when a winter storm blows up, he'll walk through it with you, pulling you close to keep you warm.

Doesn't that reality bring a smile to your face and peace to your heart? That's joy! It'll bloom through both good days and bad. And if you share it with others, it'll help them endure the winter days too.

Philippians 4 tells us to "rejoice in the Lord *always*. I will say it again: Rejoice!" (v. 4, emphasis added). Take that verse with you today, even if it's stormy. Grab your heavenly Groom's hand and spend some time with him. As you do, you'll find his joy blooming in your heart—on summer days, on winter days, always.

Planning Your Flowers

Before You Call the Florist . . .

When it comes to floral plans, it's tempting to head straight to the florist. Though it seems like the logical place to start, visiting the florist will be a waste of time if you haven't taken care of the following details first.

Check the Locations

Before you start picking out flowers, check the decorating guidelines at your ceremony and reception sites. Below are some questions to ask when you talk with site managers.

What are the site's decorating guidelines? Are there any restrictions? _____
_____
_____

Are candles permitted as decorations? What are the local fire codes? _____
_____
_____

Are any floral decorations already present at the ceremony or reception sites? _____
_____
_____
_____

Are centerpieces and/or floral decorations included in the cost of the reception site? If so, can you remove that cost from the contract if you use your own florist or provide your own decorations? _____
_____
_____
_____
_____

Is an aisle runner provided at the ceremony site? _____

What time can floral deliveries be made to the ceremony and reception sites on the day of your wedding? _____
_____

PLANNING CHECKLIST

SOON AFTER ENGAGEMENT

☐ Start gathering ideas for your floral design.

EIGHT TO TWELVE MONTHS BEFORE

☐ Create an itemized wedding flower list.

☐ Contact ceremony and reception site managers and ask about decorating guidelines.

☐ Investigate various florist options; meet with florists for estimates and ideas.

SIX TO EIGHT MONTHS BEFORE

☐ Book the florist.

☐ Finalize floral plans and get final cost breakdown from florist.

☐ Make delivery arrangements with both florist and site managers.

ONE TO THREE MONTHS BEFORE

☐ Make arrangements to borrow or rent items that were not included in your floral package (arches, aisle runner, palms and ferns, etc.).

ONE MONTH BEFORE

☐ Confirm details and delivery times with your florist.

Gather Ideas

Each bride's unique style should be reflected in the flowers that adorn her wedding day. So before you visit the florist, look for ideas that suit your taste. Bridal magazines, books, websites—all are great sources for pictures and information about wedding flowers. When certain colors and arrangements strike your eye, cut out the pictures and keep them in the cover of your wedding planner so you can bring them along to florist appointments.

Make an Itemized Wedding Flower List

As you prepare to visit florists, create an itemized list of flowers and equipment you'd like to have at your wedding.

Traditionally, flowers are used to decorate the ceremony and reception sites, to create bouquets for the bride and her attendants, and to be worn as boutonnieres by the groom and his attendants. Corsages and boutonnieres are also given to the parents, special guests, and other wedding participants. However, for musicians and officiants who are paid for their services, a flower is not required.

Use the following worksheet to create your Wedding Flower Wish List. As you get price estimates from florists, you can add those figures to the list and make adjustments to fit your budget.

Wedding Flower Wish List

Budgeted Items	Type of Flowers	Number Needed	Estimated Cost
Bouquets			
Bride			
Maid/Matron of Honor			
Flower Girl			
Bridesmaids			
Bouquet to Toss			
Corsages			
Bride's Mother			
Groom's Mother			
Grandmothers			
Special Guests/Wedding Participants			
Boutonnieres			
Groom			
Best Man			
Ushers/Groomsmen			
Ring Bearer			
Bride's Father			
Groom's Father			
Grandfathers			
Special Guests/Wedding Participants			
Headpieces			
Bride			
Bridesmaids			
Flower Girl			
Ceremony Flowers			
Main Altar			
Pews			
Entrance			
Guest Book Table			

Budgeted Items	Type of Flowers	Number Needed	Estimated Cost
Candles			
Candle Holders			
Unity Candle			
Memorial Candle/Bouquet			
Aisle Runner			
Other			
Reception Flowers			
Entrance			
Cake Topper/Cake Table			
Buffet Tables			
Head Table			
Place Card Table			
Restroom			
Candles			
Other			
Thank-You Flowers			
For Parents			
For Out-of-Town Guests			
Others			
Miscellaneous			
Ring Bearer Pillow			
Flower Girl Basket			
Ribbon			
Fabric			
Total Cost			

Choosing Flowers

There are literally hundreds of flowers to choose from. Roses, the timeless symbol of love, have been a wedding favorite for centuries. Other common wedding flowers include calla lilies, tulips, daisies, and ranunculus. Of course, each bride should incorporate her own favorites as she selects flowers for her special day. As you shop, consider the two key elements of floral design: flower availability and color.

FRESH IDEAS

Want your wedding to have some special floral flair? Try some of these ideas:

Instead of tossing petals or carrying a bouquet, your flower girl could pass out small flowers to those sitting at the end of each row.

Rather than traditional white ribbon, use colored or decorative ribbon to tie bouquet stems together.

Designate special family members and friends to sit at the end of each row with a flower in their hand. As you walk down the aisle, take the flower from each person to create your bridal bouquet.

Instead of tossing your bouquet to single women, give it to the couple that's been married the longest.

Give your maid/matron of honor a special bouquet that is different from the other bridesmaids'.

Before you toss your bouquet to the single girls, untie the stems so they will separate and "spread the luck."

Flower Availability

With modern technology, most flowers can be grown throughout the year. However, out-of-season flowers must be cultivated in greenhouses, often resulting in weaker blooms and higher prices. For the healthiest and most affordable flowers, select those that will be in season at the time of your wedding. Or choose year-round flowers, which are grown in greenhouses during their off season but are not costly or difficult to grow. Use the following list to determine flower availability during your season.

Spring flowers: apple blossom, cherry blossom, daffodil, dogwood, foxglove, hyacinth, iris, larkspur, lilac, lily of the valley, peony, ranunculus, snapdragon, statice, tulip, violet

Summer flowers: aster, clematis, cosmo, dahlia, daisy, geranium, gerbera daisy, gladiolus, hydrangea, larkspur, stock, sunflower, zinnia

Fall flowers: aster, chrysanthemum, coreopsis, cosmo, dahlia, heather, hydrangea, marigold, phlox, sunflower, zinnia

Winter flowers: poinsettia

Year-round flowers: baby's breath, bachelor button, calla lily, carnation, delphinium, freesia, gardenia, ivy, lily, orchid, rose, stephanotis, sweet pea

Flower Color

Many brides choose flowers of their favorite color or select blooms that complement the shade of their bridesmaids' dresses. To find out what flowers are available in your wedding colors, see the list below.

Purples/blues: aster, bachelor button, delphinium, heather, hydrangea, iris, lavender, lilac, sweet pea, violet

Pinks/mauves: apple blossom, aster, cherry blossom, cosmo, foxglove, hydrangea, orchid, peony, rose, sweet pea

Reds: dahlia, peony, rose, tulip

Whites: apple blossom, baby's breath, cherry blossom, daisy, dogwood, gardenia, orchid, peony, rose, stephanotis

Yellows/oranges: coreopsis, daffodil, dahlia, daisy, marigold, rose, sunflower

Various colors: calla lily, carnation, chrysanthemum, clematis, freesia, gerbera daisy, hyacinth, larkspur, lily, phlox, ranunculus, snapdragon, stock, tulip, zinnia

Wedding Candles

Candles add a soft glow to the wedding and may be used for a variety of purposes.

Decorative candles: used to decorate the altar area and/or aisle

Unity candle: lit by bride and groom during the ceremony to symbolize the joining together of two lives into one

Memorial candles: lit in memory of loved ones who have passed away

Centerpieces: used to decorate tables at the reception

Most florists can provide candles and candle holders for an additional fee, but be sure to ask about this service as you shop around. You may find it more affordable to purchase candles on your own and to borrow or rent candleholders. Rented candleholders may also be preferable if your florist does not have them in the style you like.

At the wedding, ushers or special guests should be designated to light candles before the ceremony begins. This can be done just prior to the seating of the guests or before the ceremony processional.

Finding a Florist

So you've contacted the location managers, created the itemized wedding flower list, and chosen some flowers you like—now how do you

---

COST-CUTTERS

Have attendants carry a single rose or lily rather than a bouquet.

Make your own corsages and boutonnieres.

Use bridesmaids' bouquets to decorate the head table and/or cake table at the reception.

Have ceremony flowers do double duty by transporting them to the reception site.

Use flowers that are in season.

Buy smaller numbers of expensive flowers and fill in bouquets with greens.

Use silk flowers for all or some of your decorations—they will be approximately one third the cost of real flowers.

THE LANGUAGE
OF FLOWERS

Victorians once assigned meaning to flowers, arranging bouquets with special blooms to convey a message. Although the tradition has faded, some brides may select a flower or two with special meaning for their wedding day.

apple blossom—hope

baby's breath—pure heart, constancy

bachelor's button—devotion

calla lily—feminine beauty

carnation—fidelity, deep love

daisy—youth, innocence

iris—affection

jasmine—grace

larkspur—laughter, lightness

lilac—first love

lily—purity

phlox—togetherness

pink rose—grace

red rose—love

white rose—purity

yellow rose—joy, friendship

stephanotis—happiness in marriage

tulip—fame, passion

violet—faithfulness

zinnia—thoughts of absent friends

to contact your ceremony site manager to see if they know which florists have managed your space before.

Once you've created a list of possibilities, call or visit each florist to find out if they are available to service your wedding. As you get a sense for each florist's personality, price range, and style, choose one that fits your budget *and* makes you feel comfortable. Don't settle for a disagreeable florist, or you may find yourself with wedding flowers you abhor. Instead, cut back on the number of flowers you originally planned and go with the florist you like—you may have fewer blooms, but at least they'll be the style and colors you prefer. And remember, when it comes to florists, the smaller company is often better because you'll receive more personal service.

Once you've settled on a florist, make an appointment to discuss all the details *before* you sign the final contract. Don't commit to a signed contract until you receive a cost estimate from the florist, check her references, and confirm that she can provide all the services you desire. Consider the following questions as you make your final florist selection:

Can you see photographs of previous weddings the florist has serviced? Will the florist provide references?

How big is the florist shop? Which specific designers will work on your wedding flowers? How many weddings will they be servicing on your wedding day?

What is the design style of the florist—traditional, trendy, elegant, modern? Does it fit with your style?

Is the florist knowledgeable about which flowers will be in season during your wedding

find a florist to pull it all together? Search the yellow pages for local florists or ask friends and family for recommendations. You may also want and which flowers will last the longest in wedding arrangements?

What wedding packages does the florist provide? What do they include?

Can the florist provide an itemized price breakdown before the contract is signed?

What equipment rentals can the florist provide (aisle runner, candleholders, trellis, archways, ivies, ferns, etc.)? What is the rental fee for those items?

Does the contract give guarantees for flower freshness and health?

How are flowers delivered and set up? Are delivery and setup prices included in the contract?

What is the florist's cancellation policy?

Does the florist preserve bouquets after weddings? If not, can they refer you to someone who does?

MY FLORIST

Name: _____

_____

Phone: _____

Appointment date and time: _____

_____

Meeting the Florist

To help your florist understand your preferences and needs, take the following to your appointments:

Wedding Flower Wish List

CANDLE TIPS

As you calculate the number of candles for your wedding, it's wise to include a second set for all your ceremony candles—that way you can use one set during pictures and the other during the ceremony itself.

If you are using a unity candle, burn or carve out a small hole at the top, large enough for a tea light to be slipped in. This will make it much easier to light the unity candle during the ceremony.

FLORAL AFTERTHOUGHTS

Don't forget to work out flower details that happen after the wedding. With just a little extra effort, you can ensure that your flowers are enjoyed after the big day.

Arrange to have reception centerpieces delivered to a local hospital, women's shelter, or nursing home.

Have thank-you bouquets sent to both sets of parents and any others who gave significant help with wedding plans.

Ask a local church if they'd like to use any of your floral arrangements at their services.

Investigate your options and make arrangements for the preservation of your bouquet.

---

pictures and/or diagrams of the ceremony and reception sites

photographs of your gown and attendants' gowns

color swatches of attendants' gowns, bridal
   gown, and any other fabrics being used at
   your wedding

pictures of flowers and color schemes that you
   like

addresses and times for flower delivery and
   setup—for both ceremony and reception
   sites

Bride of Peace

Let the peace of Christ rule in your hearts, since as members of one body you were called to peace.—Colossians 3:15

And those who are peacemakers will plant seeds of peace and reap a harvest of goodness.—James 3:18 NLT

And the peace of God, which transcends all understanding, will guard your hearts and your minds in Christ Jesus.
—Philippians 4:7

What the Flower Children Missed

Where does peace come from?

That's a loaded question—one that world leaders have been trying to answer for centuries. In the sixties, many people thought they had the solution. They threw out the conventional rules and embraced free love as the answer to the world's troubles. Stringing flowers in their hair, these hippies took pride in their rebellion and told the world to give peace a chance.

For all the glory of their indulgence, though, these flower children never achieved real peace. And today, we still lack a solution for world con-flicts. One glance at current events tells us that peace is still far off. We see terrorism, civil wars, famines, and epidemics across the globe. In major cities, crime and poverty are constant threats. In quiet suburbs, families are torn apart because of adultery, deceit, and divorce. Instead of peace, our "free love" world surges with uncertainty, worry, and stress.

Our personal lives also carry the burdens of an unsettled world. Sometimes it comes in a feeling—a corner of our hearts feels unsettled. Or maybe it's a nagging thought—doubts about marriage or fears that our plans may not work out. In a thousand such ways, we're crying out for peace, wishing we could take a break from the chaos of our world. Wishing we could find the peace that the flower children were searching for.

Sam was just a little boy when he decided to grow a garden. So when his mom wasn't looking, he grabbed some of her flower seeds and started digging holes in the backyard. And then he squinted at the dirt every morning, looking for tiny sprouts to push out of the ground.

The sprouts never came. And after weeks of waiting, he finally asked his mom why his seeds wouldn't grow. With one quick look at his garden plot, his mother pinpointed the problem: Sam's garden soil was dry and sandy. Without any nutrients to feed them, the little seeds never germinated.

So Sam learned an important gardening lesson: you can't get anything from a seed unless it's in the right soil. And his lesson fits for seeds of peace too. It reveals what the flower children missed: you can't grow peace if you're using bad soil.

And a lot of us use bad soil. We look to our money, our relationships, our jobs, hoping those things will help peace grow. Some of us even plant seeds of peace in humanity. We hope that somehow, if we can just be more enlightened, more loving, more *something*, we can find world peace someday.

Problem is, none of these seeds grow. Seeking security in the wrong "soil" doesn't bring any peace at all. I know because I've tried. In moments of forgetfulness I've grabbed the financial statements and tried to find peace in my bank account balance. But then a car repair cropped up, an unexpected pay cut hit—and my finances proved a poor soil for peace.

In the end, there's only one kind of soil that helps peace grow—and that's the soil of faith in God. God is the only sure thing we have in life. Looking for security in anything else will only lead to disappointment and worry. And what good does worry do?

When preaching about worry one day, Jesus essentially said, "Don't fret about life. God's got it under control." To give proof, he just pointed to the beautiful flowers growing nearby. "See how the lilies of the field grow," he said. "If that is how God clothes the grass of the field . . . will he not much more clothe you?" (Matt. 6:28–30).

So there's no need to worry—about clothes or any other issue that crops up as you plan for marriage. Instead, God offers genuine, breathe-a-sigh-of-relief peace: "Peace I leave with you; my peace I give you. I do not give to you as the world gives. Do not let your hearts be troubled and do not be afraid" (John 14:27).

Grab on to that promise today. When you're tempted to look for security in things or in people, keep looking for richer soil. And when worry fills your mind, fill your heart with the soil of God's promises. That's where you'll see the blossoms that the flower children missed—a peace that grows beautiful, green, and true.

Planting the Seeds

There's just something about flowers. The bright colors, the delicate petals, the way each flower dances in the breeze. They're the reason I put on my gardening gloves each spring. And it's amazing to see how those happy creatures start out as such tiny seeds. Before any intricate blossom appears, it's just a simple seed, put into the dirt by my own hand.

But then there are the weeds. I don't know where those seeds come from, but somehow they dive into my flower beds, and soon the ugly weeds poke their heads through the soil. If I wait too long to yank them out, those nasty weeds will take over the yard. One vine in particular seems to creep into my flower beds, twisting its way up my plants and trying to choke them out. And just like my beautiful flowers, all that weedy trouble starts out from a simple seed.

That's true in life too. Little seeds grow big results. And depending on the type of seeds we plant, what grows can be a charming flower or an invasive weed.

Sometimes we plant seeds of peace. These seeds get planted into the soil of life when we offer forgiveness, when we choose to ignore an annoying comment, or when we avoid acting stubborn and superior when we need to confront a friend. "Peacemakers who sow in peace raise a harvest of righteousness" (James 3:18). Those seeds grow into something beautiful—reconciliation in our relationships, healing in our hearts.

Often, though, we aren't holding peace seeds in our hands. During my senior year of college, I lived in a house full of girlfriends. Once, I got so fed up about unwashed dishes in the sink that I made a sign. On it, I printed a harsh message, reminding my housemates that I wasn't their mother and they should clean up after themselves. Looking back, it's laughable that I felt so mad about *dishes* of all things. But at the time, my little sign worked like an ugly seed of strife, causing tempers to flare in the house.

BIBLE BRIDE

She was just a girl, waiting for her wedding day—looking forward to a quiet, uneventful life. But one visit from an angel changed it all, tipping her world off balance. The impossible had happened: Mary, a virgin, was pregnant with the Son of God. Now she had to face the world.

Mary's head whirled as she digested the news. When word got out that she was expecting, people would start talking. Her reputation would be smeared. Her family might throw her out. And Joseph—what would he think about it all? Could he possibly believe in her faithfulness and accept this miracle?

With a mountain of reasons to worry, Mary wasn't much of a candidate for peace or joy. Yet her story bursts with both. Where some would've found only despair, Mary found a reason to rejoice. And instead of panicking over her predicament, Mary exhibited a supernatural peace and even expressed joy about being the mother of God's Son.

Things didn't get easier for her. She had to travel for miles during her last weeks of pregnancy. And when the hours of labor came, she gave birth in a stable, amid the smells and sounds of dirty animals. But even in those uncertain times, Mary had peace—"she treasured up all these things and pondered them in her heart" (Luke 2:19).

To read this bride's story of joy and peace amid challenges, check out Luke 1 and 2.

Maybe you've experienced such moments of weakness too. In frustrating situations, it's so easy to make the snide comment or say the damaging words that lead to an argument. Sometimes we don't even want to stop the fight. A friend of mine once confessed, "Sometimes I *want* to be in a bad mood." It's a confession most of us can identify with. Some days we're just plain feisty—an argument gives us a chance to blow off some steam. And it can feel pretty good to get underneath someone's skin, especially if they've already been under yours.

Problem is, those feisty moments spread some ugly seeds: anger, pride, and disrespect start growing in our relationships. Solomon warned people about this when he wrote Proverbs 30:33: "For as churning milk produces butter, and as twisting the nose produces blood, so stirring up anger produces strife." In other words, when you push someone's buttons, don't be surprised when conflicts pop up. You'll get what you plant.

When we do plant seeds of strife, those weeds have a way of spreading fast. "Starting a quarrel is like breaching a dam; so drop the matter before a dispute breaks out" (Prov. 17:14). Solomon didn't mince words with that proverb. Picking a fight, or even deciding to continue one, will eventually break the dam. So when things are heating up and your blood pressure starts to rise, drop it. Deal with it after you've had some time to cool off. Because if you don't, you'll end up planting some ugly and invasive weeds.

I don't want that weed-infested life. And neither does God. Instead, he wants our relationships to grow strong and beautiful instead of being invaded by petty arguments or angry disputes. Hebrews 12 reminds us, "See to it that no one misses the grace of God and that no bitter root grows up to cause trouble" (v. 15). So if we want peaceful relationships, we need to watch what we plant.

Of course, that's not easy when you're planning a wedding. With so many decisions to make and so many people involved, wedding plans naturally breed arguments. To avoid those "bitter roots," you may need to let an annoying comment pass. Or make an apology. You may even need to drop an issue for a while, even though it seems frustrating and unfair. Hard as it may be, those actions will plant the right seeds—and that means you'll enjoy the beautiful blossoms of peace.

So when the discussions heat up and you see the pressure building against the dam, take a good look at the seeds in your hand. Flowers or weeds. Peace or strife. What you plant is what you'll get.

7

. . . .

THE PHOTOS

*Y*ou've spent weeks getting everything just right for your wedding, so when the day finally arrives, you'll want to remember every detail. For most couples, though, the wedding day passes by in a whirl of emotions, leaving them with muddled memories. That's where wedding photos and videos rise to the occasion. Each image captures a moment in time, recording special memories that you can enjoy long after the big day.

Unlike your wedding photos, however, the virtues of faith and modesty center around things that you can't see. Whether it's having faith in a God who's invisible or modestly covering up so that you're not *too* visible, you sometimes need to focus on the unseen. So somewhere amid your busy prewedding days, carve out a few moments to consider the virtues of faith and modesty. Though they are invisible, these traits are sure to make a difference in what others see when they look at you.

Bride of Faith

I tell you the truth, if you have faith as small as a mustard seed, you can say to this mountain, "Move from here to there" and it will move. Nothing will be impossible for you. —Matthew 17:20

If you do not stand firm in your faith, you will not stand at all. —Isaiah 7:9

Dear brothers and sisters, what's the use of saying you have faith if you don't prove it by your actions?—James 2:14 NLT

Postcards from Heaven

As I kid, I loved family vacations. Each year, we'd pack up our vehicle, filling in every possible space with suitcases, food, and games. Then we'd set off from our Michigan home to explore other parts of the country. Though the destination changed each year, many things stayed the same: there were meals around the camp stove, hikes through a national park, arguments with my siblings in the car—and postcards. We sent lots of them. Nearly every night as we settled into the motel, one of us would pull out a card and write to a friend about our vacation adventures.

When it was my friends' turn to head off on vacation, I turned from postcard sender to postcard receiver. I'd watch the mailbox each day, hoping to see familiar handwriting on a card for me. I especially loved postcards from places I'd never visited. It was exciting to look at the pictures and imagine what my friends were doing there.

When I think about those postcards today, I'm reminded of the biblical definition of faith: "Now faith is being sure of what we hope for and certain of what we do not see" (Heb. 11:1). Doesn't that sound a bit like looking at a postcard? Often, the picture is of a place we've never seen—perhaps it's Hawaii, or Egypt, or Africa. And even though we've never visited those places, we don't doubt their existence. When we see that picture on the card, we feel "certain of what we do not see."

That's what faith is all about—believing in something even though you can't see it yet. With postcards, that's usually not too difficult. But it's a lot harder when it comes to our personal lives. Some women struggle to keep faith in a friend after they've been let down. Others don't have much faith in marriage because they just can't see how it can last. And all of us face situations that make it hard to keep faith in God's plan.

Abraham faced that kind of situation thousands of years ago. God asked him to move to Canaan. Then he promised to give Abraham that land and to turn his family into a great nation that would always live there. Those were big promises—and they were all things that Abraham couldn't see. He was old. He had no kids. He must've been scared to think of starting a whole new life somewhere else. If it were me, I might just ignore the whole thing.

But Abraham had faith. He trusted God to keep his promises. And that's why he followed God's call and moved to Canaan.

Not many people have that kind of faith in God today. When we watch TV or read articles from popular magazines, we find people with a different faith—rooted in the things of this world. Our culture sends "postcards," promising we'll find happiness in money, or power, or youthful-looking skin. But the pictures they send aren't real. And so we end up with the same problem Israel dealt with so long ago. We put our faith in the wrong "images"—useless idols made by our own hands (see Isa. 44:15–18).

As a bride, you face situations that require a more reliable faith, a faith no "thing" can live up to. You're committing your life to someone, not knowing what the future may bring. Maybe you're moving to a new home or a new city, and you're unsure of what it will be like. Maybe God's called you to a job or a volunteer program that you're afraid of. In each of these things, the world will offer false pictures for you to put faith in. As God's brides, we need to put our faith in what's real. We need to trust in God's promises, no matter how impossible they may seem.

And, boy, do we have a lot of promises from God! The Bible bursts with them. "I know the plans I have for you . . . plans to prosper you and not to harm you" (Jer. 29:11). "My grace is sufficient for you, for my power is made perfect in weakness" (2 Cor. 12:9). "I will strengthen you and help you; I will uphold you" (Isa. 41:10). Each of these promises comes like a postcard from heaven. And we're left to ask ourselves this question: do I have faith in those promises—in the picture God is creating for my life?

If you want to find the true answer to that question, just look at your actions. "Faith by itself, if it is not accompanied by action, is dead" (James 2:17). So if you really do have faith in God's promises, it's going to show. You'll do what he asks, even when it's scary. You'll keep working with those people God has placed on your heart, even when it seems impossible. And you'll keep hope in that project, even when you're a long way from seeing the end result.

With that kind of faith, you can survive the adventure of marriage—and the adventure of life. But without it, you'll just live in fear, losing the opportunity to see God's greatest promises become real in your life. So next time you pick up a postcard or a picture of a faraway land, think about God's promises to you. And have faith—because those postcards from heaven are more real than anything the world can offer.

Photo Albums

With old family albums laid out on the table in front of me, I was trying to select childhood photos for a slide show we'd be showing at our wedding reception. It was a trip through family history, starting with my parents' wedding album and then filling in with baby and toddler pictures of my siblings and me. Christmases, piano recitals, basketball games, graduations—as we grew, the pictures captured our family at each stage of life.

Looking again at all those photos, I wondered about my own future as a wife. Would my kids someday page through my wedding album? And what kind of history would my family pictures tell? I felt so much excitement for the future, and yet uncertainty too. Who knew what my future would hold? Yet even with those anxieties, I felt a renewed faith as I looked through my family albums. God had been faithful to my family through the years—he'd be there for my husband and me as well.

Have you ever had that experience? Looking back has a way of giving you fresh faith for today, doesn't it? Sometimes I wish I could carry those old photo albums with me all the time. That way,

when I started having doubts about what God was doing in my life, I could just glance back and remember all the ways he'd seen me through before.

Of course, we can't carry a stack of photo albums in a purse. But as God's brides, we should look back—especially when our faith wavers. It's when we're most uncertain about the present that we gain the greatest benefit from looking back.

Yet sometimes our own photo albums don't seem to cut it. Maybe you're facing struggles and stress that can't compare with anything you dealt with before. Or maybe it's still hard for you to understand some of the things God did in your past. That's OK. God knows that our individual albums sometimes fall short of what we need. And that's why he's given us the Bible—a photo album filled with pictures of God's family history.

In God's family album, we see people like David, Ruth, Elijah, and Jesus. And there are also snapshots of those with less glamorous lives, those like Moses's parents and the people who rebuilt Jerusalem's walls. In each story, we see God at work. And as we remember his faithfulness to them, we start to believe that he can do something beautiful in our lives too.

I think David was one who understood the importance of looking back. David managed to keep faith in God even when he faced some very uncertain circumstances: a king chasing after his life, a sinful mistake with Bathsheba, the rebelliousness of his sons. As we read his psalms, we can see what made his faith so strong in those trying situations: time after time he looked back to God's faithfulness in his life.

"I sought the LORD, and he answered me; he delivered me from all my fears," David wrote in Psalm 34:4. "You turned my wailing into dancing," he reminisced in Psalm 30:11. And as he remembered God's goodness in the past, David renewed his faith for the future. In fact, his faith became so strong that it lived on in future generations.

If you ever struggle to have faith in God's plans, I hope you'll follow David's example in looking back. Check out your "spiritual photo album" and revisit those memories of God's goodness in your life. Look at the memories of others too: listen to fellow believers' testimonies and take some time to read the amazing stories recorded in the Bible. As you see how God has worked things for good in the past, you'll find faith and hope growing for the future.

And that's the kind of faith you'll need as a bride. You're embarking on a new journey—one that's sure to be full of ups and downs, with many surprises along the way. Who knows what pictures will end up in your family album someday? But God will be with you every step of the way. And if you'll keep an unswerving faith in him, you'll develop the best picture you could ever pass on to future generations.

BIBLE BRIDE

Not this, God! The young Hebrew woman groaned. *Not now!*

She'd been feeling tired and unwell for several weeks. As each day passed, the truth became undeniable. It was exactly how she'd felt when she had been pregnant before. But now everything was different. Since the birth of her first child, the Egyptian king had delivered a terrible edict: all male Hebrew babies were to be killed.

As her body swelled, Jochebed hoped. *Dear Lord, please let it be a girl.* Then the labor pains came, and she delivered a baby boy. "He's beautiful," she whispered to her husband with tears in her eyes. "Let's call him Moses." Gazing at the tiny face, she felt God work in her heart. She knew what she had to do.

For three months, Jochebed hid the child from the Egyptians—not an easy task, especially when Moses cried. But even in the danger, she didn't waver from God's plan. "I don't know what God has in store for our little Moses," she would say, "but I know he wants me to keep him hidden, and that's what I'll do."

Then came the day when she had to let Moses go. She took a papyrus basket and coated it with pitch, praying it would be waterproof. And as she set Moses and the basket into the Nile River, the woman's heart pounded. *God, please let the princess see him. You asked me to put him here today, now please give my baby boy a safe home.*

Hours later, the woman's daughter came running into the house. The girl had been instructed to watch Moses's basket from a distance, and now she was back with a huge smile on her face. And Jochebed knew right then that God had honored her faith and answered her prayer.

Read the whole story of Jochebed and her unshakeable faith in Exodus 2:1–10 and Hebrews 11:23.

Planning Your Photography and Videography

Photography

Before you head out to find a photographer, consider the following photography basics.

Location—Do your ceremony and reception sites have any restrictions concerning photography? Talk to the site managers and find out before you make arrangements with a photographer. Also, determine where you want your bridal portrait taken. Some brides have their portrait taken before the wedding day, in a studio or at the location of their final dress fitting. Others prefer to wait until the wedding day, when their portrait can capture their look on the big day.

Style—Traditional wedding pictures have a "studio" style, with carefully posed shots and controlled lighting. But some couples prefer a more candid style that has a photojournalistic or artistic feel. Take some time to consider your personal style. Do you prefer pictures that are traditional, photojournalistic, artistic, or a combination of them all?

Color—While color photographs are still the norm for weddings, black and white film has gained popularity. In fact, today's photographers often shoot in both color and black and white. Color film captures the brilliant hues of your wedding and adds a touch of reality to candid shots. Black and white will give a classic, timeless look that works especially well for portraits. Some studios can even add tints to black and white photos, giving your pictures a vintage feel. If you choose to have black and white photographs, be prepared to add some money to your budget. For best quality, the film must be processed by hand, making it more expensive than machine-processed color film.

Time—Many photographers will charge a flat rate for their services, giving you a set number of hours and then charging overtime for additional hours. Other studios charge an hourly rate. As you shop around, consider the time frame for your wedding. How long will you need photographers at the wedding? Do you want them to stay for the entire reception, or can they catch highlights of just the first hour? You don't want to be surprised by overtime charges after the wedding. But there's also

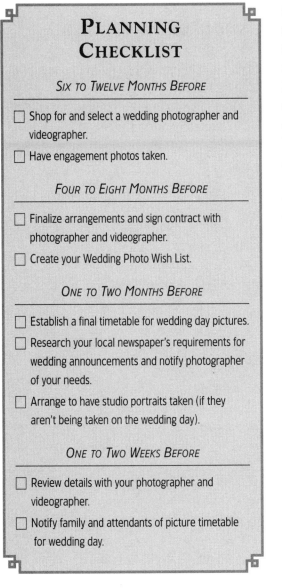

PLANNING CHECKLIST

SIX TO TWELVE MONTHS BEFORE

☐ Shop for and select a wedding photographer and videographer.

☐ Have engagement photos taken.

FOUR TO EIGHT MONTHS BEFORE

☐ Finalize arrangements and sign contract with photographer and videographer.

☐ Create your Wedding Photo Wish List.

ONE TO TWO MONTHS BEFORE

☐ Establish a final timetable for wedding day pictures.

☐ Research your local newspaper's requirements for wedding announcements and notify photographer of your needs.

☐ Arrange to have studio portraits taken (if they aren't being taken on the wedding day).

ONE TO TWO WEEKS BEFORE

☐ Review details with your photographer and videographer.

☐ Notify family and attendants of picture timetable for wedding day.

tographer? Usually, photographers include a basic number of pictures in your album and then charge for additional photos, albums, and proofs. Look for a studio that will negotiate to suit your needs. For example, if you want more pictures in your album, ask if they can substitute a number of smaller photographs for a few of the 8 x 10s. And look carefully at the pricing information. The studio may have low prices on their basic package but charge unreasonable fees for reprints and proofs—a poor deal if you need dozens of reprints for family and friends.

Finding a Photographer

Start your search with family and friends. If they've worked with a photographer at recent weddings, they can provide valuable recommendations—and steer you away from studios that provide less-than-satisfactory work. In addition to studying their finished albums, ask them to describe the photographer's personality. Was he friendly and nice or pushy and rude? As you receive recommendations, consider the source. Your friend may have adored her photographer, but if she prefers traditional photos and you really want an artistic flair, her recommendation may not be the right one for you.

If your friends can't provide recommendations, you can visit a bridal show or look through the phone book for a list of local photographers. Look for photographers who specialize in wedding photography. A studio may take lovely pictures, but if they're inexperienced with weddings, they may miss special photo opportunities.

As you make preliminary calls, ask the photographer a few basic questions:

no sense in paying a photographer who charges for seven hours if you'll only need five.

Needs—How many pictures do you want in your album? Will you need parents' albums, reprints, or any other special items from the pho-

Are you available on our wedding date?

What's your photography style and experience?

What's the price range on your wedding packages?

If their answers suit your needs, you can schedule an appointment to look more closely at their work. If not, keep looking.

At your appointments, closely examine the photographer's former work. Ask for a completed wedding album so you can get a feel for how they put it all together. Is it the quality you expect? Also, ask for the names and numbers of former clients. There's just no substitute for the honest feedback of a photographer's former customers.

Finally, be sure to meet personally with the photographer who would shoot your wedding. It's important to get a sense for someone's personality before you commit to having them at your wedding. If she makes you feel frustrated and uncomfortable, it will show in your wedding pictures. So pick a photographer who puts you at ease and who's willing to cooperate with your ideas rather than pushing her own.

Questions to Ask

When meeting with a photographer in person, ask the following questions.

What's your style (traditional, artistic, candid, journalistic, etc.)?

How long have you been taking wedding pictures?

Can I see samples of previous work?

HOW TO SPOT GOOD PHOTOGRAPHY

Not sure what to look for as you page through a photographer's work? You don't have to be an expert to sort out the good from the bad. Just keep your eyes open for the following elements of quality photography:

Photos should be framed and well centered.

There should be a variety of backgrounds and settings.

Lighting should be effective.

Photos shouldn't be over- or underexposed. (Look out for images that appear too bright or too dark.)

Photos should appear focused and crisp, not fuzzy.

People should look relaxed and comfortable.

Photos should include a balance of portraits and candid shots.

Photos should capture the emotions of the wedding day. (Look for images that portray meaningful moments or convey special relationships.)

Will you be the person actually taking the pictures? Do you have an assistant?

What will you be wearing at our wedding?

How many pictures will you take? (A good photographer will take at least three times as many pictures as you plan to have in your album.)

Do you shoot in color or black and white?

Will you take both formal and candid pictures?

What kinds of packages are available, and what's included in that price?

Do you charge by the hour, or does your package provide a set number of hours?

Are there charges for overtime? Travel costs?

What are the costs of additional photos and parents' albums?

How much time will you need to take portraits before or after the wedding?

Do you have a standard shot list?

Can you incorporate our suggestions into your shot list? Can we make substitutions for shots we don't want?

Are you familiar with our ceremony and reception sites? If not, are you willing to visit them before the wedding day?

Do you develop your own film?

How long after the wedding would we receive our proofs? Our finished album?

Do we get to keep the proofs?

Can we purchase the negatives?

What is your payment schedule?

Signing the Contract

Once you've selected a photographer and he's answered all your questions, it's time to put it in writing. Read the entire document carefully before you sign the final contract. Keep your copy of the contract with this planner, in case there are any questions about the photography package later

on. Your contract should include all the items listed in the following worksheet.

PHOTOGRAPHER

Name of studio/photographer: _____

_____

Address and phone number: _____

_____

_____

Contract date: _____

Package cost: _____

Number of hours included in package: ____

Number and size of photos included in package: _____

_____

Additional charges: _____

_____

Substitutions: _____

_____

Total contract costs: _____

Price list for additional photos, albums, proofs, upgrades: _____

_____

_____

Payment policy: _____

_____

Cancellation policy: _____

_____

Arrival time at ceremony and reception: __

_____

Date proofs will be ready: _____

Delivery date for completed album: _____
_____

Name of newspaper(s): _____
_____
_____

Required information: _____
_____
_____
_____

Required photo size: _____

Arrangements with photographer: _____
_____
_____
_____

Videography

Wedding photos will show the look and feel of your special day. But if you want to capture the sounds and action of your wedding, you'll also want to arrange for a videographer to record the events. As you start your search, consider these videography basics.

Location—Do your ceremony and reception sites have any restrictions concerning videography? Talk to the site managers and find out before you make arrangements with a videographer.

Style—Wedding videos can have a variety of looks and feels. The simplest, and usually least expensive, style presents events in a direct format, simply recording them as they unfold. A nostalgic format may include pictures of you and your fiancé from childhood to the present, footage from the ceremony and reception, and a photo montage that highlights special moments of the day. If you want your video to include shots of wedding preparations and interviews with attendants and guests, you'll want to look for a videographer who offers a documentary style.

Cameras—How many video cameras will you need at your wedding? The answer to that question depends on the video style you choose. One camera can't be everywhere at once, so if you want your finished video to have a documentary feel, you'll need two or more cameras. Keep in mind that each additional camera will probably add to your costs.

Sound—A good videographer provides wireless microphones to capture sound for your video. Consider how many microphones you'll need—most likely you'll want at least one for the pastor and one that can be clipped by the groom's boutonniere. If your wedding is outdoors or in a large space that carries echoes, you'll probably want microphones for the readers and soloists as well.

Finding a Videographer

When it comes to choosing a videographer, follow the same guidelines that you used to locate a photographer. Talk to friends and family. Ask to see sample tapes of each videographer's work. And watch for signs of quality editing and camera work—crisp images, good color, and clear sound.

As you shop, ask videographers about their cameras and editing equipment. Is it up-to-date equipment? Can they show you both finished

SPECIAL TOUCHES

Want to add extra flair to the images of your wedding day? Try these ideas:

Disposable Cameras—Set disposable cameras on tables at the reception. Your guests can snap photos, capturing moments you may not otherwise see.

Polaroids—Ask a friend to take some Polaroid shots throughout the wedding day. That way, you'll have pictures to enjoy during the honeymoon.

Make a Wedding Documentary—Use a video camera to record various aspects of your wedding plans: dress fittings, food sampling, favor assembly, etc. Ask someone to be the "host," narrating during the scenes and conducting interviews. You can show the film at your rehearsal, reception, or post-wedding party.

Guest Greetings—Have someone take a Polaroid picture of each guest (or couple). Insert them into album pages and have guests write a short message beside their picture.

Hire an Artist—Ask an artist (or art student) to paint or sketch the reception as it unfolds. Or take a Polaroid picture of the bride and groom and have the artist re-create it as a drawing or painting. Guests can stop to watch the artist work, and you'll have a special memento from your wedding day.

Photo Thank-Yous—Make your own thank-you notes, using a picture of you surrounded by your gifts. If you're feeling especially industrious, you can personalize each thank-you with a photo of yourself opening that person's gift.

tapes and raw footage? (That will give you a sense for how much editing they'll do to your video.) You may not understand some of the technical jargon they use, but as you ask questions about the editing process, you can gain a sense of the videographer's level of expertise.

Finally, be sure to select someone who will make you feel comfortable on your wedding day. Choose a cameraperson who is unobtrusive and friendly—not one who is barking orders to you and the guests.

Questions to Ask

When meeting in person with a videographer, ask the following questions.

What's your style (direct, nostalgic, documentary)?

How long have you provided videography services for weddings?

Can we see samples of previous work?

Will you be the person actually taking the video? Do you have an assistant?

What will you be wearing at our wedding?

Will you have backup equipment with you in case of emergency?

Will you provide microphones and/or coordinate the use of equipment with the site managers?

What kind of packages are available? What's included in that price?

Do you charge by the hour, or does your package provide a set number of hours?

Are there charges for overtime? Travel costs?

What are the costs of additional videos?

Are you familiar with our ceremony and reception sites? If not, are you willing to visit them before the wedding day?

Can we preview the raw footage and make suggestions for what to include in the edited video?

Can we purchase the raw footage?

How long after the wedding will we see a finished video?

What is your payment schedule?

Signing the Contract

Once you've selected a videographer, ask to get the details confirmed in a written contract. Read the document carefully before signing and keep your copy of the contract with this planner. The contract should include all the items listed in the following worksheet.

VIDEOGRAPHER

Name of studio/videographer: _____

_____

Address and phone number: _____

_____

_____

Contract date: _____

Package cost: _____

Length of shooting period: _____

Number of videos included in package: ____

_____

Additional charges: _____

_____

Substitutions: _____

_____

Total contract costs: _____

Payment policy: _____

Cancellation policy: _____

Arrival time at ceremony and reception: __

_____

Delivery date of finished video: _____

Picture Wish List

Several months before your wedding you should create an itemized list of the pictures you'd like. Be honest about your preferences as you discuss this wish list with your photographer and

GOING DIGITAL

With current advances in technology, many photographers and videographers now take their shots with digital equipment. Going digital provides several advantages over film. Shots can be previewed on-scene, video and proofs can be previewed on a secure website (saving time and cost of developing proofs), and digital photos and videos can be stored easily on a CD or DVD. If you're interested in digital images of your wedding, talk to your photographer and videographer about these options.

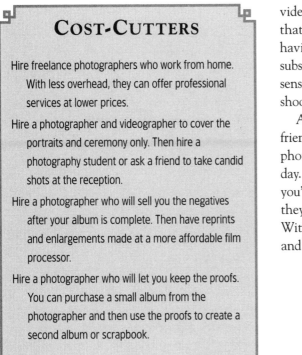

COST-CUTTERS

Hire freelance photographers who work from home. With less overhead, they can offer professional services at lower prices.

Hire a photographer and videographer to cover the portraits and ceremony only. Then hire a photography student or ask a friend to take candid shots at the reception.

Hire a photographer who will sell you the negatives after your album is complete. Then have reprints and enlargements made at a more affordable film processor.

Hire a photographer who will let you keep the proofs. You can purchase a small album from the photographer and then use the proofs to create a second album or scrapbook.

videographer. If there are some traditional shots that you don't want, don't feel pressured into having them; perhaps your photographer could substitute some extra candids instead. There's no sense wasting precious time with unwanted photo shoots on your wedding day.

A week or two before the wedding, designate a friend or relative to review the wish list with your photographer and videographer on the wedding day. Give this person a list of special guests whom you'd like to include in the wedding pictures so they can point them out to the photographers. With these details taken care of, you can relax and enjoy your big day.

Wedding Photo/Video Wish List

	Photo	Video
Preparation Photographs		
Bride Getting Ready		
Groom Getting Ready		
Other		
Other		
Ceremony Photographs		
Bride and Father Walking Down Aisle		
Attendants Walking Down Aisle		
Groom's Expression as Bride Walks Down Aisle		
Bride and Groom Exchanging Vows		
Bride and Groom Kneeling at Altar and/or Lighting Unity Candle		

	Photo	Video
Bride and Groom Kissing		
Bride and Groom Recessional		
Guests in Receiving Line		
Other		
Other		
Portraits		
Bride Alone		
Bride with Maid/Matron of Honor		
Bride with Parents		
Bride with Bridesmaids (as a group and/or individually)		
Bride with Flower Girl		
Bride with Grandparents		
Bride with Siblings		
Bride with Family		
Groom Alone		
Groom with Best Man		
Groom with Parents		
Groom with Ushers/Groomsmen (as group and/or individually)		
Groom with Ring Bearer		
Groom with Grandparents		
Groom with Siblings		
Groom with Family		
Bride and Groom Together		
Bride and Groom with Best Man and Maid/Matron of Honor		
Bride and Groom with Attendants		
Bride and Groom with Flower Girl and Ring Bearer		
Bride and Groom with His Parents		
Bride and Groom with Her Parents		
Bride and Groom with His Family		
Bride and Groom with Her Family		
Bride and Groom with Officiant		
Musicians		
Special Guests (list names)		
Other		
Other		

	Photo	Video
Reception Pictures		
Bride and Groom's Arrival		
Best Man's Toast		
Bride and Groom Cutting Cake		
Bride and Groom Feeding Each Other Cake		
Bride and Groom's First Dance		
Groom Dancing with Mother		
Bride Dancing with Father		
Bride Tossing Bouquet		
Groom Tossing Garter		
Other		
Other		

Bride of Modesty

Charm is deceptive and beauty is fleeting; but a woman who fears the LORD is to be praised.—Proverbs 31:30

Daughters of Jerusalem, I charge you . . . Do not arouse or awaken love until it so desires.—Song of Songs 2:7

I also want women to dress modestly, with decency and propriety, not with braided hair or gold or pearls or expensive clothes, but with good deeds, appropriate for women who profess to worship God.—1 Timothy 2:9–10

False Advertising

We live in a world of images. On billboards, in stores, on TV—I've even seen advertisements posted in public restroom stalls. Some images are disturbing, though. And there's one in particular that causes women a lot of grief. It's an image we find all over the place. It's an image that many of us have started to worship. And it's an image that can really mess up a bride's priorities. This awful image I speak of? It's beauty.

Beauty, of course, isn't the real problem. In fact, God both created and desires beauty. He filled his creation with it. And he designed women to possess deep beauty—a beauty that men adore. So beauty isn't the evil. But it can be distorted. And that's when we have a problem.

In today's culture, women face a staggering mountain when it comes to beauty. Magazines burst with articles about smooth skin, white teeth, and toned muscles. The television and music stars gain admiration for their tiny figures and revealing clothing—an image that millions of women try to achieve.

We hear a distorted message about sexuality undergirding all these messages about beauty. We're told to flaunt what we've got and leave modesty to the prudes. If we really want to look attractive, we should loosen up. Show some shoulder. Bare some of that back. Let those legs show. Beauty needs to be sexy, or so we're told.

But in the real world, we don't have three hours to spend with cosmetics and hair stylists every morning. When we walk down the street, there's no airbrushing to hide our trouble spots. And when we dress immodestly, we have to settle for interested stares instead of the gentle attention we crave in our souls. The sexy brand of beauty takes a ton of work—but it turns us into cheap objects instead of valuable people.

As God's brides, we should look at beauty differently. "Your beauty should not come from outward adornment, such as braided hair and the wearing of gold jewelry and fine clothes. Instead, it should be that of your inner self, the unfading beauty of a gentle and quiet spirit, which is of great worth in God's sight" (1 Peter 3:3–4). No matter what we wear, how toned our bodies are, or how good we look in a swimsuit, our true beauty doesn't lie on the outside. What's most beautiful about a woman lies within.

Most of us nod our heads in agreement with that idea. Yet as we look around, it's hard to distinguish much difference between God's brides and everyone else. Many believers don the revealing dresses and figure-hugging clothes that have become so popular with the world. They're showing more skin, just like everyone else. But is that how

it should be? Should God's brides really join the world in throwing modesty to the wind?

Speaking to the heart of immodesty, Proverbs 31:30 reminds us that "charm is deceptive, and beauty is fleeting; but a woman who fears the LORD is to be praised." When a woman dresses in suggestive clothing, she's advertising something—she's displaying her body in a way that's going to tempt men. But what a deceptive advertisement! We're not for sale—and God calls us to reserve our bodies for the enjoyment of just one man.

No matter how charming the look may be, we're guilty of false advertising when we dress immodestly. And it's especially deceptive when we're God's brides. We can't proclaim to live for him and then ignore his commands to save our bodies for one man. Sure, a lot of women say they don't mean to be immodest—they're just trying to follow the trends. But at what price should a woman purchase beauty? If the trends lead her to tempt men and disobey God, isn't that price too high?

It's time for God's brides to reclaim real beauty—instead of accepting the distorted images of our culture. The models may display stunning figures beneath revealing clothes, but we must recognize the ugliness of turning women into objects to be gawked at. And the new trends may turn guys' heads, but we must acknowledge that enticing men to sinful thoughts is not a beautiful thing. It's the woman who understands the power of her body and saves it for marriage who displays true beauty. And in her modesty, people can appreciate her inner character instead of getting distracted by her outer curves.

So as you consider the clothes you'll be wearing today, don't forget about God's love for modesty.

If you dress to please your heavenly Groom, that will be a beautiful picture indeed.

Snapshots

As the high school yearbook editor, I faced a barrage of snapshots. I'd heard about the foibles of previous editors—who'd arrogantly placed pictures of themselves on page after page. With no desire to plaster my own face all over the yearbook, I became intent on finding snapshots that included a wide variety of students.

I still love looking through snapshots—but I still avoid photos of myself. The tiny eye of a camera captures so much, telling incredible stories about the people depicted there. But sometimes it shows too much! And I'm afraid of what others will think when they see that image of me with messed-up hair or a crazy smile. Maybe you've groaned at pictures too, wishing you weren't in the snapshot. It seems like natural instinct to worry about our image.

But when I read through the story of creation, I start to wonder if we have it all wrong when it comes to the picture thing. "God created man in his own image, in the image of God he created him; male and female he created them" (Gen. 1:27). That means we're supposed to be snapshots of God—images of his love for the world to see. When I think of life from that perspective, it changes things. Instead of worrying so much about what others think of me, I start asking myself, *Can they see God in my snapshot?*

The world looks at us for snapshots of God—often with some skepticism in their stare. They're watching our words, noting how we respond to the situations around us. And they're examining

LOVE STORY FROM GOD

The armor was ridiculously large. "I won't wear it." David shrugged off the heavy pieces. He'd come to fight Goliath—the vicious giant who dared to taunt God. And once King Saul realized David was serious, he'd tried to give him this armor.

But David planned a more modest method of protection. Picking up five smooth stones, he grabbed a simple slingshot and headed toward the field where the giant stood mocking the Israelite God. "I know it's not much," he prayed, "but I've used this slingshot during all my years as a shepherd. And if you'll help me, God, I know I can hit the target again today."

Standing in awe, the other Israelite soldiers watched David. "That boy's got faith," one commented. "And it may just kill him," another soldier sneered. Moments later, the giant started yelling again, berating the entire Israelite army for sending out a scrawny shepherd to fight him.

David couldn't listen to the giant belittling his faith. "You may have superior weapons and more strength, but I've got God!" he shouted. And then he hurled a rock, waiting until it hit the mark. *Praise God!* David thought as he saw the giant fall. *Praise God! Today he's given the whole world a picture of his power!*

Read the entire story of David's faith, and see how his modest attitude allowed God's power to shine through in 1 Samuel 17.

our every action, trying to see if God is for real in our lives.

Unfortunately, though, our snapshots sometimes show God in the shadows. Our human instincts seem to turn us into yearbook editors who litter the book with pictures of themselves. We want people to notice *us*, to like *us*, to listen to *our* thoughts. And so, instead of being modest about our accomplishments and giving credit to God, we sometimes boast about them and seek the spotlight for ourselves.

Some of you may struggle with this pride more than others, but I think it's a temptation for every bride. And pride creeps up in subtle ways. Your relationship with your fiancé, your creativity with wedding plans, your designs for the future—it's tempting to take credit for your talents and good taste in these areas, rather than acknowledging God's hand in it all.

But when we take the credit, we create snapshots that don't do justice to our Creator—snapshots that show little of him and an awful lot of us. Truth be told, God does want people to appreciate who he's created them to be. But instead of seeing a picture that only glorifies ourselves, he wants us to point to him. He wants the world to notice his love through the one-of-a-kind snapshot that is you.

"What do you have that you did not receive? And if you did receive it, why do you boast as though you did not?" (1 Cor. 4:7). Those questions drive us to the heart of practicing modesty. Because no matter how many talents we have, no matter how put together we may be, no matter how great our family is—we still can't take credit for it ourselves.

So take an honest look at your life today. Are there any areas where you could give more credit to God? If there are, think of some inventive ways to show others how much God has been working behind the scenes. That kind of modesty looks beautiful on any bride. And it ensures that your wedding pictures are complete—including the heavenly Groom who's captured your heart.

8

· · · · · · · · · · · ·

THE WEDDING
ATTIRE

As you face the dress racks, you may feel overwhelmed—somewhere amid all the silk, taffeta, tulle, and lace, your dream dress is waiting. But how do you actually find it? This chapter will prepare you for the task. Once you're armed with some helpful information and ideas, your dress-shopping experience will become a special memory rather than a stressful experience. Soon you'll be staring at your reflection in the mirror and whispering, "I think this is the one."

As you search for that perfect gown, you'll also have a great opportunity to consider the attitudes you'll be wearing as your wedding approaches. They aren't as showy as a wedding gown, but the virtues of humility and honesty can make a big impression on those around you. Guests will always compliment the bride's lovely gown. But when you become a humble and honest bride, people will also admire something else: your beautiful heart.

Bride of Humility

Let him who boasts boast in the Lord.—1 Corinthians 1:31

If you reject criticism, you only harm yourself; but if you listen to correction, you grow in understanding.
—Proverbs 15:32 NLT

God opposes the proud but gives grace to the humble.
—James 4:6

Making Alterations

Seamstresses can work wonders!

That's what I was thinking after each of my bridesmaids' dress fittings. One by one, they slipped on their dress and stood in front of the mirror. The seamstress made straightforward suggestions for adjustments, and each bridesmaid added a few ideas of her own. A few weeks later, the dresses were finished. And what a difference a few alterations made! Instead of wearing dresses that hung loosely and puddled on the floor, my bridesmaids now looked gorgeous in gowns that fit just right.

I'm sure my bridesmaids felt funny standing in front of the mirror during that first fitting. It's a humbling ritual most bridesmaids endure—becoming an object of scrutiny as several people offer suggestions for changes to the dress. But in the end, those adjustments create a better fit. And that's true of our character too—humility helps us make much-needed personal alterations. With it, we can listen to the advice of others and pinpoint areas that need adjustment—perhaps in our attitudes, words, or actions. In the end, those changes make our character look better than it did before.

Pride puts a kink in this system of alterations, however. It shoves us into defense mode whenever someone tries to make a suggestion. It yells into our ears, "Who are they to give me advice?" And it turns our finger back toward their problems, instead of taking an honest look at our own.

The Bible warns about this kind of behavior: "The arrogant one will stumble and fall and no one will help her up" (Jer. 50:32). Do you envision someone as you read this passage? A prideful person whom everyone is silently hoping to see fall and put in their place? Most of us know someone who fits that description. But without humility, *we* become that person. Consumed by the beast of pride, we can be blinded to our faults, deaf to advice—and bound to make mistakes.

Humility tames that beast of pride, opening our eyes to both the beauty and the blemishes. Where there's beauty—physical, emotional, or spiritual—we can feel a sense of pride that's focused on our Creator instead of ourselves. And where there are blemishes, we can be open to the well-meaning suggestions of those who love us. With a healthy perspective on both our strengths and weaknesses, we can be proud of who God has created us to be while also being humble about our faults and our need for adjustments.

With pride put in its proper place, the alterations begin. And those alterations play a crucial part in the life of a bride. Proverbs says that "he who ignores discipline despises himself, but whoever heeds correction gains understanding" (15:32). When I think of those words, I picture one bride who refused any alterations, standing in a dress that falls off her shoulders with a skirt that sags to the floor. And then I picture another bride, looking slim and beautiful because her alterations created a perfect fit.

Obviously, we'd rather be the bride who heeds correction than the one who walks down the aisle in a poorly fitted dress. But when we ignore truthful advice about our actions and decisions, we act like the first bride, who looks ridiculous. Instead of making the alterations we badly need, we live with character flaws that look poor on God's brides.

It would be wonderful if those flaws just didn't exist. And pride tempts us to hide or ignore those problem areas. But in reality, we all have areas where some adjustments are needed. Maybe your temper needs to be taken in, or perhaps your patience needs to be lengthened a bit as you plan for your wedding. It's tough to swallow your pride and listen to someone's advice, but the alterations they suggest may be just what you need.

Take a look in the mirror today. What do you see? Are there strengths that have made you boastful? Are there weaknesses you've ignored? Ask a close friend to give you honest advice about what alterations could improve your character. Or think about the suggestions you've heard from your family in recent weeks. With an attitude of humility, you'll discover areas that need adjustment or repair. But just like a seamstress altering masterpieces of silk and lace, God can work wonders with your character. And as you pinpoint the changes you'd like to make, he'll reassure you that he can do the job: "He who began a good work in you will carry it on to completion" (Phil. 1:6).

It's All about the Shoes . . .

As week-old newlyweds, my husband and I were enjoying our move into an apartment, joking around as we organized our new home. When

LOVE STORY FROM GOD

She took another look at the house where Jesus and his disciples were eating, then glanced at the perfume in her hands. *Maybe I shouldn't bother with this,* Mary thought to herself. *Jesus and his friends may think I'm crazy if I decide to wash his feet with perfume.*

Filled with uncertainty, Mary considered turning around and walking away. And yet, her heart was tugging her toward Jesus, the man she recognized as the promised Messiah. She knew that the religious leaders were plotting to kill him. And she longed to make a special gesture—to show Jesus that she loved him and believed in him.

But she doubted the others would appreciate her actions. She could already see their eyes rolling at her dramatics. *Maybe I should just go in and act like Martha.* Martha—such a calm and grounded person. She never got fanciful notions about washing Jesus's feet with perfume. She was inside the house even now, serving Jesus his meal without attracting any attention.

But Mary couldn't pretend to be someone she wasn't. And she longed for everyone to see the truth—that Jesus was God himself. So she followed through with her plan. And just as she'd expected, she heard derogatory comments about her foot-washing being "a waste of good perfume."

Even as she noticed the disapproving looks, though, Mary felt peace. She'd been true to herself—and to her God. And Jesus looked pleased. In fact, he told everyone that "wherever the gospel is preached throughout the world, what she has done will also be told, in memory of her." Hearing those words from the Messiah she loved, Mary felt her heart skip for joy. Apparently, he loved her just the way she was.

To read the entire story of this woman who humbly exposed her true feelings, read Matthew 26:6–13 and John 12:1–11.

it came time to put away our shoes, Brian quickly stowed his three pairs in the closet. Meanwhile, I pulled a couple shelves into my closet and started unloading three crates of footwear. I tried to explain why a woman needs so many shoes, but Brian just rolled his eyes and laughed at my large collection.

I'm not sure I ever convinced my husband why shoes are so necessary. But I've found consolation in knowing that most women share my passion for lovely footwear. We love our shoes, don't we? And I suppose that's why brides spend millions of dollars on wedding shoes each year—despite the fact that most people will never see their feet!

We're not the only ones thinking about footwear, though. Have you ever noticed how much the Bible mentions feet? I searched an online Bible and found dozens of references to these funny-looking appendages. Here's a few of them that really stuck out: "How beautiful on the mountains are the feet of those who bring good news, who proclaim peace" (Isa. 52:7), and "Stand firm then . . . with your feet fitted with the readiness that comes from the gospel of peace" (Eph. 6:14–15).

Those verses speak of footwear—but not the kind we can purchase at the mall. Instead, we're prompted to think about our "spiritual" feet. Do they look beautiful right now? Are they fitted with the right kind of shoes?

I recently purchased new tennis shoes based on the recommendation of a friend. When I put them on, my feet felt heavenly. I'm not much of an athlete, but these shoes made me feel like I could run a marathon. I was amazed at the difference they made. I wanted to run, jump, and take on the world!

That's exactly what our spiritual shoes should feel like. They should make us feel excited and energetic about our faith. And they should fill us with readiness—to hit the pavement and put our faith into action. But where exactly should our feet be taking us?

God answered that question in an interesting way. He decided literally to "walk in our shoes" for a while. So he became a human and lived for thirty-three years on this earth. And he did it so we'd have a living picture of where to walk—how to move our feet in the ways that please God.

Jesus moved his feet a lot. Just read through the Gospels and take note of how often he and the disciples moved from one town to another. After putting in miles on foot, Jesus would still find energy to teach, heal, and share the good news of salvation with those he encountered. And one day, Jesus walked a crowded pathway through Jerusalem to die on a cross for our sin.

The path Jesus chose—the footwork he laid—shows humility in action. One night near the end of his life, he even performed the lowly task of washing his disciples' feet. Here he was, a man who'd developed celebrity status as a great teacher, and he was stooping to wash the feet of his inferiors. In that quiet action, Jesus showed us how to walk—in paths of service. And he also showed us what kind of shoes to wear: shoes of humility, that make us ready for any task—even those that seem beneath us.

These shoes are especially important when it comes to marriage, because the devil tries so hard to fill our relationships with demands and insults. Without an attitude of humility and service, it's easy for couples to get upset with each other about trivial tasks. Instead, we need to promote peace by being ready to serve each other. We need to use our hands and feet to show God's love to our spouses.

So keep shopping for those wedding shoes. And as you do, take a look at your spiritual feet. Are they fitted with readiness to serve? Are they beautiful feet that proclaim peace? If not, you may need to look for a new pair of shoes—a new attitude of humility and eagerness to serve. Rest assured, though, that's one pair of shoes that your fiancé will love to add to the closet.

Planning Your Wedding Attire

Dressing the Men

When it comes to wedding attire, guys have it pretty easy. In most cases, they simply head to the tuxedo shop, pick out a style they like, and have their measurements taken. Depending on the formality of the wedding, they may even wear a nice suit that they already own.

Finding the Tuxedo

If you need to rent tuxedos, and most grooms do, seek out a reputable rental agency. Ask your friends and family for recommendations and evaluate the professionalism of the stores you visit. It's fine to compare prices, but don't forget to consider the service as well. Can the tuxedo shop do alterations on site if one of the tuxes needs last-minute adjustments? Do they provide shoes, gloves, and other accessories? Can they replace a tux quickly if something goes wrong with one of the rentals? It may be worth a few extra dollars to rent from a business that provides top-notch service.

As you choose a tuxedo, make a selection that will match the style and formality of the bridal gown. Bring dress swatches to the store; then select cummerbund or vest colors that match or complement the bridesmaids' dresses and choose a shirt color that matches the shade of your dress. Groomsmen should also wear matching shoes, so ask the rental agency if shoes are included in your rental package.

Fittings and Pickup

Once the tuxes have been selected, make arrangements with the groomsmen to have their measurements taken. Generally, the fathers of bride and groom are invited to rent tuxedos as well. Out-of-town attendants can get their measurements from a tailor or tux shop in their town. Just make sure that a professional takes all measurements, otherwise your groomsmen may end up with ill-fitting tuxedos.

Remind the groom and his attendants to pick up their tuxedos the day before the wedding. They should allow enough time to try on the tux in the shop, in case last-minute adjustments need to be made.

Groom's and Attendants' Attire

TUXEDO STORE INFORMATION

Name of store: _____

Phone number: _____

Contact person: _____

RENTAL SPECIFICS

Tuxedo style: _____

Shirt: _____

Vest: _____

Cummerbund: _____

Tie: _____

Dress socks: _____

Shoes: _____

Gloves: _____

Cuff links: _____

Other: _____

Total cost: _____

IMPORTANT DATES

Fitting date: _____

Pickup date: _____

Return date: _____

Dressing the Ladies

From the flower girl to the mother of the bride, every lady wants to look pretty at your wedding. As the bride, your challenge is to select colors and styles that will complement everyone involved. But before you start shopping, talk with your officiant and the wedding site manager about any religious requirements for attire. You don't want to select that gorgeous spaghetti-strap gown only to discover that the church requires all dresses to have sleeves!

PLANNING CHECKLIST

NINE TO TWELVE MONTHS BEFORE

☐ Shop for and order your bridal gown.

SIX TO NINE MONTHS BEFORE

☐ Order bridesmaids' dresses.

☐ If dresses are being made, choose a seamstress and have measurements taken.

☐ Shop for headpiece, veil, and other bridal accessories.

FOUR TO SIX MONTHS BEFORE

☐ Select tuxedos for groom and his attendants. Have their measurements taken.

ONE TO TWO MONTHS BEFORE

☐ Arrange final fittings for you and the bridesmaids.

☐ Set appointments with hairdresser and makeup artist.

TWO TO FOUR WEEKS BEFORE

☐ Confirm appointments with hairdresser and makeup artist.

☐ Confirm that groom and attendants have finished rentals and fittings.

Mothers

Mothers of the bride and groom usually select their own gowns. But the bride should provide them with suggestions for colors and styles that will complement the overall wedding style. Encourage your mother and future mother-in-law to shop several months in advance.

Bridal Attendants

As you shop for the attendants' attire, look for gowns that will flatter the shapes and sizes of all. If possible, have an attendant try on some dresses and ask her opinion. Of course, the final choice is yours, but try to be flexible as you consider your bridesmaids' feedback. Also, be considerate about the dress price, as the bridesmaids generally pay for the dresses themselves.

DRESSES

Traditionally, bridesmaids wear identical dresses, while flower girls wear white dresses similar to the style of the bridesmaids' but in a shorter length. Variations in style or color are acceptable, however, and can create a lovely bridal party, especially if your attendants' body shapes vary.

Once you've selected the gowns, have each woman measured for her dress. When possible, protect their privacy while measurements are taken. As your bridesmaids consider what dress size to order, keep in mind that their weight could fluctuate in the months before your wedding. It's wise to err on the side of ordering too big—a dress that's too big can always be taken in. After measurements are complete, you should order all the dresses together to avoid any variation in the dye color or design.

WHAT TO WEAR?

Wedding attire should match the formality of your wedding. Here are a few guidelines to help you out:

Informal Wedding

Bride—Wears a formal suit, tea- or street-length dress, or floor-length gown. Wears no veil or train.

Groom—Wears a simple suit, a white shirt, and a tie.

Semiformal Wedding

Bride—Wears a floor-length gown with chapel or fingertip veil. May wear a tea-length or ballerina gown with shorter veil or hat.

Groom—Wears a formal dinner jacket (tuxedo), dark trousers, a cummerbund or vest, white dress shirt, and bow tie. For daytime weddings, a suit jacket and four-in-hand tie may be worn instead.

Formal Wedding

Bride—Wears a traditional floor-length gown with a chapel or sweep train and gloves. Veil is usually fingertip length (for daytime) or longer (for evening). Very formal brides may wear cathedral-length train and veil.

Groom—Wears cutaways or tailcoats, a stiff white shirt, a white or gray tie, and a white or gray waistcoat.

ALTERATIONS

Since few women will fit perfectly into the gown you've selected, some alterations probably will be needed. As the dresses are hemmed, make sure that all the bridesmaids' hemlines fall the same distance from the floor. Take measurements from the floor to the hem of your tallest attendant; then match the other attendants' dresses to that length.

Some bridal shops include alterations in the dress price, but usually they cost extra. You may find it more affordable to have dresses altered by a seamstress. But regardless of who alters the dresses, be sure to have your bridesmaids wear the lingerie and shoes they'll be wearing for the wedding when they have their fittings. Final fittings should occur at least one month before the wedding.

SHOES AND HOSIERY

Ask your attendants to buy shoes well ahead of the wedding. Heel heights may vary according to the bridesmaids' height, but your attendants should wear shoes of a similar style and color. You may select a particular shoe, order shoes to be dyed, or simply ask your attendants to purchase their own. If the shoes are being dyed, have them dyed together to avoid any variations in color.

When the attendants' gowns are floor-length, matching hosiery may not be necessary—each bridesmaid can purchase her own in the shade she prefers. However, when dresses are shorter, you should make sure the bridesmaids have matching hose. Don't forget to purchase an extra pair of panty-hose for each bridesmaid, in case of emergencies.

HAIR, MAKEUP, AND ACCESSORIES

If you would like your bridesmaids to have their hair styled by a professional, tell them of your preferences several months before your wedding. They may have a favorite stylist or want to schedule their own appointment. But as a courtesy, offer to schedule appointments for those who do not

usually use a professional stylist. Or hire a stylist to come to the wedding site as a convenient option for your attendants. Again, be considerate of costs as the bridesmaids generally pay for this service themselves.

Generally, bridesmaids take care of their own makeup application. But you should use fabric swatches from the dresses to coordinate their lipstick colors and nail polish. Accessories—such as gloves, hats, floral wreaths, and jewelry—should be of a similar style. Inform your bridesmaids if any accessories need to be purchased by them ahead of time.

Bridal Attendants' Attire

STORE/SEAMSTRESS INFORMATION

Name of store/seamstress: _____

_____

Phone number: _____

Other: _____

DRESSES

Bridesmaid dress manufacturer: _____

_____

Bridesmaid dress color(s): _____

Bridesmaid dress style number(s): _____

Bridesmaid dress description: _____

_____

Bridesmaid dress cost: _____

Flower girl dress description: _____

_____

Flower girl dress cost: _____

Shoes: _____

Hosiery: _____

Hat: _____

Jewelry: _____

Hair: _____

Makeup: _____

Total accessories cost: _____

First fitting time and location: _____

_____

Second fitting time and location: _____

_____

Final fitting time and location: _____

_____

Pickup date: _____

Here Comes the Bride

If you're like most brides, you can't wait to find the gown that you'll wear on your wedding day. With images of satin and pearls in your head, you're eager to visit the bridal stores. As you head off on this memorable journey, keep in mind the following ideas.

Prepare to Shop

Before you travel to the bridal store, take some time to think about your personal style. Envision yourself walking down the aisle. Do you want to look elegant? Dramatic? Simple? Like a princess? As you think about your unique style, bear in mind that your dress should match the degree of formality in your wedding.

Next, look through magazines and bridal books for pictures of dresses that appeal to you. Or attend and take pictures at bridal shows, which are often held in the spring and fall. Show these pictures to sales associates as you visit bridal shops so that they can quickly and easily pull out dresses that suit your taste.

At the Store

Many dresses take months to deliver after they're ordered, so it's a good idea to shop early, if possible—about nine to twelve months before your big day. As you head to the store, wear clothes that easily slip on and off. Take a friend or two with you to give honest opinions about the dresses you try on. If possible, have a friend take pictures of gowns as you try them on. That way, you can consider your options in privacy once you get home.

Stores carry hundreds of dresses, and it can be difficult to sort through them all. Keep in mind that some dresses will look better on you than they do on the hanger. Even if you have doubts about a particular dress, it might be worth trying on. Once you have the sample dress on, take note of how comfortable it feels. Can you lift your arms? Does it feel too heavy? Try crumpling a section of the fabric in your hands to see if it wrinkles easily. Each of these factors can play a deciding role in you final dress selection.

As you work with sales associates, be honest about your budget. You don't want to fall in love with a gown that costs far more than you can afford. And if you look carefully, you'll find just the right gown in your price range. Also, ask questions about hidden costs as you shop. Does the shop include alterations in the price of its dresses, or do alterations cost extra? How much do alterations generally run? How much will the crinoline or petticoat cost? Will they press the dress for you, or will you have to pay a dry cleaner to do it for you? Asking these questions could save you lots of time and money, so shop around for the best deal.

Time to Order

Once you've finally settled on a particular gown, order it as soon as possible. The store will take your measurements and help you determine what size to order. Remember, you may gain or lose several pounds before your wedding day, so choose a dress size that can be altered if necessary.

You'll have to make a deposit when you order the dress—often about one half of the total dress cost. Before you put money down, ask a few final questions to make sure this is the store for you. When exactly will they order your dress? Can they guarantee its arrival at least two months before the wedding? What will be the expected delivery date? Are they willing to put all the details in writing?

Once the contract is signed, keep a copy of it in your wedding planner. You may want to make periodic phone calls to check on the status of your order. Once the dress has arrived, schedule a fitting to see if alterations are needed.

All the Extras

You've found the perfect dress; now you can pick out all the extras that go with it. From the

SEW EASY

It's usually more affordable to have your dress and/or the bridesmaids' dresses sewn by a local seamstress. If you choose this option, ask fabric stores for recommendations and check the seamstress's references to ensure that other customers have been satisfied with her work. A few questions to ask before hiring a seamstress:

Do you need a pattern or can you create custom designs?

How far before our wedding will you start sewing the dresses? (You'll want them ready for a final fitting at least one month before your wedding.)

Can you give me advice about fabrics and patterns?

What materials do you expect me to supply?

Can I see samples of your work?

veil on your head to the shoes that cover your toes, you'll want to make sure that every accessory is just right.

Veil—Veils come in a variety of lengths and styles, so choose one that complements both you and the style of your dress. Consider a detachable veil that can be removed from the headpiece after the ceremony. That way, you won't need to worry about having your veil snagged during all those hugs and dances.

Headpiece—Whether it's a wreath of flowers, a simple headband, or a glittering tiara, your headpiece marks the finishing touch to your veil and hair. Try to pick something that won't overpower you or your dress. And if you're purchasing a headpiece, give yourself at least ten weeks for it to arrive after it's ordered.

Shoes—Your shoes may never be seen beneath all the layers of your gown, but you'll still want your feet to have some flair for your wedding. Today's brides try everything from satin slippers to tennis shoes adorned with ribbons. Look for shoes that will keep your feet comfortable throughout the day, and then wear them around the house for a few days to break them in before the wedding.

Crinoline/Petticoat—Many dresses require a crinoline, or petticoat, worn beneath the skirt to add fullness to the gown. While crinolines can be purchased, many bridal salons rent them for a small fee.

Lingerie—It's time to splurge on some pretty undergarments for your wedding day. Some gowns require a special bra, and you may also want to wear a corset or stomach-minimizing underwear. Shop for these items early—you'll want them ready so you can wear them to your first fitting.

Jewelry—Before you drop a lot of money on new jewels, you may want to look through the jewelry collections of your friends and relatives. Your grandmother may have the perfect necklace, and if she's willing to loan it to you, it's sure to be a meaningful part of your special day. As you look for necklaces, earrings, and bracelets, keep in mind that your jewelry should not overshadow your hairstyle, face, or gown.

Accessories—Handbags, gloves, hats, cloaks— the list of bridal accessories goes on and on. Look through department stores and bridal salons for items that can put the finishing touch on your ensemble.

Hair—You may be skilled at styling your own hair, but if you're like most brides, you'll want a little help with this detail on your wedding day.

PRESERVING YOUR GOWN

The wedding dress is probably the most expensive item of clothing most women will ever own. So after the big day, many brides will want to store it properly and make sure that it lasts for years to come.

Dry cleaners and bridal salons often provide cleaning and preserving services. Look for cleaners who specialize in gown preservation, and try to get your dress to them within six months of the wedding. Go over the gown with the cleaner, pointing out any stains, holes, or tears.

Once your gown is returned, follow the store's instructions for storage. If you're given a special preserving box, keep it sealed and store it in a climate-controlled environment. If your dress is not in a box, purchase some white sheets that are free of perfumes or dyes. Wrap the dress securely in these sheets and then store it in a place that will not get damp, hot, cold, or brightly lit. If possible, store your dress lying down—hanging your dress causes pulling on the shoulder seams and waistline.

If you plan to use a professional stylist, schedule the appointment at least two months before your wedding day. If possible, set a trial appointment as well so that the stylist can see your headpiece and experiment with various styles.

Makeup—Visit a department store cosmetic counter to ask for advice about your wedding makeup. They'll try to sell you products, but their pointers can give you confidence in buying and applying your wedding makeup. If you prefer, you can schedule an appointment with a cosmetologist on your wedding day. Don't hesitate to tell them when they use colors or products that you dislike. They can easily change your makeup, but you live with the wedding pictures forever.

Nails—Don't forget about those fingers! Unless they're covered by gloves, your hands will be on display throughout the day. Apply a soft-colored nail polish. Or treat yourself to a manicure and pedicure during the week of your wedding.

Bridal Style

As you shop for your wedding attire, you'll probably run in to a few words and terms you've never heard before. Don't worry! Here's the low-down on bridal style.

Gown Styles

A-line—A fitted bodice that flares out from the waistline, creating the shape of an A. Also called a princess line.

Ball Gown—A very full skirt that falls to a formal length, creating a "Cinderella" look.

Basque—A dropped waist that starts several inches below the natural waistline and forms a U or V shape.

Empire—A high-waisted dress with a bodice that ends just below the bust and a skirt that flares from the high waist.

Sheath—A form-fitting bodice with a straight, close-fitting skirt.

Trumpet—A fitted bodice with a skirt that hugs the body and then flares out at or above the knee. Also called mermaid style.

Necklines

Ballerina—Low neckline, usually found on strapless or spaghetti-strap dresses.

Bateau—High, wide neckline that runs straight across the front and back and meets at the shoulders.

Rounded—Neckline is open and forms a U shape.

Square Neck—Open neckline shaped like a half square.

Sweetheart—Neckline shaped like the top of a heart.

V-neck—An open neck forming a V shape in the bodice.

Trains

Sweep Train—Train that barely sweeps the floor.

Chapel Train—Train that flows three to five feet behind the gown.

Cathedral Train—Train that flows six to eight feet behind the gown. Also called a monarch train.

Watteau Train—Train that drapes from the shoulders.

Veils

Blusher—Short veil that is worn over the face.

Fingertip Veil—Veil that falls somewhere around the fingers.

Sweep Veil—Veil that barely sweeps the floor.

Chapel Veil—Veil that trails one or two feet from the gown.

Cathedral Veil—Veil that trails three to eight feet from the gown.

Mantilla—Veil that drapes over the head and shoulders like a scarf, of varying lengths.

Getting Dressed on the Big Day

Both you and your attendants should allow plenty of time to get dressed before your wedding. Plan on being completely dressed at least fifteen minutes before photography begins. To avoid any mishaps or weather problems, it's wise to get dressed at your wedding site.

If your dress is close-fitting, have your hair styled after the gown is put on. Avoid makeup application after you're dressed, however. You don't want to stain your wedding dress with bright cosmetics. Instead, apply makeup before dressing and wear a scarf or towel over your face as the gown is put on.

Before your wedding day, make sure the bride's dressing room has been outfitted with a large mirror. You might also add a low stool that you can sit on before the wedding begins. That way, you can spread your skirt around the stool as you sit, avoiding getting any wrinkles in your dress. It's also helpful to pack an "emergencies" kit for the women's dressing room. A few items to include are:

safety pins

hairspray

COST-CUTTERS

Look for tuxedo rental packages that offer the groom a free rental if the groomsmen rent through their agency.

Shop for bridesmaids' dresses at or right after prom season. Prom dresses offer formal attire at a much lower price. And prom accessories and shoes may be more affordable than those found at your bridal salon.

Order bridesmaids' dresses and/or your dress through a discount bridal outlet.

Wear a vintage wedding dress. Whether it's from your family or found at an antiques store, you may be able to refurbish an old dress for much less than the price of a new one.

Borrow a dress from a friend or rent a dress from a local rental store.

Shop for your dress at a consignment store, which sells once-worn dresses. You'll enjoy a lower price but still get to keep your dress after the wedding day.

hair dryer (can be used to dry any liquid spills on clothing)

breath mints

extra pantyhose

straws (to sip drinks without ruining your lipstick)

feminine napkins/tampons

aspirin/pain reliever/antacid tablets

white chalk (can cover spills on your white dress)

THE RIGHT FIT

Finding a wedding dress can be frustrating, especially if the dresses don't flatter your figure. Fortunately, these fashion guidelines can help you find the dress that's just right for you:

Triangle Shape (small bust, bigger hips)—Try an A-line or empire dress with a bodice that has more embellishment than the skirt. Avoid V-necks, heavily decorated skirts, and dresses that hug the hips.

Rectangle Shape (narrow body shape with bust, waist, and hips that are similar size)—Try an empire or A-line dress with a full skirt. You will also look good in a ball-gown-shaped dress.

Hourglass Shape (bust and hips nearly the same, smaller waist)—Try a straight skirt or trumpet-style gown and look for strapless dresses and V-necklines. Avoid dresses with lots of ruffles and ornamentation that will make you look heavier than you actually are.

Pear Shape (bust and waist smaller than hips)—Try ball gowns that accentuate your waist and conceal your hips. Look for off-the-shoulder necklines, embellished bodices, and plain skirts. Avoid dresses with bows in the back at hip height.

Full Figures—Try A-line dresses or basque dresses with a full skirt and open neckline. Ornamentation by the neckline will draw attention to your face rather than your full figure.

Petite—Try straight A-line or empire gowns with high necklines that are short-sleeved or sleeveless. Avoid very full gowns or basque gowns with a low waist.

extra bobby pins

needle and thread

scissors

Bride's Wedding Attire

MEMORIES

How many dresses I tried on before finding mine: _____

How many stores I visited before finding the dress: _____

What I thought when I saw the dress on the hanger: _____
_____
_____

What I felt when I first saw myself in my dress: _____
_____
_____

What my friends and family said about my dress: _____
_____
_____

Why I chose this dress: _____
_____
_____

GOWN INFORMATION

Shop/seamstress name: _____
_____

Phone number: _____

Contact person: _____

Gown style number: _____

Gown description: _____

_____

Gown cost: _____

Deposit paid: _____

Expected delivery date: _____

Crinoline: _____

ALTERATIONS

First fitting date/time: _____

Final fitting date/time: _____

Cost: _____

VEIL AND HEADPIECE

Veil style: _____

Veil cost: _____

Veil delivery date: _____

Headpiece style: _____

Headpiece cost: _____

Headpiece delivery date: _____

ACCESSORIES

Shoes: _____

Lingerie: _____

Gloves: _____

Jewelry: _____

Other: _____

Total cost: _____

HAIR AND MAKEUP

Hair stylist/salon: _____

_____

Phone number: _____

Appointment time(s): _____

_____

Cost: _____

Makeup artist: _____

_____

Phone number: _____

Appointment time: _____

Cost: _____

Bride of Honesty

Who may ascend the hill of the LORD? Who may stand in his holy place? He who has clean hands and a pure heart, who does not lift up his soul to an idol or swear by what is false.
—Psalm 24:3–4

The LORD detests lying lips, but he delights in men who are truthful.—Proverbs 12:22

Truth for Sale

Shopping for the wedding dress—it's a memorable experience for any bride. I visited numerous shops in my own quest for a gown, searching through row after row of silk, satin, and tulle. I tried on various dress styles, laughing at some of them and putting others into my mental "maybe" category. Yet something about each dress made me unsure. I still hadn't found "the one."

Maybe you're one of the lucky few who will love the first dress you try on. But more likely, you will search for a while before discovering the perfect gown. Everyone's different, but eventually, we all find the right dress. I knew I'd finally found mine when every other dress seemed to pale in comparison.

Sometimes, searching for truth feels like our search for a wedding gown. In today's culture, it seems like truth is for sale on every corner. This person buys into one belief; that person tries out something different. And we're told it doesn't matter—that truth is whatever you want it to be. In the end, most people end up trying on truth after truth, hoping they'll eventually find the one that really fits.

Sad thing is, a lot of these "truths" are really lies. Like the "truth" that money and popularity will give you fulfillment. Or that it's OK to use others to get ahead. Or that happiness comes from indulging in your desires. Looking around at these mixed-up beliefs, Isaiah made a prophecy that still seems relevant today: "Truth has stumbled in the streets . . . Truth is nowhere to be found" (59:14–15).

Amid these contorted values, honest brides need to defend the truth. Proverbs 31:8–9 challenges us to "speak up for those who cannot speak for themselves, for the rights of all who are destitute. Speak up and judge fairly." And that's just what an honest bride does—she confronts those who ignore the truth. And she challenges the false truths that hurt and destroy others.

Sometimes those false truths will stand out in black and white: it's wrong to take advantage of the poor, to kill an unborn child, to judge someone by the color of their skin. When the truth is clear, we need to be champions of the cause, defending what's right even when others try to silence us.

More often, though, we're confronted with situations that seem gray. Many times, we just aren't sure what's right and what's wrong. And we're left with this dilemma: how can we promote honesty when we don't know what's true?

Jesus gave us an answer to that question. Here's what he said: "I am the way and the *truth* and the life" (John 14:6, emphasis added). "Everyone on the side of truth listens to me" (John 18:37). In these simple words, Jesus tells us the secret to truth—it's found when we listen to him.

And there's a lot for us to listen to. God's Word bursts with the truth, if we'll take the time to read it. Jesus often said the words "I tell you the truth" as he preached sermons and parables to his followers. In fact, that phrase is used over seventy times in the Gospels. The truth really is out there—in the Word of our heavenly Groom.

As a new bride, you'll face many different values and ideas. They're in the bridal magazines at the store. They're in the sitcoms about married life that you watch on television. They're in the friendly words of advice from family and friends. Just as with bridal gowns, there are thousands of "truths" for sale. But be careful. Most of them are counterfeits—lies hidden in innocent-sounding words. Weigh things carefully. Compare ideas to the eternal Truth that God lays out in his Word. Listen for his voice in prayer.

And when you do find the truth, hang on! Protect it from any distortions, just as you guard your pristine wedding gown from any blemish or stain. And don't let it slip away. Because when your wedding day comes—and the marriage that follows—you'll want to be more than a woman in a pretty dress. You'll want to be a bride who is forever sold on the truth of God.

Unveiled

What a great spot, I silently congratulated myself. I was lying flat on the roof of our tree house, plotting my next move in our neighborhood game of hide-and-seek. Since the roof sloped toward the back of the yard, it was a great hiding place. Unless someone looked up from behind, I was invisible.

It's been years since I've lain on that tree house roof. In fact, the tree house is gone, just like my childhood days of hide-and-seek. Sometimes, though, I'm still hiding. And I've gotten more clever with my hiding places as the years go by. Steering conversations in a certain direction, keeping certain thoughts and beliefs to myself, pretending to like something I don't—those are just a few of the ways I keep people from seeing the real me.

Do you ever hide like that? Most of us do. We pull our masks on each morning—and we just keep changing them to fit the occasion. In little ways, we hide parts of ourselves or pretend to be someone we're not.

I think of a robber who stood near the convenience store as cops arrived on the scene. He'd heard the sirens in the distance, exited the store, and dodged into the shadows to pull off his jacket and mask. Quickly slipping back toward the scene of his own crime, he put a frightened look on his face and pretended to be a customer who had fled the store. The cops asked him if he'd seen the robber running by, and he replied with a simple no. Inwardly, he snickered as he realized he was telling the truth.

That's the problem with masks. They cause us to distort truth, even when we're not overtly lying. Beneath our masks, we hide things—our mistakes, our fears, our beliefs. Maybe we hide our faith in front of certain people instead of acknowledging how much we love God. Or maybe we hide our faults instead of coming clean about our mistakes. But whenever we put up a front with others, we keep them from seeing who God made us to be. And often, it's the things we *don't* say that distort the truth the most.

Honesty pulls back all those masks. And honesty is a trademark of true love: "Love does not delight in evil but rejoices with the truth" (1 Cor. 13:6). Maybe you've experienced that kind of honesty with your fiancé. I hope you have. Maybe you even experience it with your close family and friends. Yet all too often, we hide things even

BIBLE BRIDE

What a mess it had been. Abigail still remembered the incident like it was yesterday.

Her husband, Nabal, had always been selfish and mean. They had thousands of goats and sheep, more than enough to keep them satisfied. Yet one day when David's men had come and asked Nabal to spare some food, he had refused to help. Acting like an arrogant fool, he belittled David and his supposed destiny as Israel's next king.

David became furious. And when Nabal's servants heard about David's plan to destroy their household, they rushed off to talk to Abigail about the ordeal. Abigail was always the sensible one—the one who bailed her husband out of trouble.

As soon as she heard the news, she got to work. Gathering up an abundance of food, she took off to find David. And when she reached him, she came with humility, acknowledging her husband's poor behavior and wanting to make things right. Several times, she mentioned her desire to serve David—and her belief that he'd become Israel's next king.

But she also spoke the truth to this powerful man, reminding David how wrong it would be to kill Nabal. "You don't want murder on your conscience when God finally puts you on the throne," she said. "Don't you remember that God will take care of your enemies for you?" Her honesty hit the mark—and David had accepted her meal in peace.

Not only that, but after Nabal's death, David asked Abigail to be his wife. What an amazing twist of events that was! Since then, David became the king. And because of her simple humility and honesty, Abigail now stood by his side.

Check out Abigail's full story in 1 Samuel 25.

from those we love. We justify it, saying that we don't want to hurt them by telling the truth. But dishonesty can't be part of real love.

And dishonest masks don't work with the God of love either. We may ignore a sin rather than confess it. We may move forward with our own plans while claiming to follow God. Or we may soothe our troubles with things—relationships, alcohol, shopping—instead of taking them to God. But God sees all our hiding places. In Jeremiah 23:24, he says "Can anyone hide in secret places so that I cannot see him?"

God is so in love with us that he knows our hearts better than we know them ourselves. He can handle whatever we bring to him, whether it's sin, pain, guilt, or doubt. And he feels frustrated when we hide beneath a mask, because all he wants to do is reach in and wipe the tears from our eyes.

Maybe you're wearing a mask today. Maybe you've been holding back the truth from someone—or from God. Or maybe you've been hiding your faith. Perhaps you've even used dishonest actions and words to keep yourself veiled. But God sees beneath the veil and loves you anyway. And he can give you all the strength you'll need to unmask and reveal who you really are.

Once you take off that mask and let honesty be your guide, you'll be amazed at the results. Truth and love are forever linked, and as you seek to be truthful, you'll notice yourself beginning to look a lot like love. It's the trademark look of all of God's brides. As Paul put it, "We, who with unveiled faces all reflect the Lord's glory, are being transformed into his likeness with ever-increasing glory" (2 Cor. 3:18).

So why not quit your game of hide-and-seek? After all, you're God's bride. And as you stand in your regal gown, with a sparkling necklace adorning your neck and a glow in your cheeks, your Groom can't wait to flip back your veil and reveal the beautiful woman beneath.

9

THE INVITATIONS

When it comes to wedding plans, invitations often get treated as an afterthought. But they actually play a key role in your wedding, giving guests their first impression of your special day. Though it's tedious work to address and stuff all those envelopes, your invitations provide family and friends with a helpful reminder of the wedding date and time. With careful planning, they'll also become a practical way to track which invitees can actually attend.

Like wedding invitations, the virtues of prayer and courage invite others to share a special part of your life. Prayer invites God inside, giving him the opportunity to mold your life into something better than you could achieve on your own. And with courage, you share your faith with others, inviting them to accept God's transforming love. As your wedding day approaches, keep these important virtues in mind—prayer and courage may just become the most important invitations you'll ever send.

Bride of Prayer

In the morning, O LORD, you hear my voice; in the morning I lay my requests before you and wait in expectation.
—Psalm 5:3

Be glad for all God is planning for you . . . and always be prayerful.—Romans 12:12 NLT

I urge, then, first of all, that requests, prayers, intercession and thanksgiving be made for everyone . . . This is good, and pleases God our Savior.—1 Timothy 2:1, 3

Chat Sessions

I love watching the classic movie *Anne of Green Gables*. In one particularly funny scene, Anne invites her best friend, Diana, over for a tea party. Wanting everything to be perfect, Anne arranges pastries on a tray and pulls a bottle of raspberry cordial from the cupboard. Diana arrives, and the young ladies spend their first few moments acting formal, pretending to be grand ladies conversing at a social. Unbeknownst to them both, however, Anne's "raspberry cordial" turns out to be a bottle

of alcohol. And as Diana drinks glass after glass, she gets intoxicated, giggling and hiccupping along the way.

The incident makes me laugh out loud. But it also reminds me of my own real-life antics.

I remember a time when I got all dressed up and invited my boyfriend over for a fancy dinner. Amid candlelight and soft music, we felt very sophisticated—for a little while anyway. Neither one of us got drunk, but despite the fancy atmosphere, we couldn't act formal for long. We were still just boyfriend and girlfriend, laughing together and letting our defenses down. We ended up renting a funny movie and cuddling on the couch.

Hopefully you enjoy moments like that too—the kind where you can let your guard down and forget about social protocol. The kind where you end up laughing and chatting with your best friend for hours. Those moments make all the stress and anticipation of wedding plans bearable. And no matter how crazy life may be right now, hopefully you and your groom still find time to create those relaxed times together.

But there's another Groom who'd also love to be invited for a chat: God relishes those wonderful moments when we talk to him in prayer. Those moments can be difficult to find, though. It's hard enough for a bride to spend time with her fiancé, much less God!

And it's especially difficult to carve out time for prayer if those prayers feel awkward. Maybe you heard a sermon about the right "formula" for prayer, but when you tried it out, it felt too stiff and formal. We're often told to make prayers with a spoonful of thanks, a dash of confession, heaping mounds of praise, and then a few requests to finish. But that recipe just doesn't taste right in everyone's mouths.

There's certainly validity to some of these theories on prayer. It *is* good to include thanks, praise, and confession when we talk with God. But God isn't expecting our prayers to feel like a formal dinner. He doesn't want us to act like Anne and Diana. He doesn't want us to act all proper and sophisticated. In fact, he doesn't want us to act at all.

He's just interested in having a chat with his girl.

Prayer lets you invite God over for that chat. Then you can let your defenses down and pour out your heart to God. In fact, our Groom invites us to kick back with him: "Come to me all you who are weary and burdened, and I will give you rest" (Matt. 11:28). Does that sound at all like you right now? Burdened? Busy? Stressed? Why not invite God over so you can talk about it?

Just be prepared to end up like Diana. Because when you spend quiet moments with the guy you love, you end up feeling intoxicated. And prayer can have the same effect. In fact, brides of prayerfulness will always be "under the influence," because as we draw close to God in prayer, we'll feel his influence in our lives. And what a sweet influence it is. Instead of those unsettling worries and anxious feelings that brides so often experience, our hearts can be at rest.

If prayer has been in the backseat since your wedding plans started, maybe it's time to send out that invitation to God. Driving to work, exercising at the gym, eating dinner—he doesn't care what you're doing as long as you're being genuine with him. So go ahead. Be a bride of prayer and have a chat with your Groom.

God in the Dirt

It's always an adventure when I decide to invite friends over for dinner. The activity begins a few hours before my guests arrive. That's when I start working double time to clean my home. I wipe down the bathroom, vacuum the rugs, and pick up papers from counters and tables. Usually I'm still bustling around minutes before guests arrive, trying to straighten a few last details so everything looks just right.

My charade seems to work. Several people have commented on our nice home, and I always smile. Meanwhile, I'm thinking, *Thank goodness I had time to clean things up and get it looking like this!*

Have you ever played that game? The one where you clean up your life before inviting someone to have a look? As a bride, you're probably playing the game right now. When acquaintances ask how the wedding plans are going, you may smile and say, "Fine." But in reality your head spins with details you still need to plan, and your heart aches over the argument you had with Mom last night.

It's a game we all play at times. Cleaning everything up and making it look just right—it's a natural part of wedding plans, and dinner parties, and life. Of course, it's not such a great game when it comes to God.

God knows that life is messy. He knows *your* life is messy. Whether it's the overwhelming task of keeping your family happy while you plan a wedding, or the supposedly "easy" task of getting along with your fiancé, life gets complicated. Sometimes we make mistakes—or someone else messes up. Sometimes our hearts feel like a chaotic mess—filled with anxious and flustered feelings.

Does that sound like you right now? God won't be surprised if you answer yes. But you know what he says about the mess of life? "Do not be anxious about *anything*, but in everything, by prayer and petition, with thanksgiving, present your requests to God" (Phil. 4:6, emphasis added). I think that's his way of saying, "Hey, you don't have to clean up the mess for me. You can ask me about *anything*. I'd love to help."

That sounds simple enough, doesn't it? God longs for us to pray about everything—even the

LOVE STORY FROM GOD

It wasn't looking good for King Hezekiah. He'd lived a good life, striving to please God in his role as Judah's king. But today he faced some daunting news: a prophet had told him he would soon die. Though he felt sick in body and heart, Hezekiah knew what to do. Turning his face to the temple wall, Hezekiah prayed. "Remember how I've been faithful and devoted to you," he cried and pleaded with God. "Dear Lord, please save my life."

Hezekiah didn't know how God would answer, but he was confident that God would hear. He'd seen God respond to prayer before. At a time when it had seemed all but certain that Jerusalem would fall to the overwhelming and brutal power of the Assyrians, Hezekiah hadn't given up in despair—he'd turned to God in prayer.

And what an answer he'd gotten! The next morning, the Assyrians woke up to find 185,000 of their soldiers dead. The Assyrian king had withdrawn to his own land, unable to conquer Jerusalem or the one true God.

Remembering that miraculous answer to prayer, Hezekiah gained new hope in his prayers for healing. As he continued to pray, the prophet Isaiah came to him with words from God: "This is what the Lord, the God of your father David, says: I have heard your prayer and seen your tears; I will heal you . . . I will add fifteen years to your life" (2 Kings 20:5–6). Listening to those sweet words, Hezekiah sighed with joy and relief. Once again, God had responded to his prayers with a miracle.

To read the whole story of Hezekiah's powerful prayer, see 2 Kings 19:1–20:11.

dirt. But for some reason, we still try to hide the messes when it comes to prayer. Sometimes it's overt: we just refuse to pray about certain parts of our lives—a relationship, a past sin, a present temptation. In those situations, we actually prefer the mess. We don't really want God to do anything about it.

Most of the time, though, I don't think we really mean to hide our messes from God. It's just that we think we can handle them on our own. When trouble strikes, our first instinct is to clean it up using our own genius. By the time we get around to praying, we think it's already under control. And so we've played the "clean up" game with God—asking him to bless what *we've* done, instead of inviting *him* to deal with our messes.

This brings us to almost comical situations. I picture it like this: God walks into my house for a dinner party and quickly notices supper boiling over on the stove, magazines peeking out from under the couch, and a pile of dirt that escaped from under the rug. Meanwhile, I smile and say, "Well, hello. Don't you think I've done a good job of keeping my life in order?"

Truth is, we're not so good at keeping life in order. And that's exactly why we need prayer. It's our chance to invite God into the dirt. To admit that we need his help in dealing with the mess. The apostle Paul understood this dynamic well. When writing about the messes of life, he said that God's strength "is made perfect in weakness," and he went on to say, "For when I am weak, then I am strong" (2 Cor. 12:9–10).

At the very moments when we feel weakest—when we stop trying to fix the mess ourselves and give it over to God in prayer—that's when we become strong. That's when God gets to work. And then we really experience God's power in our lives.

So as your wedding day approaches and the messes crop up, stop trying to fix them by yourself. Instead, invite God into the dirt. He's better at cleaning than we are anyway.

Planning Your Wedding Stationery

Choosing Invitations

Invitations should match the style and tone of the wedding. For formal weddings, traditional third-person wording and black ink should be used, and printing should be engraved or thermographed onto ivory or white paper. If you're planning a semiformal or informal affair, invitations with personal wording and colored papers and inks are acceptable; printing may be thermographed or laser printed. For small, intimate weddings, handwritten invitations are the preferred option.

As you consider invitation styles, you'll also need to select inner and outer envelopes. Lined envelopes provide a touch of elegance and color, but they also add to the overall cost of your invitations. Since your guests will most likely throw envelopes away, you may opt for unlined envelopes if you're in a budget crunch. Eliminating the inner envelope altogether provides another easy cost-cutter.

Once you have an idea of what style you'd like, start looking through sample invitations at local printers and stationery stores. Most brides select their wedding stationery from the catalogs of a few large printers. While it's impossible to create a personal design when selecting from a

catalog, this method boasts several advantages. Catalogs usually include samples that give you an exact feel for the weight and color of each invitation. Also, since the catalogs come from well-established printers that specialize in wedding invitations, you can generally be assured of good quality while also enjoying a lower price. To be sure of quality, however, you should always ask the stationery store if they've experienced any problems when ordering from the company you are considering.

If you'd like a unique invitation design or want to have your invitations engraved, you'll need to investigate smaller printers rather than the large catalog companies. Be prepared to spend more money if you decide on this route. And as you talk to potential printers, request samples of their work so you can look for quality workmanship. Make sure they have expertise in both printing and designing wedding invitations.

Whether you choose a large company or a local printer, always request an itemized cost breakdown before you order anything. Also, ask what their policy is regarding printer error. How quickly can they provide replacements? They should guarantee a firm delivery date that will give you plenty of time to proofread the printed items before they need to be addressed and mailed.

Wording

As you write out your wedding invitations, be sure to include the following details: full name of bride and groom, time, date, and location of ceremony. Before you finalize the order with your printer, double-check that words are spelled correctly and all necessary information has been accurately given.

Below, you'll find traditional wordings for wedding invitations. Keep in mind, though, that a few changes to the "traditional" wording are perfectly acceptable, particularly for semi-formal and informal invitations. Also, though stepparents are not mentioned in the examples below, you may choose to include their names in the wedding invitation as well.

Wedding Given by Bride's Mother and Father

Mr. and Mrs. James McCleland
request the honour of your presence
at the marriage of their daughter
Teresa Ann
to
Mr. Benjamin David Stevens
Friday, the third of September
two thousand six
at half after six o'clock
Lakeview Baptist Church
Smithville, Minnesota

PLANNING CHECKLIST

SIX TO NINE MONTHS BEFORE

- [ ] Research cost and options for invitations and other wedding stationery.
- [ ] Finalize guest list and determine how many invitations are needed.
- [ ] Select printer and invitation style. Determine what enclosures you will need.
- [ ] Finalize wording for invitations and enclosures.
- [ ] If necessary, create maps, directions, and travel information for out-of-town guests.
- [ ] Order invitations and other wedding stationery.
- [ ] Compile addresses and phone numbers of guests.

THREE TO FIVE MONTHS BEFORE

- [ ] Make arrangements with friends and family to address invitations, or hire a calligrapher.
- [ ] Double-check that you have contact information for each guest.
- [ ] Proofread each item when your printed order arrives.

TWO TO THREE MONTHS BEFORE

- [ ] Weigh invitations and purchase postage.
- [ ] Address envelopes and assemble invitations.

FOUR TO EIGHT WEEKS BEFORE

- [ ] Mail invitations, preferably at least six weeks in advance.

TWO TO FOUR WEEKS BEFORE

- [ ] Make follow-up phone calls to those who have not sent an RSVP.

A PRINTING PRIMER

Does all that printing terminology have you confused? Don't fret. The following explanations will help you understand your printing options:

Handwritten—This one's pretty straightforward. Though it takes a lot of time to write out each invitation by hand, it's great for your budget. If you plan a small wedding, this may be the perfect option for you. Just purchase quality pens and recruit helpers with beautiful penmanship.

Flat/Offset Printing—This method doesn't provide the raised effect of thermography or engraving, but it allows you to incorporate multiple ink colors into your design. The finished look is flat and can generally be achieved at a lower cost than thermography or engraving.

Laser Printing—With a large number of laser printers on the market today, laser printing can be done quite inexpensively with a home computer. Many stationers provide blank invitations and software that can be used to print your own invitations.

Thermography—Using a special press that heats the ink, thermography results in a raised-letter effect. This method provides a look that is almost identical to engraving but at about half the price.

Engraving—Considered the most elegant form of printing, engraving uses metal plates that stamp the paper from the back as the printing is done. The result is a raised-letter effect that can be felt on both the front and back of the paper. Engraving also results in print that is less shiny than that of thermography.

Wedding Given by Both Bride's Parents and Groom's Parents

Mr. and Mrs. George Stanley

and

Mr. and Mrs. Miguel Lopez

request the honour of your presence

at the marriage of

Jessica Marie Stanley

and

Alexander Miguel Lopez

Saturday, the twenty-second of June

two thousand six

at three o'clock

Hoffman United Methodist Church

Hoffman, Colorado

Wedding Given by Bride and Groom

The honour of your presence

is requested

at the marriage of

Miss Christine Sue Lawrence

to

Mr. Michael James Fisher

Saturday, the twelfth of July

two thousand five

at half after ten o'clock

Northgate Central Park

Northgate, Georgia

Wedding Given by Mother, Father Deceased

Mrs. Anne Jacobs
requests the honour of your presence
at the marriage of her daughter
Allison Renee
(etc.)

Wedding Given by Mother, Divorced

Use mother's current or maiden name and father's last name:

Mrs. Anne Smithfield Jacobs
requests the honour of your presence
at the marriage of her daughter
Allison Renee
(etc.)

Wedding Given by Both Parents, Divorced

Use mother's and father's current name:

Mrs. Anne Smithfield and Mr. Alan Jacobs
request the honour of your presence
at the marriage of their daughter
Allison Renee
(etc.)

Wedding Given by Remarried Mother

Use present husband's name:

Mr. and Mrs. Anne Bradley
request the honour of your presence
at the marriage of her daughter
Allison Renee Jacobs
(etc.)

Wedding Given by Father, Mother Deceased or Divorced

Mr. Alan Jacobs
requests the honour of your presence
at the marriage of his daughter
Allison Renee
(etc.)

Wedding Given by Remarried Father

Mr. and Mrs. Alan Jacobs
request the honour of your presence
at the marriage of his daughter
Allison Renee
(etc.)

Military Weddings

If rank is lower than sergeant, do not list rank but list branch of service below name:

Mr. and Mrs. Timothy Davidson
request the honour of your presence
at the marriage of their daughter
Monica Jane
United States Navy
to
James Allen Smith
United States Navy
(etc.)

If rank is higher than lieutenant, place rank before name and put branch of service below line. Junior officer's titles are placed below their name, along with the branch of service.

Mr. and Mrs. Timothy Davidson
request the honour of your presence
at the marriage of their daughter
Monica Jane
Lieutenant, United States Navy
to
Captain James Allen Smith
United States Navy
(etc.)

Assembling Your Invitations

Now that the invitations have been delivered, it's time to start the long process of addressing and assembly. If you have some friends or family members with lovely penmanship, you may want to recruit their help for an "invitation assembly party."

Envelopes should be addressed according to the following guidelines.

Outer Envelope

Formal titles should be used. For example, "Mr. and Mrs. Robert Johnson" instead of "Bob and Jane Johnson."

Titles such as doctor, reverend, father, and captain are written out.

The titles Mr., Mrs., and Ms. should be abbreviated.

PROOFREADING CHECKLIST

Before you order invitations, proofread everything you've given to the printer. The following list will help you double-check the details. And once your order has arrived, you should go through the list a second time to check for printer errors.

☐ Are all names and places spelled correctly, with no abbreviations or nicknames (unless that was the person's preference)? Are titles accurate?

☐ Are the date and time correctly written out? Do they correspond with the calendar?

☐ Is all address information accurate?

☐ Is punctuation in correct places?

☐ Do the lines break correctly, with the hosts' names, the bride's name, the groom's name, the date, the year, the ceremony site, and the location all getting their own line?

☐ Are the words properly spaced and centered?

☐ After delivery: does the invitation match the sample in weight, color, size, and design?

☐ After delivery: are the correct font and style used on all items?

☐ After delivery: is the return address correctly printed on envelopes and/or response cards?

☐ After delivery: do all cards and enclosures fit into the proper envelopes?

City and state names are written out without abbreviation, along with address words such as street, court, avenue, and boulevard.

When inviting a family, the words "and family" can be added behind the husband and wife's titles and name.

Inner Envelope

Write out titles and last names of invited adults, such as "Mr. and Mrs. Johnson."

If children are invited, include their first names on a line below their parents' names. Do not use the phrase "and family" on inner envelopes.

For a more casual approach, first names of friends and family members may be used. For example, "Bob and Jane Johnson" or "Uncle Bob and Aunt Jane."

Envelopes sent to single guests should include their name, followed by the phrase "and guest."

Assembly

Start by placing the response card inside its envelope.

Place the reception card, response card and envelope, and any other inserts (maps, rain cards, etc.) inside the invitation (or behind, if invitation is printed on single sheet).

Position tissue paper over the invitation printing to avoid smudging.

Place the invitation into the inner envelope, folded edge down and print facing the back so it's visible upon opening. Do not seal the inner envelope.

Tuck the inner envelope inside the outer envelope, with the guest's name facing the back so it's visible upon opening.

Postage

While most invitations can be sent with standard-rate stamps, the addition of several inserts may require added postage. Take a fully assembled invitation to the post office and have it weighed so you can purchase the right postage. You may also need to add postage if your invitations are square or some other nonrectangular shape. For a nice touch, purchase special stamps that have a floral or wedding motif.

Inserts

When ordering invitations, you should also order the necessary inserts. Consider the following options.

Response Cards—Response cards can be printed in postcard style, with your return address directly on the card. Or they can be ordered with small envelopes that bear your return address. In either case, you should provide postage for this item. To avoid any confusion, provide a deadline for guests' responses and use wording similar to the following example:

> *The favor of a reply*
> *is requested before*
> *August twenty-four*
>
> *M*_____
> *will*_____ *will not* _____ *attend.*
> *Number of persons* _____

Reception Cards—These cards include the time and place of the reception and can be inserted into the invitations of guests who are invited to join you at the reception.

Maps—For out-of-town guests, a map showing the locations of both your ceremony and reception sites will prove helpful. Include written directions to accompany the map.

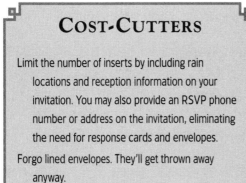

Cost-Cutters

Limit the number of inserts by including rain locations and reception information on your invitation. You may also provide an RSVP phone number or address on the invitation, eliminating the need for response cards and envelopes.

Forgo lined envelopes. They'll get thrown away anyway.

Use cheaper printing methods, such as thermography and offset printing.

Avoid reorders by proofreading items carefully before submitting your order.

Purchase extra invitations and envelopes. Since much of the printing cost is due to setup costs, it's much less expensive to order extras with your original order than to place a second order.

Eliminate inner envelopes.

Create your own invitations, using a laser printer and invitation packages and/or materials that are available at many stationery or computer supply stores.

Choose simple designs, basic fonts, and black ink.

Pew Cards—Pew cards usually include a simple note saying "Reserved Seating." They can be enclosed with invitations to close family and special guests and then handed to the ushers at your wedding so that these guests can be seated in the reserved areas at the front.

Rain Cards—If your ceremony or reception is being held outside, you may want to include a card listing the alternate location in case of rain.

Ceremony Cards—When weddings are held in a public location, such as a museum or garden, ceremony cards give them admission and distinguish them from tourists visiting the site.

Travel Information—If many out-of-town guests are expected, it's thoughtful to include information about local hotels, airports, train stations, and restaurants. If a block of hotel rooms has been reserved, this information should be included with the invitation.

Additional Items

Most printers and stationers also provide other wedding-related items. While it's not necessary to order these items with your invitations, it may be cost-effective to do so. Many companies provide invitation packages that offer discounts when greater quantities are ordered. Of course, if you have a creative flair, you can make many of these items yourself using materials from stationery stores. Look over the following list to determine which items you'll need.

Thank-You Cards—Also called informals, thank-you notes usually include the name or initials of the bride and groom on the cover. Inside, the notes are blank.

Wedding Announcements—If your space and budget are limited, there may be friends, acquaintances, and co-workers who couldn't be invited to the wedding. If you'd like to include them in a small way, send them a wedding announcement. Announcements traditionally include the same wording as your invitations, with the substitution of "proudly announce the marriage of" instead of "request the honour of your presence at the marriage of."

Place Cards—If reception seating will be assigned, you should order or make place cards telling guests where they are to be seated.

Programs—Ceremony programs usually include the order of your ceremony, along with any special readings or song lyrics. You'll want to print the names of attendants and other wedding participants, noting their relationship to the bride or groom. Your program also provides a great place to write a thank-you to your guests or to incorporate a special Bible verse.

Personalized Items—A variety of items can be personalized by printers today—from napkins and matchbooks to keepsake candy boxes and candles. Ask your stationer or printer for a catalog of items that they offer.

Ordering

Before placing your final order, finalize your guest list and determine the exact number of invitations you'll need. Ideally, you should send an invitation to each couple, single guest, and child who is eighteen or older. Remember to include invitations for the wedding party, officiant, and musicians as well.

Once you have a final number, add a few extras to your order. You'll want a few invitations to save as keepsakes or to use for last-minute additions to the guest list. A good rule of thumb is to add 5 percent of your original number to the order. It's also wise to order additional envelopes in case mistakes are made while addressing invitations.

Finally, review your other stationery needs before placing an order for invitations. Often, you can get a better price if additional items—such as response cards, wedding announcements, and thank-yous—are ordered at the same time as your invitations. Fill out the Wedding Stationery List to help you pick out the necessary items.

Wedding Stationery List

	Number Needed	Cost
Invitations		
Outer envelopes		
Inner envelopes		
Reception cards		
Response cards		
Response envelopes		
Maps		
Pew cards		
Ceremony cards		
Rain cards		
Announcements		
Place cards		
Programs		
Thank-you cards		
Other		
Postage		

WEDDING STATIONERY

Name of stationer/printer: _____

_____

Contact information: _____

_____

_____

Invitation style: _____

Font/typeface style: _____

_____

Total cost: _____

Deposit paid: _____

Delivery date: _____

GET CREATIVE

There are many ways to add a special touch to your invitation. Try one of the following:

Create a personalized logo to appear on your invitations, inserts, and wedding programs.

Lightly spray each invitation with an inviting perfume.

Put a few dried rose petals or some confetti in each envelope, so they will sprinkle out when the invitation is opened.

Add the words of your favorite Bible verse to the invitation.

Make your own invitations, using your engagement photo and materials found at scrapbooking stores.

Add ribbon to your invitations by punching holes on the top or side and weaving a decorative ribbon through the holes.

Seal your invitations with a hot wax stamp or a decorative stamp.

Bride of Courage

Be strong and courageous. Do not be terrified; do not be discouraged, for the LORD your God will be with you wherever you go.—Joshua 1:9

But encourage one another daily, as long as it is called Today, so that none of you may be hardened by sin's deceitfulness. —Hebrews 3:13

RSVP

When I think of courage, I often picture great biblical heroes, people like Abraham, David, and Peter. These were men who followed God with gusto. They moved to strange lands, fought giants, and walked on water. And compared to such courageous heroes, I feel small.

I often lack confidence to do simple things—like apologizing to a friend, considering a new job, or sharing my faith with a neighbor. My fear stands in the way, and instead of accepting God's invitation to a new adventure, I tend to run toward the safety of the status quo. My RSVP gets stuck in a corner of my heart that's afraid to say yes to God's call. And I feel like the lion from *The Wizard of Oz*—my courage has been lost.

I don't think I'm alone, though. Fear lives among us all, often choking out our passion to follow God. Fear tells us we could never live like those heroes of the faith—that we shouldn't even try. But those biblical heroes weren't superhuman. They faced fear too, just like you and me.

While living in Egypt, Abraham feared the king would be jealous of his beautiful wife, so he lied and called Sarah his sister. David expressed a mountain of different fears throughout the Psalms. And Peter? He became so terrified that he denied knowing Jesus three times during one night. These heroes were no strangers to fear. But when they trusted in God, they accomplished great triumphs.

173

Just imagine for a moment what would've happened if they hadn't had that trust. Abraham never would've been the spiritual father of God's chosen people. David would've missed his opportunity to be a king. And Peter would've stayed in the boat instead of walking on waves. Without courage, they would've missed the wonders of God at work in their lives. And they'd have failed in their mission to show the world who God really is.

When fears overwhelm us today, we need to pause and remember what's at stake. God invites us all to do different things, some wonderful and some scary. But whatever the situation, it's always an invitation for God to work in our lives. And when we lack the courage to respond, we not only lose the opportunity to see God's wonders in us, but we also present the world with a very weak faith.

Among God's brides, courage should never be rare. Yet so often we walk around like scared, powerless people. Like the *Wizard of Oz* lion, we let fear distort reality, and we forget who we really are. And in reality, we are even mightier than a lion! We're brides of a powerful Groom. The God who walked beside Abraham, David, and Peter—that's the same God who walks with us. So why should we ever let fear win the day?

Yes, fear's a natural human response. But we live in the grace of a supernatural God. If we'll remember who we are—and more important, who God is—we can move forward in faith. Not because fear has vanished. But because our God is bigger than the fear. And instead of letting fear strangle our lives, we can press through it with a courage born of faith.

"Be strong and courageous. Do not be terrified; do not be discouraged, for the LORD your God will be with you wherever you go" (Josh. 1:9). That's God's challenge for you. And no matter where he calls you or how uncertain or frightening things may seem, God will always walk with you. So consider his invitation today. And as you sort through all those wedding RSVPs, start considering your own all-important response. When God invites you to take a step of faith, will you have the courage to trust in him?

God's Guest List

Who's invited to the wedding? As you've ordered invitations and created your guest list, you've probably asked that question a dozen times. Should you invite that old childhood buddy? What about your new neighbors or the great-aunt you haven't seen in five years?

Deciding which friends and acquaintances will make the final cut isn't easy, especially when you have limited space. That's probably why dozens of advice columns have been written on the topic. Yet despite their best efforts, no one has discovered the magic formula for a perfect guest list. And until they do, we'll keep scrutinizing each name and hoping we don't offend anyone.

I'm grateful that God doesn't go through that kind of process when he invites people to trust in him. Can you imagine if he did? He could've taken one look at any of us, considered all our sins, and left us off his guest list.

Fortunately, that's not how God operates.

Revelation 19:9 proclaims, "Blessed are those who are invited to the wedding supper of the Lamb!" Blessed. That's exactly what we are. Just think of everything God has given us—hope for the future, salvation from sin, peace about eter-

BIBLE BRIDE

Esther took a deep breath. Those who entered the king's inner court without invitation could be sentenced to death. And even though Esther was the queen, she hadn't been summoned here today.

Yet here she was, ready to risk her life by walking inside. And as fear gripped her stomach, she remembered her cousin Mordecai's words: "Perhaps you have come to royal position for such a time as this."

Esther understood this monumental moment. Her entire race was at stake. One of the king's officials, Haman, had gotten terribly angry when Mordecai would not bow down to him as other officials did. In a fit of rage, Haman had stormed off to the king, convinced him that the Jews were a troublemaking group, and talked him into killing the whole race.

Now Esther stood between the life and death of her people. And the king didn't even know she was a Jew. Revealing her identity and pleading for her people could mean her death. So Esther had fasted and prayed for three days, desperately seeking the courage to go before the king.

Now, as she stepped into the king's court to make her plea, Esther knew that God had answered her prayer for courage. And when the king nodded his approval at her presence and promised to grant her request, she realized something else—one simple act of courage had just saved an entire nation.

To read the rest of Esther's story, check out Esther 5–8.

nity, joy that doesn't change with circumstances. Yet millions of people live without these things. They face life day in and day out without that kind of assurance.

All of those hopeless people need to hear God's invitation. They need to know about the wedding day that's coming and the deep love of the Groom. And God is inviting them—through his Word, through his Spirit, and through his creation. But he also tries a more personal approach to his invitations: he uses people like you and me.

When you consider the materials he's working with, it's pretty amazing that God uses average people to send out his invitations. Most of us aren't experts on evangelism. Many of us fumble for words when we try to share our faith. All of us struggle with sin. And somehow, God works through all of that, asking us to "go out into all the world and preach the good news to all creation" (Mark 16:15).

Following those words takes courage. The world doesn't understand our beliefs or our God—and many will laugh at us or hurl insults when we speak out about our faith. On a personal level, witnessing raises fears too. We don't want our witnessing to offend people. We may feel awkward about sharing our testimony. We might lose a friend, or a job, or our social status.

Yet people all around us are dying, both physically and spiritually. And if we don't find courage to tell them about our faith, they'll never get invited to God's wedding feast. We're fighting for the most important thing in life: people's souls. And for such a sacred task, we must find the courage to act.

Just think of all the courageous acts that took place on September 11. As airplanes crashed and the Twin Towers fell, we saw hundreds of courageous people in action. These were people who rose to the occasion, and their courage captured our attention. As survivors were interviewed, reporters often asked, "What got you through? What gave you the courage?" Instinctively, we all wanted to know where we could find such courage for ourselves.

And that's what happened for the apostles too. When they risked their lives to preach about Jesus, people noticed their courage and looked for its source. "When [the crowd] saw the courage of Peter and John and realized that they were unschooled, ordinary men, they were astonished and they took note that these men had been with Jesus" (Acts 4:13). By sharing courageously, those apostles spread the gospel throughout the world. And when we step out in courage, we can capture someone's attention too.

As a bride today, it may be hard to think about courage or sharing your faith. There are so many distractions in your life at the moment, and you need to plan your future. Yet even now, there are neighbors, friends, co-workers, and strangers who live in hopelessness around you. And if you don't have the courage to share the Good News, they may never find their way to God's wedding feast.

Think of God's guest list today. And then ask the simple question: is there anyone you need to invite?

10

THE CEREMONY

Flowers, cakes, gowns—these details may fill the pages of popular wedding magazines, but the real heart of a wedding happens at the ceremony. That's when you and your fiancé stand before family and friends to make lifetime promises to each other. And that's the sacred moment when God blends two lives into one.

As you plan your wedding day, don't let ceremony details wait until the last minute. Choose vows, songs, and Scriptures that reflect what you believe in and Whom you depend on. Then consider creative ways to worship God on your special day. When you and your fiancé weave the virtues of worship and dependence into your wedding plans, your ceremony will give a delightful glimpse of who you are—and the marriage you hope to build.

Bride of Worship

How good it is to sing praises to our God, how pleasant and fitting to praise him!—Psalm 147:1

Therefore I urge you, brothers, in view of God's mercy, to offer your bodies as living sacrifices, holy and pleasing to God—this is your spiritual act of worship.—Romans 12:1

Out with Eddie

As a kid, I watched many reruns of *Leave It to Beaver*. It had the novelty of a black-and-white TV program and the appeal of simple, lovable characters. And besides these charming features, I thought Wally Cleaver was kind of cute. Yet there was one character who always got on my nerves: Eddie Haskell, the mischievous teen who always sweet-talked the adults. Eddie took the credit for other people's good deeds, shining like a star while the real do-gooder went unnoticed. I felt like shouting to the two-dimensional adults on the screen: "Don't praise Eddie! He doesn't deserve it!"

Unfortunately, Eddie Haskell doesn't just exist on the TV screen. We run into Eddies all the time in real life. Recently, a friend expressed frustration over a co-worker. This person would listen to everyone's ideas and then present them to the boss as if they were her own. There's an Eddie Haskell for you—taking all the credit but deserving none of it.

Eddie Haskells work in the wedding business too. But I'm not talking about the annoying salesperson who tries to sweet-talk you into their products. I'm actually thinking about some blissful couples—the ones who take all the credit for their love.

Just flip on the television during a wedding scene and you'll see what I mean. On nearly every show, the wedding vows will sound the same. Their basic message usually amounts to this: "Look at us! We've been through so much and worked so hard to be here. Today, we celebrate our love for each other and promise to keep loving each other forever!"

Now, I don't have any problems with love, or with couples who celebrate their unique journey to love. I'm just frustrated by Eddie Haskells—those brides and grooms who forget to give credit to the One who created their love. The One who *is* love.

The writer of Psalm 100 tells us who really deserves the credit. "Worship the LORD with gladness . . . It is he who made us, and we are his . . . For the LORD is good and his love endures forever; his faithfulness continues through all generations" (vv. 1–2, 5). In these brief words, the psalmist reminds us why God deserves the praise. He's the one who made us—and the love we share. Only he can create a love that endures forever, the kind that can draw a man and woman together for a lifetime.

When we stop to consider who's really responsible for our love, those TV weddings look ridiculous. Sure, the couple may have gone through a lot of twists and turns to get to the wedding chapel, but as they celebrate themselves, they forget about Love himself. And without giving any mention of him, those weddings have an Eddie Haskell feel—everything is sugary sweet but kind of empty underneath it all.

Sadly, many real-life couples do the same thing—even those who believe in God. Their ceremonies are filled with sweet talk and secular songs that focus on *their* love, but they never take time to honor the *creator* of their love. They pull an Eddie Haskell, taking credit for everything themselves.

Hopefully, you'll decide to give God credit at your wedding. But maybe you're wondering how exactly to do that. How can you let others know that this day isn't just a celebration of your love, but that it's also a celebration of God's love?

The angels of heaven are shouting out the answer even now: "Worship him who made the heavens, the earth, the sea and the springs of water" (Rev. 14:7). Worship. It helps us overcome Eddie Haskell syndrome. It gives praise to God instead of focusing it on ourselves. And even though the world may not put weddings and worship together, they're actually a perfect pair. What better time to honor God than at an event where we celebrate the love he's given?

So as you plan your own celebration, don't forget about worship. Ask the congregation to join in a praise song, have a parent offer prayers of thanksgiving, or try another creative way to honor God. In these little ways, you'll push Eddie Haskell right out the door. And he'll have to sweet-talk someone else. Because at your wedding, the credit's going to the One who deserves it.

The Heart of Worship

Marlena had an amazing voice. Working as the worship coordinator at a small church, she had lots of opportunities to use it. She spent hours each week attending practices and planning worship services. And when Sunday morning came around, her powerful voice led the congregation in beautiful worship songs.

From the outside, anyone would've thought Marlena offered sincere worship. But the church members doubted it. Marlena had gained a reputation for her heartless criticism of other singers—and anyone who challenged her worship plans. She'd started voicing her desire to move from "this Hicksville church," as she called it, "to a place where they have some musical talent to work with." Things had gotten so bad that church leaders were planning to fire her.

Marlena certainly knew *how* to worship. She could sing praises with the best of them. And when it came to worship plans, she had a lot to offer with her talent and her ideas. But Marlena was missing something crucial: she forgot to bring her heart. Her worship became a Sunday show quickly forgotten during everyday life.

We may shake our heads at her story, but could there be a little piece of Marlena in us too? Have you ever sung praise hymns on Sunday and then shouted an insult on Wednesday? Ever raised your hands during a song of commitment and then made a poor judgment call later the same day? We're all guilty to some degree. It's a constant struggle to keep our hearts in the right place—not just during worship services but all week long.

The people of Israel had the same problem. Isaiah didn't mince any words when he challenged them about it. "The Lord says: 'These people come near to me with their mouth and honor me with their lips, but their hearts are far from me'" (29:13). Later, the apostle James shared a similar complaint with the early Christians. "Out of the same mouth come praise and cursing. My brothers, this should not be" (James 3:10).

BIBLE BRIDE

"Where's my tambourine?" Miriam muttered to herself as she hurriedly searched through her belongings. Everything had been haphazardly thrown together when Moses told the Israelites to prepare for their exit from Egypt. As she'd packed, Miriam had felt nervous. They'd been slaves for so long, and it seemed impossible that Pharaoh would just let them walk away now. Something was bound to go wrong.

Miriam was right. Pharaoh had been scared by a plague from Israel's God—scared enough to let the Israelites leave. But before long, he'd changed his mind. As the Israelites approached the Red Sea, Pharaoh's troops had been right on their heels.

But God sent a miracle. Before her very eyes, Miriam watched the Red Sea part. She stared in amazement while she walked through the watery walls. And now her people were safely on the other side, while Pharaoh's men were drowned when the waters crashed in. Filled with awe and gratitude, Miriam wanted to give praise to God for their safe crossing.

Spotting her tambourine at last, Miriam grabbed it and began to sing, "Sing to the Lord, for he is highly exalted!" Soon the rest of the women were joining in, singing, laughing, and dancing. At a time when the future was uncertain, it still felt good to worship their powerful God.

Read Miriam's story in Exodus 14 and 15.

Isaiah's and Paul's words cut to the heart of the matter—they cut to *our* hearts. When it comes to worship, God wants more than just lip service. He wants our worship to be alive. He wants us to offer him all that we have—in a way that impacts our lives far beyond a weekly worship service. In short, God wants our hearts.

Maybe the best picture of this concept can be found at a wedding ceremony. That's where a bride and groom give their hearts away—to each other. Often, they say those very words in their wedding vows or through the songs that are sung. Sometimes, the couple even uses a picture of two entwined hearts on their wedding programs. And in worship, we should offer our hearts in the same vulnerable and heartfelt way.

Just imagine how horrible it would be if the bride or groom didn't have their heart in it. Picture the groom whispering to the pastor, "I know we have to go through these vows to make things legal, but could we hurry it along so I can golf this afternoon?" Or worse yet, picture a bride in silent tears because her heart still belongs to another man. At a wedding like that, our hearts would ache for the person who's stuck with a halfhearted spouse.

That's exactly how God feels about halfhearted worship. When he sees worship that vanishes after Sunday, his heart aches. He longs for a bride who'll honor him in her heart—every day of the week.

Are you that kind of bride? Do you find time to worship God in everyday life, or are you too busy finding a place to live or picking the colors of your wedding flowers? When it comes to life outside of church, can others see that you've given your heart to God?

Maybe you have some weaknesses in this area, but starting today, you can renew your heart for worship. Try something symbolic, like putting your wedding planner in the pajama drawer on Sundays—so you can take a day off from wedding plans to focus on praising God. Or try blending worship experiences into daily life—listening to a worship CD in the car, reading a psalm of praise each morning at work, or offering prayers of praise with your fiancé before dinner.

Through these simple actions, you'll plant a worshipful attitude that spreads into every part of your life. But more important, worship will put your heart right where it's always belonged—in the hands of your heavenly Groom.

Planning Your Ceremony

Meeting with the Officiant

Hopefully you selected an officiant for your wedding ceremony shortly after the engagement was announced. (See chapter 4 for more information on choosing an officiant.) Once you've confirmed your officiant's availability for your wedding day, schedule an appointment with him or her to go over ceremony details. If possible, arrange for this appointment at least three months prior to your wedding. This will allow plenty of time to plan the ceremony while also coordinating details with other wedding participants. If your officiant doesn't work for the church where you'll be married, you may need to schedule a separate meeting with someone from the ceremony location as well.

Read through the following list of questions and put a mark by those you wish to ask during your meeting with the officiant and/or ceremony site manager.

What are the requirements for getting married in this church/synagogue/religious tradition?

Is premarital counseling required and/or available from you? If so, when can our counseling sessions be scheduled?

Are we allowed to write all or parts of the ceremony (readings, vows, etc.) or must we follow prescribed elements?

What ceremony order would you recommend? How much latitude do we have in changing or adding to the traditional ceremony order?

Can additional clergy take part in the ceremony? If so, who will be responsible for which parts?

Are there any restrictions on decorations? On music?

What musical instruments are available at the church (organ, piano, other)?

Does the church or synagogue have musicians available to play or sing for weddings?

Is an aisle runner available at the church?

Are there any restrictions on throwing rice, bird seed, or rose petals outside the church?

Can the flower girl toss real rose petals inside the church?

Are there any photography or videography restrictions?

Are there any restrictions concerning bridal attire? Bare shoulders or arms? Head coverings?

Are rooms available for dressing prior to the service? If so, is a large mirror available in the bridal dressing room or will I need to bring my own?

What time can I get into the ceremony site for decorations and setup?

Will another wedding be held on the same day as ours? If so, how much time is there between ceremonies for setup and cleanup?

What arrangements need to be made for heating/air-conditioning on the wedding day?

Will the ceremony site provide a sound technician or must we find someone on our own?

What's the total cost for officiant fees and the use of the facilities? Are janitorial services included in this price or must we clean up after the ceremony ourselves?

What are parking arrangements at the church? If parking is limited, can you recommend nearby locations where guests can park?

Musicians, Take Your Places

To ensure your musicians' availability, contact them several months before the wedding. Whether it's a close friend or the longtime church organist, never assume that musicians will be

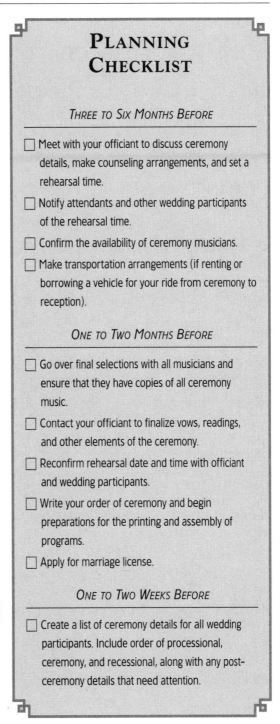

PLANNING CHECKLIST

THREE TO SIX MONTHS BEFORE

☐ Meet with your officiant to discuss ceremony details, make counseling arrangements, and set a rehearsal time.

☐ Notify attendants and other wedding participants of the rehearsal time.

☐ Confirm the availability of ceremony musicians.

☐ Make transportation arrangements (if renting or borrowing a vehicle for your ride from ceremony to reception).

ONE TO TWO MONTHS BEFORE

☐ Go over final selections with all musicians and ensure that they have copies of all ceremony music.

☐ Contact your officiant to finalize vows, readings, and other elements of the ceremony.

☐ Reconfirm rehearsal date and time with officiant and wedding participants.

☐ Write your order of ceremony and begin preparations for the printing and assembly of programs.

☐ Apply for marriage license.

ONE TO TWO WEEKS BEFORE

☐ Create a list of ceremony details for all wedding participants. Include order of processional, ceremony, and recessional, along with any post-ceremony details that need attention.

THE REHEARSAL

Rehearsals are generally held the night before the wedding, giving the wedding participants a chance to meet each other and allowing the officiant to review ceremony details with everyone involved. If you want to make the most of your rehearsal, keep the following ideas in mind.

Who to Invite—When it comes to the rehearsal (and rehearsal dinner), you should invite all members of the wedding party, the officiant, readers, sound technicians, and musicians, along with their spouses or significant others. You'll also want to invite parents and grandparents of both bride and groom.

What to Bring—Bring a copy of the ceremony order and a wedding day schedule that can be distributed to all wedding participants. (Include diagrams of the processional and recessional, as well as the time that each participant should arrive on your wedding day.) Also bring diagrams that show the placement of attendants and a roll of tape that can be used to mark their positions at the front of church. You might also bring along items for the wedding day such as programs, candles, the guest book, and the marriage license.

What to Do—If your wedding participants do not know each other, be sure to include a round of introductions, explaining how each person will be participating in the ceremony. After introductions, the officiant will guide everyone through the elements of the ceremony, explaining any special details, wordings, or last-minute changes. If time allows, have the wedding party walk through the processional and recessional; track how much time this takes so the musicians can plan accordingly. Finish your rehearsal by reminding participants of their arrival time on the wedding day.

able to participate in your special day. It's both wise and courteous to ask for their participation several months before the wedding, leaving them with plenty of time to prepare music and reserve the date.

If you're unsure where to find the musicians you need, ask your officiant, friends, and family members for suggestions. You can also consult local music shops or the music department of a nearby university for the names of talented musicians.

Once you've selected musicians, schedule a meeting with them to go over musical selections for the wedding. Ask the musicians for recommendations. If they've played for weddings before, they'll have a good idea of what works and what doesn't.

As you finalize the list of songs for your special day, ask each musician if they have the music they need. If there's a song they've never played or sung before, you may need to find and pay for the sheet music yourself. Be sure to deliver all music to musicians at least one month before the wedding. This will give them time to polish those songs for your special day.

Wedding Musicians

ORGANIST

Name: _____

Meeting time: _____

Music needed: _____

_____

_____

Fee: _____

PIANIST

Name: _____

Meeting time: _____

Music needed: _____

_____

_____

_____

Fee: _____

SOLOIST

Name: _____

Meeting time: _____

Music needed: _____

_____

_____

_____

Fee: _____

OTHER MUSICIANS

Names: _____

Meeting time: _____

Music needed: _____

_____

_____

Fee: _____

Planning the Ceremony

While wedding "rules" differ from one religious tradition to the next, certain elements are part of every tradition—including the processional, special placement of guests and attendants, the ceremony, and the recessional. The following sections will give you a good idea of what to expect at Protestant, Catholic, and Orthodox ceremonies. I've also included information about the Jewish ceremony, for those who wish to honor the Jewish roots of their faith by incorporating Jewish elements into their wedding. Keep in mind that your particular congregation may vary on some points from this general overview. To ensure that you'll meet the religious requirements of your church, discuss ceremony details with your officiant.

Protestant and Catholic Weddings

PROCESSIONAL

Before the procession, the grandparents and parents are seated (starting with groom's grandparents, then bride's grandparents, groom's parents, and ending with the mother of bride).

Officiant, groom, and best man enter and wait at the altar as procession begins.

Groomsmen enter from the side or accompany the bridesmaids.

Bridesmaids enter, beginning with the attendant who will stand farthest from the bride and ending with the honor attendant.

Ring bearer and flower girl enter together or with ring bearer walking first.

Bride enters, accompanied by her father or other special person.

MUSICAL NOTES

Need some ideas for ceremony music? Check out the following list of popular songs.

PRELUDE/CANDLE LIGHTING/ATTENDANTS' PROCESSIONAL

"Air" from *Water Music* (Handel)

"Air on the G String" (Bach)

"Rondo" (Mozart)

"Jesu, Joy of Man's Desiring" (Bach)

"Largo" (Handel)

"Gymnopedies" (Satie)

"Moonlight Sonata" (Beethoven)

"Reverie" (Debussy)

"Sheep May Safely Graze" (Bach)

"Ave Maria" (Franz Schubert, Bach)

"Canon in D Major" (Pachelbel)

PROCESSIONAL AND RECESSIONAL

"The Bridal Chorus" from *Lohengrin* (Wagner)

"Wedding March" from *A Midsummer Night's Dream* (Mendelssohn)

"Wedding March" (Guilmant)

"Trumpet Voluntary" (Clarke, also called "Prince of Denmark's March")

"Trumpet Tune" (Purcell)

"Ode to Joy" (Beethoven)

"Spring" from *The Four Seasons* (Vivaldi)

"Hornpipe" from *Water Music* (Handel)

"Allegro" from *Water Music* (Handel)

"Rondeau" (Mouret)

PLACEMENT

The bride's guests sit on the left side and the groom's guests sit on the right, looking from the back of the church.

During the ceremony, the officiant stands at the altar or front of the church, with the bride and groom standing before him.

The rest of the attendants stand next to the bride and groom, creating a V shape with the bride and groom at the center.

Attendants can stand in pairs (except for the honor attendants, who remain next to the bride or groom) or they may be grouped together with bridesmaids on the left and groomsmen on the right.

ORDER OF CEREMONY

Protestant ceremonies generally include the following elements:

Prelude

Processional

Welcome and opening prayer

Giving away of the bride

Special music/Scripture readings/words about purpose of marriage

Wedding message by officiant

Exchange of vows and rings

Communion

Lighting of unity candle

Special music/prayer/reading

Declaration of marriage and kiss

Benediction

Presentation of bride and groom

Processional

Catholic ceremonies differ slightly from the Protestant, usually including these elements:

Prelude

Processional

Introductory rites/prayer

Liturgy of the Word

Rite of marriage/exchange of vows (while congregation stands)

Exchange of rings (while congregation stands)

Mass

Nuptial blessings/final prayer

Processional

RECESSIONAL

Bride and groom exit first, followed by the flower girl and ring bearer.

The attendants exit next (beginning with those who stood closest to the bride and groom), followed by the officiant.

The ushers return to the front of the church to usher out parents and grandparents (bride's parents first, followed by groom's parents, bride's grandparents, and groom's grandparents).

For large weddings, the ushers will also dismiss guests row by row. At smaller weddings (less than 250), the bride and groom may return

to the sanctuary and dismiss their guests themselves.

Orthodox Weddings

PROCESSIONAL

Groom, best man, and priest enter from the side before processional begins.

Ushers escort groom's family and bride's mother to their seats.

Procession begins with the bridesmaids, usually escorted by the groomsmen.

Flower girl and ring bearer enter, followed by the maid of honor.

Bride enters, accompanied by her father.

PLACEMENT

Same as Catholic and Protestant weddings.

ORDER OF CEREMONY

Betrothal—priest blesses rings, and best man exchanges rings between bride and groom's fingers three times to represent the Trinity.

Candle lighting—priest presents bride and groom with lit candles, which they hold throughout the ceremony.

Sacrament of marriage—priest prays, petitions, and reads from Scripture, then joins the couple's hands together.

Crowning—best man gives two wreaths to couple that are connected by a white ribbon to symbolize their unity. Priest places these "crowns" on their heads, and best man switches the crowns three times. These crowns symbolize the glory with which God crowns his people.

Common cup—couple shares a glass of wine as priest reads from the Bible.

Ceremonial walk—the priest and the couple circle a table three times as the choir sings three hymns, symbolizing the journey of marriage.

Final blessings—priest says a blessing to the bride and a blessing to the groom.

RECESSIONAL

The couple exits first, followed by honor attendants.

Flower girl and ring bearer exit next, followed by the rest of the bridesmaids and groomsmen.

Parents exit after the wedding party.

Jewish Weddings

PROCESSIONAL

Rabbi and/or cantor enters first.

Bride's grandparents and then groom's grandparents follow (with wives standing to the right of their husbands).

Groomsmen enter in pairs, followed by the best man.

The groom enters with his father on his left and his mother on his right.

Bridesmaids enter in pairs, followed by the maid/matron of honor.

Flower girl and ring bearer enter together.

Bride enters, her father on her left and her mother on her right.

PLACEMENT

The bride's guests sit on the right side and the groom's guests sit on the left, looking from the back of the synagogue.

Under the chuppah—a canopy symbolizes the home that the couple will build—the bride and groom stand in the center, with the rabbi and/or cantor in front of them. The couple is surrounded by their parents and honor attendants.

Other attendants line up next to the chuppah (or under it, if space permits), with bridesmaids on the right and groomsmen on the left.

ORDER OF CEREMONY

The Jewish ceremony generally includes the following elements.

Processional

Greeting and invocation

First cup of wine/betrothal blessing (signifying betrothal)

Vows

Ring ceremony

Reading of the Ketubah (much like a marriage contract)

Second cup of wine (signifying the nuptial ceremony)

Lifting of the veil

Special music/prayers/readings by family and friends

Seven marriage blessings

Pronouncement and benediction

The broken glass (as guests shout "Mazel tov!")

Recessional

Yichud (bride and groom spend ten or fifteen minutes alone in a separate room)

RECESSIONAL

Bride and groom exit first.

Bride's parents exit, followed by groom's parents.

Bride's grandparents exit, followed by groom's grandparents.

Ring bearer and flower girl exit.

Maid/matron of honor and best man exit, followed by bridesmaids and groomsmen.

The rabbi and/or cantor exits last.

Making It Yours

As you plan the ceremony, look for ways to make it uniquely yours. While many elements will be based on tradition and religious requirements, there are still many ways to add special meaning to your ceremony.

Poetry/Scripture readings—Is there a poem that captures your hopes for the future? A Bible verse that has special meaning to you as a couple?

LICENSE TO MARRY

Marriage license requirements vary from state to state, but one thing is common to them all: you have to get a license to make your marriage legal. Here's the marriage license scoop.

When to Apply—Start the license process at least one month before the wedding to allow ample time for fulfilling the requirements. Don't wait until the week of the wedding, as many states require a waiting period between the application and receipt of the license. But don't apply too early either—marriage licenses do expire.

Where to Apply—Marriage licenses are usually acquired at the city clerk's office.

What to Bring—When you apply for a marriage license, you'll need to bring required paperwork (birth certificates, driver's license, proof of citizenship), certification of blood tests or consultations from your doctors, and a fee (usually somewhere between fifteen and thirty dollars).

Signing—Sign the license on your wedding day, using your married names. Two witnesses must also sign (usually the best man and maid/matron of honor).

Making It Official—Leave the signed license with your officiant after the ceremony. They will validate it and send it back to the proper office.

Ask a friend or family member to share this reading at your ceremony.

Music—If you love music, have fun selecting musical pieces for your ceremony. Favorite classical

THERE THEY GO!

As you head off to the reception, you'll want to leave with style. Here are a few suggestions to make sure your departure is memorable.

Ask the bridesmaids to distribute birdseed or rose petals for guests to toss as you leave the church. For a more dramatic flare, you may have guests light sparklers, blow bubbles, or release butterflies into the air. Whatever you choose, ask the church about any restrictions beforehand.

Rent a limo, vintage car, or trolley to whisk you away to the reception.

If you can't afford a rental, ask friends and family members if they know of anyone who owns a nice sports car that they're willing to loan out for a special occasion.

pieces could be incorporated into the prelude, or you might invite guests to join in singing a meaningful hymn during the ceremony. Asking a soloist to sing a special song adds a beautiful touch as well. Keep in mind that even though many secular songs contain beautiful expressions of love, they may be better reserved for the reception. Your wedding ceremony is a sacred moment—shared with God—and the music you choose should celebrate his presence at the beginning of your marriage.

Vows—Depending on your religious background, you may have the freedom to choose, or even write, your own wedding vows. You'll find material for vows in a variety of places, from poetry books to love letters and the Internet. Be careful as you read through the options. Many vows give a romantic expression of human love but are completely devoid of spiritual accountability or meaning. As you pull ideas together, remember the true purpose of your vows and make sure the following elements are included: (1) a promise to be exclusive to each other's only partner in life; (2) a commitment to a lifelong relationship; (3) a pledge to fulfill the specific role of a husband or a wife (and if you want, also mention specific actions that define those roles); (4) a promise to respect and honor each other; and (5) a commitment to seeking God's help in order to fulfill your vows.

After the Ceremony

Once the ceremony is over, you can breathe a sigh of relief. You're finally married, and it's time for the celebration to begin! But before you head off to the reception, take care of the items listed on the Ceremony Details worksheet.

CEREMONY DETAILS

Assign someone to clean out dressing rooms and bring any forgotten items to the reception.

Person assigned: _____

_____

Assign someone to remove flowers from the church and transport them to reception site (if you're reusing ceremony flowers).

Person assigned: _____

_____

Assign someone to bring the guest book to the reception, along with any gifts that were brought to the church.

Person assigned: _____

_____

Assign someone who will remind you to sign the marriage license.

Person assigned: _____

_____

Bride of
Dependence

But this happened that we might not rely on ourselves but on God, who raises the dead.—2 Corinthians 1:9

I said to the LORD, "You are my Lord; apart from you I have no good thing."—Psalm 16:2

Trusting oneself is foolish, but those who walk in wisdom are safe.—Proverbs 28:26 NLT

Dependence Isn't a Four-Letter Word

In a twenty-first-century world, the independent woman gets the attention. Television shows portray assertive women who can push ahead without the help of a man. And news programs tout the "wisdom" of women who have financial and social independence in their marriages.

Meanwhile, *dependence* has become a dirty word. With frowns on their faces, experts look at the era of 1950s housewives as if it were an embarrassing aunt who needs to be locked away. *Dependent* is a word reserved for needy women who

don't live up to their potential—the kind who become clingy girlfriends and timid wives.

But is that picture of dependence accurate? Is dependence really such a horrible thing? In a world of independent living, dependence has certainly gotten a bad rap. But according to God's plan for marriage, it's not always a bad idea. In fact, when it's viewed the right way, dependence becomes a noble character trait—making you stronger than any independent woman could ever be.

Of course, absolute dependence should never be put on any human, even a husband. A bride should reserve that kind of dependence for just one person—her heavenly Groom. When she seeks her ultimate fulfillment and identity in a man, she has carried dependence to an unhealthy extreme that strangles God's potential in her life.

But the opposite extreme—total independence—doesn't work either. In 1 Corinthians we read that "in the Lord, however, woman is not independent of man, nor is man independent of woman" (11:11). This verse reminds us that God created men and women with unique characteristics, characteristics that complement each other. When we live independently, focusing on our goals at the expense of our spouses', we end up with a shaky love. And we miss out on the real joy of marriage—two lives joined into one.

Instead of the independent woman, we need to be brides who live out a special kind of dependence—*inter*dependence. This kind of dependence shouldn't be a dirty word. And it won't leave you helpless and weak. Rather, it transforms both husband and wife into a whole that's better than two independent parts.

Holly bushes give a unique picture of this interdependence. Those bright berries we see at Christmas don't grow under just any circumstances. Unlike most other plants, a holly bush is either "male" or "female." If you pick up a trio of male holly bushes at the nursery and plant them in your garden, you'll have some pretty foliage and healthy plants, but you'll never see any berries. Likewise if you plant only the female variety. The male and female need to be planted together for berries to grow.

Just like those holly bushes, God designed men and women for interdependence too. A husband and wife each bring unique strengths and weaknesses to their relationship. Sure, they may have some nice "foliage" individually. But when they work together, they're even better. As a couple meets each other's needs, they grow a special love—like those bright holly berries.

This kind of relationship doesn't have the flashy appeal of independent living. While an independent woman can push ahead at her own pace, interdependent couples take the time to look out for each other. They show their dependence in quiet ways, such as offering each other back rubs, holding each other spiritually accountable, and asking for each other's input before scheduling the social calendar. And in these simple gestures, they willingly give up a bit of their independence so that they can become something special together.

It takes two willing people for this interdependence to work. Two people who will truly love, honor, and cherish each other above themselves. And two people who rely on God above all else.

As you look to your future marriage, can you say that you and your fiancé are those two people? If you'll take God's cue and give interdependence a try, you'll find that *dependence* isn't such a dirty word after all. Because when you lean on each other and God, you'll walk farther than you could ever go alone.

Declaration of Dependence

Greg looked into his wife's tear-filled eyes and kissed her on the forehead. "It's going to be OK," he whispered. "You'll be better in no time. And five years from now, we're going to live in that dream house and have a couple of kids to keep us on our toes. I promise you, Lizzie, it's going to be fine."

But it wasn't fine. Lizzie had been feeling a lot of chest pain and sometimes struggled to catch her breath. And the doctor had just diagnosed a rare disease that was affecting her heart. Over the next six years, doctors tried various treatments but with little success. And with all the hospital bills and health concerns to deal with, Greg and Lizzie had to put their dream house and family plans on hold. Finally, after an experimental heart operation, Lizzie began to improve. A year later she was thrilled to receive a clean bill of health. But it certainly hadn't been the quick recovery Greg had promised.

Promises. We make them so easily—and often with the best of intentions. Yet so often they're impossible to keep. Like Greg, we desperately want to make someone feel better, so we promise them it'll all work out. Or we just love someone so much that we want to promise them the world. Yet the world's not ours to promise. And we can't guarantee that everything will get better. We depend on Someone else to work those things out.

Marriage promises fit in this category too. We really can't depend on ourselves to keep them. That's a revolutionary idea in today's wedding culture, though. A lot of couples assume that loving, honoring, and cherishing will always come naturally to them—that they can depend on themselves to keep their love alive for better or worse.

But can anyone really handle that job? As I look around at marriages today, I see a lot of people who struggle to keep their wedding vows. What sounded so simple on their wedding day

LOVE STORY FROM GOD

Elijah wasn't very popular at the moment. He'd been calling on his fellow Israelites to turn from their pagan gods for years. When they didn't, God revealed to Elijah that he would punish Israel with a severe drought. Elijah warned King Ahab, but his efforts at reforming the king only brought him Ahab's anger. So God led Elijah to a hideout in the Kerith Ravine. It was on the east side of the Jordan, a safe distance from King Ahab and his murderous wife—hopefully.

The ravine had a pleasant brook—water to satisfy Elijah's thirst. And each morning, the ravens brought Elijah some bread and meat to eat, returning with more in the evening. To Elijah, the brook and the birds were miracles sent from heaven—a sign that God hadn't forgotten about him. But even more than that, they reminded him of how much he depended on God—for bread, for meat, for his very life.

Back in Israel, Ahab was depending on other things—wealth, power, pagan gods. None of those things brought rain, though. And for all his apparent strength and independence, Ahab could do nothing to stop the drought. The land withered away.

In the end, it would be Elijah—the man who depended on God for everything—who had the power to bring rain. During a showdown on Mount Carmel, he confronted Ahab and hundreds of pagan prophets, calling on God for help. God responded—first with a miraculous fire, and then with rain. And as the raindrops started to fall, some people understood the truth—that a man of God has greater power than a king.

Check out the whole story in 1 Kings 17–18.

turns out to be a difficult task. And as the days go by, they don't always treat each other with love and respect. Sometimes it's all they can do to keep from shouting at each other, much less cherishing each other.

You probably think "these people" I'm talking about are the thousands of couples who give up and get divorced. But they're not. I know friends and family who are strongly committed to their marriage, yet they readily admit that keeping those wedding vows doesn't always come naturally. They're just like my husband and me. As much as we want to honor those wedding day promises, we mess up from time to time.

So we're facing the same struggle as Lizzie and Greg. We have a heart problem. Despite our best promises, our hearts just aren't strong enough to keep us from messing up. There will be moments when our good intentions break down and we hurt the one we promised to love and cherish. There will be times when we can't keep those wedding vows—not on our own, anyway.

It's a good thing we don't have to do it alone! "Do not fear; for I am with you . . . I will strengthen you and help you" (Isa. 41:10). When it comes to making those wedding vows, you don't have to fear the divorce statistics or worry about your own weaknesses. God can give couples the strength to keep their promises. You can—and should—depend on him.

That may sound weak to you—maybe you feel that your love alone should be enough to carry you through. But in reality, admitting your dependence on God will make your love stronger. "Apart from me you can do *nothing*" (John 15:5, emphasis added). According to that verse, you need God's help to keep those wedding vows—whether you're star-crossed lovers or a down-to-earth pair.

Maybe it's time to write a declaration of dependence in your own wedding vows. It doesn't have to be a lengthy piece—the words "God helping us" may say it all. But they'll be words that make all the difference. Because as you declare your dependence on God, your wedding vows will be more than beautiful words and hopeful intentions—they'll also be promises that you can keep.

11

. . . .

THE RECEPTION

After the ceremony, you can breathe a sigh of relief. You'll finally be husband and wife, and that's reason to celebrate at the reception. Before you can relax, however, you'll put a lot of work into your reception plans. Wedding receptions usually eat up more money and time than any other aspect of the wedding plans. So whether you're planning a formal gala at the country club or a relaxed barbeque in the backyard, be prepared: it will take careful planning and discernment to make everything just right.

In a world where the line between good and bad often gets blurred, you'll need discernment for more than just planning your reception. With a discerning mind, you can also build a life characterized by goodness. So as you pick out the perfect details for your wedding reception, put those discerning skills to work in your life as well. They're the key to becoming a bride of both goodness and wisdom.

Bride of Goodness

In everything set them an example by doing what is good.
—Titus 2:7–8

Hate what is evil; cling to what is good.—Romans 12:9

So don't get tired of doing what is good. Don't get discouraged and
give up.—Galatians 6:9 NLT

The Good Things

Have you ever watched the Steve Martin film *Father of the Bride*? It's filled with hilarious scenes as a father copes with his daughter's upcoming marriage. But the most impressive part comes at the end, when everyone gathers at the parents' house for the wedding reception.

It's a picture-perfect affair—an elegant tent in the backyard, twinkling candlelight, sparkling crystal, beautiful china, band music, and splendid flowers spread everywhere. As I watched the movie for the first time, I hoped with all my heart that I could someday have such a beautiful wedding reception. And when it finally came time to plan my own reception, I still pictured the *Father of the Bride* gala in my dreams.

Maybe your dream wedding reception doesn't come from a Hollywood film, but you probably hope for the same things I did—a reception filled with good things. That's why we spend hours looking for the perfect caterer, sampling foods, and agonizing over menu selections. And that's why we spend a lot of money on beautiful centerpieces and a delicious cake. When it comes to the wedding reception, we want everything to be polished and perfect.

198

Wouldn't it be great if we treated our spiritual lives the same way? What if we filled our minds with all the good things of life? And what if we polished the ideas and desires that fill our hearts?

That's exactly what Paul challenged the Philippians to do: "Whatever is true, whatever is noble, whatever is right, whatever is pure, whatever is lovely, whatever is admirable—if anything is excellent or praiseworthy—think about such things" (Phil. 4:8).

I don't know about you, but that verse strikes me hard every time I read it. When I think about some of the conversations I've participated in, or some of the television programs I've watched, the words *true*, *noble*, and *lovely* don't exactly come to mind. Sometimes I'm entertained by things that aren't excellent or praiseworthy at all.

But just like everyone else, I can come up with some good justifications for my behavior. As humans, we seem to have a special knack for this. We tell ourselves that it's all in good fun—that we can filter through the bad stuff and block out negative influences from our minds. But when we put our lives up to the standard of Philippians 4:8, those justifications fall apart. Sure, watching movies filled with promiscuous sex won't necessarily make us start sleeping around, but will it fill us with desire to be faithful to one man? A violent song won't always make us hit someone, but will it encourage us to listen to a friend in need?

There's a fundamental problem with letting these bad things into our minds. And it's not so much that they'll always cause us to do bad things (though sometimes they do), but that they distract us from seeing the good things. It's like eating a diet of junk food—it may not kill us right away, but it won't leave us with an appetite for anything healthy, either. And instead of being spurred toward goodness, we'll get bogged down with the baseness of life.

As women of God, we need to feed ourselves good things. And we can't expect our goodness to grow in a healthy way if we're constantly taking in junk. That's like trying to create a good reception when you've booked a lousy caterer and a mediocre band. It just doesn't work. Instead, we need to seek out the good things for our hearts and minds—and push the mediocre out.

Next time you're hanging out with friends, reading a book, or watching a movie, hold those things up to the standard of Philippians 4:8: Are they true? Noble? Admirable? Praiseworthy? If the answer is no, you're probably feeding on some unhealthy food. And if you want a healthy spiritual life, you may need to let those things go.

In their place, look for ideas that inspire you to live for God. Search out friends who will encourage you in your faith. Spend some spare time helping a neighbor in need. These things may not be glitzy or glamorous, but they are the good things of life. And they satisfy better than any junk food can.

Copycats

I know some people who seem really good. They look good; they're good with words; they have good ideas; they make other people feel good. Even when facing tough times, they talk about good things, quoting Bible verses and talking about God. Truthfully, these "good" people sometimes get on my nerves: Do they have to be good all the time? Couldn't they mess up just once?

I don't know about you, but I'm not that good. I have my moods—and sometimes I pick a fight just to blow off steam. Some days, I don't feel like looking for anything good. So instead I focus on everything that's going bad. Yet I know God has called me to something bigger than those petty fights and moody scowls. Goodness is tucked right in the middle of the fruits of the Spirit (see Gal. 5:22). And it's been drilled into my head since Sunday school days. A woman of God needs to be good—and that can't happen when I'm wallowing in a bad mood.

So in my own spiritual quest, I used to look at those good people I mentioned earlier. And I became a copycat. Remember that childhood game in which a sibling would mimic your every word and action? That was me. I copied people's words and actions, trying to act just as good as them. But in the end, I could never catch up to their goodness. Somehow, those other people still seemed to be better than me—and I wound up feeling frustrated with trying to be someone I wasn't.

Since that time, I've noticed that I'm not the only copycat. I see a lot of people trying to act like someone else. Sometimes they copy a hairstyle they see in a magazine. Sometimes they copy the actions of an charismatic personality on TV. Sometimes they just copy a friend or a relative so they can fit in. And in the end, all us copycats are searching for the same thing. We just want others to think we have something good—whether it's our personality, our hairstyle, or our faith.

When it comes to real goodness, though, the copycat approach doesn't work very well—at least not when we're just comparing ourselves to another person. God has created us all to express goodness in our own unique way. And we can't

BIBLE BRIDE

What a glorious day. Sunshine sparkled off the river flowing through the garden, and the flowers looked splendid in full bloom. Eve smiled as she saw her reflection in the water. Standing behind her was the man she loved. Her perfect fit—Adam.

Life in Eden was just so good. That was the word God had used to describe everything when he created it. And as she looked around, Eve agreed. This paradise, this amazing man, this peace and delight that welled up in her soul—it was all so very good.

Taking in all the goodness around her, she couldn't help but let it flow from herself too. Thoughts of anger, jealousy, or discontent were foreign to Eve. Every word she said, every decision she made, every thought and action—they were always good.

But Eve felt no arrogance about this goodness. She knew where it came from—her wonderful God. She loved to walk with him through the garden in the cool hours of the evening. Soaking in all the good things he said and did, Eve felt a deep love for God. And with no bad thing to poison her mind or her life, she lived on in the glory of paradise.

Before Eve sinned, Eden was a beautiful picture of humans in true goodness. Read more about it in Genesis 1–3.

find real goodness just by copying someone's actions. We may do some good *things* that way, but we won't be transformed into good *people*. Eventually we'll be back to where we started—fighting the "bad girl" within.

To find true goodness, we need to copy Someone else. Someone who embodies goodness. When we think about God, we see that kind of Someone. "The LORD is good" (Ps. 135:3), and the Bible affirms that in dozens of psalms. God's not good just because of what he does. He's good because of who he is. So if we want to be good, we should fill our lives with him instead of trying to act like someone we're not.

Have wedding plans brought out the worst in you lately? Are you feeling like a "bad girl"? You may look at some other women and feel frustrated because you can't seem to measure up to their goodness. But instead of looking outward, try looking upward. Your heavenly Groom has the kind of goodness you're looking for. Read the Bible. Pray. Look for signs of goodness in everyday life. And as you fill up with God, you'll find his goodness filling you up too.

Whether it's bad moods, bad attitudes, or bad girls, anything can be turned to good when we look to God. And since Ephesians 5:1 tells us to "be imitators of God," I think it's safe to say that he doesn't mind having a few copycats around.

Planning Your Reception

Meeting with the Site Manager

Once you've reserved a reception location (see chapter 4 for more details on this), arrange an on-site meeting with the site manager. This will give you an opportunity to ask important questions and get a closer look at the site.

Take note of the room's lighting, acoustics, and air circulation. If the lighting doesn't quite suit your tastes, you can make special arrangements with the site manager, such as unscrewing a few lightbulbs or adding strands of Christmas lights in certain areas. If the room has poor acoustics or is quite large, you may need to rent a microphone and speaker system. And in a stuffy setting, you'll need to bring additional fans for air circulation.

You should also start planning the reception layout. Where can the head table be placed? How about the guest tables, DJ, and dance floor? Are there good places for the cake table, gift table, place card table, and receiving line? As you look around, create a diagram of the way you'd like each item positioned.

Plan to ask a lot of questions during this visit. Here are a few to get you started.

What kind of wedding packages are available? What do they include and what do they cost? Are substitutions allowed?

What kind of deposit is required?

Are taxes and gratuities included in the price?

Is an in-house catering service available? If so, do we still have the option of bringing in our own caterer?

Does the site have a fully equipped kitchen?

Does the site have a liquor license? What are the laws regarding alcohol service?

Are there any restrictions on food, decorations, or music?

How many hours is the site available for? Are there overtime charges if the reception is extended?

What time will we (and our wedding vendors) have access to the site on our wedding day?

PLANNING CHECKLIST

NINE MONTHS TO ONE YEAR BEFORE

☐ Select and reserve a reception location. (For peak times, begin looking even earlier.)

☐ Make arrangements to use on-site caterer or hire an outside caterer.

☐ If renting a limo or other vehicle for transportation of the wedding party, reserve your wedding date with the rental agency.

SIX TO NINE MONTHS BEFORE

☐ Choose your menu and type of food service (sit-down, buffet, or passed trays).

☐ Visit the reception location with site manager.

☐ Book a band or DJ.

☐ Rent linens and place settings (if they're not available from the reception location or caterer).

THREE TO SIX MONTHS BEFORE

☐ Coordinate with reception site manager, caterer, and/or florist to create table centerpieces and other reception decorations.

☐ Investigate parking options at your reception site. If necessary, arrange a shuttle service to transport guests from a nearby parking lot to the reception location.

☐ Select a baker to create your wedding cake. Coordinate the delivery time of the wedding cake with the baker and reception site manager.

ONE TO THREE MONTHS BEFORE

☐ Create a schedule of reception events to distribute to caterer, reception site manager, and DJ. Include clearly delegated responsibilities and approximate times of reception events.

☐ Confirm delivery arrangements for any outside vendors and coordinate with reception site manager.

TWO TO THREE WEEKS BEFORE

☐ Create seating arrangements.

☐ Submit final guest count to caterer.

☐ Confirm final details with reception site manager, caterer, baker, florist, DJ, and limousine service.

What is the room capacity for guests? How big is the dance floor?

Are tables and chairs provided? How about table linens and place settings?

What decorations will already be in place?

What are the parking arrangements for the site? Is valet parking available? Can we make arrangements to pay parking fees for our guests ahead of time?

Does the facility have more than one reception site? If so, will we have adequate privacy in our area?

Is a dressing room available where we can change into going-away clothes?

What audio-visual equipment is available at the site (microphones, speakers, screen, projector, etc.)? Does the site have enough cords and outlets to accommodate rented sound equipment?

Food and Such

By the time your guests have attended the wedding and traveled to your reception site, they'll be ready to eat! Depending on the time of day and the degree of formality at your wedding, your reception could feature anything from breakfast quiches on a tray to a five-course meal served at the table. Before you investigate caterers and start planning the menu, though, you'll need to decide what type of service you'd prefer.

Seated Meal—Guests are seated at the table and then served by hired waitstaff. Guests may receive plated service, when the foods

SPECIAL TOUCHES

Want to make your reception a unique event? Consider the following ideas.

Table Themes—Instead of using simple table numbers, organize a theme for each table and then decorate accordingly. Theme ideas could include famous cities, legendary movie stars, sports teams, or types of flowers. Your guests will be delighted to find "The London Table" printed on their seating cards, instead of the traditional "Table #4."

Ethnic Traditions—Does the bride or groom come from a unique ethnic background? If so, incorporate those ethnic traditions into the reception events.

Rename Entrées—Instead of printing the menu with traditional food names, spruce things up a bit. Rename your entrees by incorporating wedding terms or the names of special guests.

Make a Groom's Cake—Ask the baker to create a small groom's cake that can be displayed with the wedding cake. Groom's cakes are often designed and decorated to reflect one of his hobbies.

Add Your Personality—Add personal touches to your wedding reception by sharing your interests with the guests. Did you go to a movie on your first date? Rent an old-fashioned popcorn machine and serve fresh popcorn as the guests leave. Do you love to golf? Hand out golf balls as wedding favors. Enjoy hiking? Why not print up a reception program that looks like a trail book?

are arranged on a plate and then brought to the table. For a more formal touch, the plates can be at the guests' places and wait-staff will serve each food item separately from a platter. (This is called Russian or French service, depending on the number of waiters.)

Buffet—Guests bring their plates to a table where all the food items have been arranged. Or, instead of placing plates at the table setting, dinnerware can be stacked at the buffet table and retrieved as guests come up for food. Guests either serve themselves or receive the assistance of buffet servers.

Food Stations—A variation of the single-table buffet, food stations each feature one type of food (meat carving station, pasta station, salad station, etc.). Guests move around to select foods from the stations they prefer. Sometimes dessert food stations are set up at the conclusion of a sit-down meal.

Passed Tray—Waiters walk throughout the room, carrying trays of hors d'oeuvres or desserts and offering them to guests. Passed tray service can be used alone or in conjunction with a buffet or sit-down meal.

Picking a Caterer

Unless you're hosting a very small reception (fifty or fewer guests), it's wise to hire a caterer for the food and beverage services. Many reception sites offer in-house caterers—a great option that usually saves both time and money. However, some brides may need or prefer to use an outside caterer. Either way, you should check a caterer's references before agreeing to use their services. And if possible, try to sample some of their foods.

As you investigate caterers, run through the following checklist of questions.

What types of meal service are offered (sit-down, buffet, food stations, etc.)?

What's the range of your food prices (usually offered as a per-person charge that varies based on your final menu selections)?

Are meal and beverage prices lower for children?

What's the cost of an open bar for the entire reception? For the first hour of the reception?

Do you have a liquor license?

Do you include gratuities in your quoted price?

How many meal options do you offer? Do you specialize in any cuisine?

Are wedding packages available? What do they cost, and can substitutions be made?

What size and style of wedding do you usually cater?

What is the ratio of servers to guests?

Do you provide other services such as coatroom attendants and valet parking personnel?

Do you provide linens and place settings? If so, are there a variety of colors and styles to choose from?

Is insurance against breakage of china or crystal included in the costs?

How many guests can be seated at each table?

Do you provide a wedding cake? If so, are we still allowed to use a cake from an outside bakery?

When must the final guest count be provided?

THE CATERER

Caterer's name: _____

_____

Phone number: _____

Type of reception: _____

_____

Approximate food costs (per person): _____

_____

Items/services included in cost: _____

_____

_____

_____

Items/services available for additional fee:

_____

Taxes and gratuities: _____

Deposit required: _____

Total cost: _____

Balance due: _____

Menu

Once you've selected a caterer, schedule a meeting to discuss the menu. Ask your caterer for a complete price list so you can make menu decisions that fit your budget. For instance, you may be hoping for smoked salmon served Russian style, but if the funds are tight, you'll probably prefer a buffet meal including chicken or pork. Also, keep in mind that your menu should appeal to a wide range of personal tastes. You don't want your guests to wrinkle their noses at unusual food selections.

If funds are especially tight, consider hosting your reception between meal times. A breakfast reception could include quiches, croissants, and fresh fruits. For the midafternoon, try a tea party with finger sandwiches, scones, fruits, and cheeses. Or for an evening affair, host a dessert reception with passed-tray service offering tarts, tortes, and chocolate-covered fruits. Such options provide both taste and elegance but at a fraction of the cost you will pay for a full meal.

In addition to the food, you'll need to consider beverages. Generally the caterer will provide some basic beverage options such as lemonade, sodas, and coffee. You may or may not want to serve alcoholic beverages as well. If you do serve liquor at the reception, consider how much to serve and what kind of service to provide. While some families may offer an open bar throughout the entire night, others prefer to serve only wine and champagne at dinnertime. Discuss the options with your caterer and select one that will suit both your guests and your budget.

THE MENU

Punch and mints/nuts: _____

_____

Hors d'oeuvres: _____

_____

Salad: _____

Entrée: _____
_____

Side dishes: _____
_____
_____

Breads: _____
_____

Desserts: _____
_____

Food stations: _____
_____

Beverages: _____
_____
_____

Getting There

Before any reception festivities can begin, you and the rest of the guests will need to travel from the ceremony to the reception site. While guests drive their own vehicles, you'll probably want a special ride to whisk you away from the church. Some vehicles can accommodate the entire wedding party, but it may be nice to share the ride alone—it could be the only time you have to yourselves during the day.

If you plan to rent a limousine or some other vehicle, make arrangements at least nine months before the wedding. Otherwise, you may find that the vehicle you wanted is unavailable. As a cost-saving alternative, borrow a special car from a friend or decorate your own vehicle. Whatever you choose, be sure to arrange a driver for your

---

RECEPTION DECOR

As you plan for your wedding reception, don't forget those added touches to enhance the reception space:

Flowers—Whether you transport them from the ceremony or ask your florist to create special pieces for the reception, flowers add an elegant and festive touch to the reception décor. Try placing bouquets on the head table, gift table, and cake table, and in the restrooms.

Lighting—To create an air of romance, ask the reception site manager to dim the lights. Add candles to your table centerpieces or try stringing white Christmas lights around doorways or along the head table.

Fabric—Use soft fabrics, such as tulle netting, to create billowing drapes around windows and doorways. Select table linens that will complement your overall wedding scheme.

Centerpieces—Add drama to the tables through beautiful centerpieces. You might consider fresh floral arrangements or an array of candles arranged atop a mirror. For themed tables, creative objects could be used, such as a miniature Eiffel Tower for a "Paris Table" or a football helmet for the "Chicago Bears Table."

Wedding Favors—Small boxes of mints, tulle-wrapped votive candles, little silver bells—these and dozens of other wedding favors can add a special touch when placed at each person's table setting.

vehicle and let the attendants know whether they will ride with you or follow in separate cars.

Don't assume that your guests are familiar with the reception site. Include a map and parking instructions with the invitations (or make them available at the church immediately following the ceremony). At the reception site, investigate the parking situation ahead of time. Depending on parking availability, you may want to offer valet parking or a shuttle service that can transport guests from faraway parking areas. In places where parking is only available for a fee, you might make special arrangements to pay for your guests' parking ahead of time.

TRANSPORTATION

Rental agency: _____

Agency phone number: _____

Type of vehicle rented: _____

Length of rental time: _____

Vehicle arrival time at ceremony site: _____

_____

Rental cost: _____

PARKING

Parking areas available: _____

_____

Parking costs: _____

   Amount paid ahead: _____

   Amount guests will pay: _____

Cost of parking attendants/valets: _____

Seating Arrangements

Without assigned seating, guests usually feel uncomfortable. So if your reception will involve a seated meal, it's a good idea to create a seating plan. Keep in mind the following tips as you make seating assignments.

- The bride, groom, and attendants usually sit at a rectangular or U-shaped head table that faces the guests. Bride and groom sit in the center, with the bride to the groom's right. The maid/matron of honor is seated next to the groom, with the best man sitting beside the bride. Next to them, the bridesmaids and groomsmen alternate along either side of the table. When room allows, attendants' significant others should be seated at the head table as well.

- The bride's and groom's parents usually sit at separate tables, along with grandparents or close friends. If you prefer, both sets of parents can be seated at the same table, along with the officiant, special family members, and/or friends. Divorced parents are usually seated at separate tables, but both should be near the head table.

- Determine the number of guests that can be comfortably seated at a table by visiting the reception site and looking at a set table. Then determine the total number of tables you will need to comfortably seat your guests.

- Don't create seating assignments until all the reception cards have been returned.

COST-CUTTERS

Instead of hiring live musicians or a DJ, make a CD of your favorite tunes and play them during the reception.

Ask your baker to make a small, decorative wedding cake and serve your guests from inexpensive sheet cakes.

Ask a catering staff to cook the food and then pack it up for you. Since a large portion of catering costs goes toward the service, you can save money by picking up the food yourself and providing your own servers.

If your caterer will allow it, purchase your own alcohol and simply pay them a per-bottle fee to serve it.

Order a small cake for each table. It can do double duty as a lovely centerpiece.

Hold your wedding between meal times. By doing so, you can serve fewer, and less expensive, foods.

Offer an open bar for the first hour only. Not only will this cut your costs, but it can also save guests from having too much to drink before they head home.

Have a soft bar (which serves only beer, wines, and sodas) instead of a full bar that offers mixed drinks.

Whenever possible, try to seat guests with at least one person or couple that they know. Ask both sets of parents for suggestions as you add their family members and friends to the seating plan.

Before finalizing your seating plan, look through your response cards and double-check that each attending guest has been assigned a seat.

At formal weddings, place cards should be set at the table setting of each guest. If you're planning a less formal wedding, you may use place cards only at the head table. In either case, it's wise to place table cards somewhere near the reception entrance. Table cards simply list a guest's name and table number so they can easily find their seating assignment.

The Wedding Cake

Since most bakeries create a limited number of wedding cakes each week, you should order your wedding cake at least two months in advance (preferably more) to ensure your baker's availability. When it comes to cakes, you'll have a few basic choices to make: flavor, filling, and design. Ask your baker for a list of flavors and fillings that they provide and then look through pictures of previous cakes they have designed.

Before signing a contract with any baker, be sure to discuss the following:

Can you tell us what size cake should be made for the number of guests we expect?

Do you specialize in a particular flavor or design of cake?

Can a "show" cake be decorated and less expensive sheet cakes be made to serve guests?

Can different flavors be made for each layer of the cake?

Can you provide sauces or toppings to spruce

RECEPTION ACTIVITIES

Reception customs vary greatly from one place to the next, but here's a few traditions included at most receptions today.

Receiving Line—The receiving line offers your guests a chance to personally congratulate you and the groom. While all wedding attendants can be included in the receiving line, many couples invite only their parents and/or honor attendants to participate. As you stand in the receiving line, be sure to welcome your guests, thank them for coming, and introduce them to other members of the receiving line whom they do not know. If you prefer, the receiving line can be formed at the church rather than the reception.

Announcing the Wedding Party—Once the guests have arrived and been seated, the master of ceremonies should introduce each member of the wedding party, ending with the announcement of the bride and groom. Since many guests do not personally know your attendants, it's nice to provide brief background information in their introduction, such as their relationship to you, their current endeavors, and the reason you wanted them to be in your wedding.

Toasts—The best man traditionally offers the first toast before your meal is served. Other toasts may be given throughout the evening, including the maid/matron of honor toasting the couple, the bride toasting the groom, the groom toasting the bride, parents toasting the couple, and the couple toasting their parents.

Entertainment—As guests finish their meal, some sort of entertainment is usually offered. It could be a hired comedian or a simple invitation for friends to share stories about the happy couple. Sometimes the bride and groom present a short slide show featuring pictures of their past.

Cake Cutting—Before dessert is served, the bride and groom go through the traditional cake-cutting ceremony. The groom places his hand over the bride's as they cut the first slice. Then they feed each other their first bites as guests cheer and applaud.

Opening Dances—If dancing will be a part of your reception, the first dance should be reserved for the bride and groom. After this romantic moment, the bride usually dances with her father, followed by the groom and his mother. Other opening dances might include the bride dancing with her father-in-law, the groom dancing with his mother-in-law, or the bridesmaids and groomsmen dancing with each other.

Bouquet/Garter Toss—All the single women gather behind the bride as she tosses her bouquet. (Many brides purchase a small bouquet for this, rather than tossing their own.) Legend has it that the lucky winner will be the next woman married. This ritual is followed by a similar one, when the eligible bachelors gather and the groom tosses the bride's garter.

up the served cake (ice cream, fruit, chocolate sauce, etc.)?

What is the cost of the cake? What's included in that cost? Are there additional charges for delivery, setup, or tier separators?

How much time will you need for delivery and setup of cake?

As you discuss the wedding cake with your baker, you'll need to provide the following information as well.

Number of expected guests

Other dessert plans

Wedding party colors

Floral scheme and linen colors

Kitchen equipment available

Contact information for reception site, caterer, and florist

You should confirm delivery times with both the baker and the reception site coordinator several weeks before your wedding day. Also, be sure to give clear driving directions to the baker so he or she will be able to find the reception site.

THE WEDDING CAKE

Bakery name: _____

Phone number: _____

Contact person: _____

Number of expected guests: _____

Cake flavor: _____

Cake filling: _____

Cake design: _____

Colors: _____

Sheet cakes needed: _____

Cost: _____

Deposit paid: _____

Balance due: _____

Musical Notes

Live band, DJ, or previously recorded tunes—any of these musical options can add a celebratory air to your wedding reception. Depending on your personal tastes and the style of your wedding, you could choose anything from the soft sounds of a piano or violin to the lively beat of a swing band. Keep in mind, though, that your musical selections should be pleasing to your guests as well. Instead of a playlist with songs known only to you, it's nice to incorporate tunes that will be familiar to all.

Start your musical search with a sober look at your budget. You'll need to know how much you're willing to pay before you can wisely book a musician. Whether it's a pianist, a DJ, or a live band that you're after, start by asking your friends and family for recommendations. If they're not helpful, look in the phone book or ask the reception site manager for suggestions.

As you consider various people, try to find a time when you can see them in action, or ask them if you can review a tape of their performances. Pay attention to the variety of songs that they offer. Do they know how to play familiar songs? Do they offer a mix of fast and slow songs? Do they take requests? Also, take note of their personality. Could they act as the master of ceremonies at your reception? Would they make guests feel comfortable?

Once you've found the musical talent you want, sign a contract that includes the following: the musician's attire, the musician's arrival time at the reception, equipment provided, the total cost, and what is/is not included in that cost. Also, be sure to specify the exact location of your wedding reception and offer driving directions if needed.

If necessary, you may need to rent additional sound equipment that is unavailable from the band or reception hall. Check with your reception site manager for suggested rental agencies.

Reception Music

Name of musician/band/DJ: _____
_____

Phone number: _____

Contact person: _____

Type of music: _____

Equipment provided: _____
_____
_____

Number of hours: _____

Services provided: _____

Special songs requested: _____
_____
_____
_____

Afterthoughts

Even after the guests have slowly filtered out of the reception hall, there's still work to be done. Don't forget to make arrangements for the following post-reception details.

Assign a person or two to transport gifts from the reception location to your home.

Assign people to return any items that were rented for the reception.

Ask your caterer to prepare a small honeymoon basket of reception foods. Since most couples don't have time to eat at their own reception, it's nice to have a basket of food that you can enjoy together in the privacy of your hotel room.

Musician's attire: _____
_____

Arrival time at reception: _____

Total cost: _____

Deposit paid: _____

Amount due: _____

Rental equipment needed: _____
_____

Rental equipment delivery time: _____
_____

Rental equipment cost: _____

Bride of Wisdom

Test everything. Hold on to the good. Avoid every kind of evil.
—1 Thessalonians 5:21–22

If you are wise and understand God's ways, live a life of steady goodness so that only good deeds will pour forth.
—James 3:13 NLT

Choose my instruction instead of silver, knowledge rather than choice gold, for wisdom is more precious than rubies, and nothing you desire can compare with her.—Proverbs 8:10–11

Sweeter than Honey

During my junior year of college, a set of twins lived on my floor. They were tall, beautiful, and friendly. And for the life of me, I couldn't tell them apart! While I greeted other people by name, I'd always say a simple "hi" when one of the twins walked up—I didn't want to risk blurting out the wrong name.

I eventually learned how to tell them apart. But when it comes to sorting out right from wrong, sometimes I still feel that kind of confusion. I can't always tell what's what. Sometimes all my options seem equally good (or bad), and I really have no idea how to move forward.

Have you dealt with such situations lately? Most brides do, especially since they're making so many important decisions about their future. The "right" path isn't always very clear, and it takes a woman of great wisdom to figure it all out.

Of course, it's one thing to know that we need wisdom. It's another thing altogether to find it.

If you're like me, you get sick of all this talk and just shout, "OK, I want wisdom already. Now tell me how I can get it!" Fortunately, God hasn't left us clueless when it comes to seeking wisdom. In Psalm 119, we see the way:

> Oh, how I love your law!
>   I meditate on it all day long.
> Your commands make me wiser than
>   my enemies . . .
> How sweet are your words to my taste,
>   sweeter than honey to my mouth!
>
>   verses 97, 103

Meditating on God's commands brings wisdom. Makes sense, doesn't it? If we really want wisdom, we need to go to the source: God's Word. It's like my experience with the twins. It wasn't until I got to know them better that I was able to tell them apart. And it's not until we get to know God better—by reading his Word and taking the time to reflect on it—that we're able to tell the good from the bad in our lives.

What a challenge, though. The psalmist said that God's Word was "sweeter than honey to my mouth." And when I read that, I'm challenged to ask myself, "Do I love God's Word that much? Do I crave his Word as much as a delightful food?"

I love popcorn. The way I smother it with butter doesn't exactly make it a healthy snack, but it's a snack I crave. So I eat popcorn nearly every night. I just can't resist.

I wish I could write a psalm saying that I love God's Word more than popcorn—that I crave it with the same intensity. But I have to admit, sometimes I treat Bible-reading like a chore rather than a treat. And instead of savoring my quiet

moments in the Word, I often rush through it as if I'm trying to swallow my least-favorite casserole. I hate to think how many times I've missed out on God's wisdom because I've been too busy to really meditate on his Word.

James wrote, "If any of you lacks wisdom, he should ask God, who gives generously to all without finding fault, and it will be given to him" (1:5). That's a beautiful promise for God's brides, especially since it takes so much wisdom to make it through this life. But as we ask him for wisdom, we must realize that God offers most of it through his Word. If we're serious about discerning right from wrong, it's time to start searching the Scriptures and listening to what God has to say.

Starting today, ask God for a hunger to dig into his Word. It's the place where you can learn to discern right from wrong. And for God's brides it really is sweeter than honey, or any of our favorite foods. In God's words, we can find wisdom—and that is something sweet indeed.

Seating Charts

Gretchen rubbed her aching temples. "This seating chart is driving me insane!" she shouted to no one in particular. She'd been reshuffling the table arrangements for hours, trying to find places where each guest would feel comfortable. And when she'd asked her mom and sister for help, their suggestions had just made everything more complicated. Grabbing the bottle of aspirin, she started muttering to herself, "It'll take the wisdom of Solomon to figure this chart out."

Poor Gretchen. She's just run into the tricky task that every bride dreads: the infamous seating chart. Hopefully your charting adventure hasn't caused you any splitting headaches. But for most brides, deciding how to seat guests at the reception can get a little complicated. Certain people just won't mix well. And it takes some insight and wisdom to sort through it all.

As difficult as those seating charts can be, however, they're nothing compared to the complications of everyday life. Life is messy. There's good and bad out there, but the two don't mix well. So we're left to sort through everything, trying to figure out right from wrong. Sometimes our task is simple: we know murder is wrong, for example. But most of life's decisions aren't so clear-cut. Is lying OK if it protects the well-being of a friend? Can we watch a violent movie that has a good underlying theme? What's the right decision when you're facing a choice about the future?

It's tough to make decisions when the right thing to do isn't clear. With a lot of different ideas and values out there, it's difficult to sort out the truth. And it's tempting to just go along with the crowd as long as they're not doing anything blatantly wrong. That's why we need a special kind of wisdom—the wisdom to discern. Discernment doesn't settle for a wishy-washy approach to life. It looks to the core of each decision and seeks out God's best. And it always asks the question: is this thing good or bad?

That's a natural question for most brides—at least when it comes to the wedding. As they plan out their receptions, they ask lots of discerning questions: "Will those linens match the color of the bridesmaids' dresses?" "Will this DJ be friendly toward my guests?" "Will the guests prefer roast beef or salmon?" Sifting through all the details, brides seek the best things for their wedding.

But do we practice that kind of discernment in the rest of life? When it comes to our conversa-

LOVE STORY FROM GOD

As she walked home from the court, Deborah felt reflective. She still couldn't believe that God had put her in a position of such power. Israel didn't have a king yet, so the judges maintained order. And for now, Deborah was that judge, trying to lead her people well.

It was a job requiring great wisdom. As she listened to disputes, it was hard to separate fact from fiction. But always, Deborah looked to God for the help she needed. She'd been a prophetess before becoming judge, so she was used to listening for God's voice. As she heard case after case, she just kept listening for that voice.

Today, Deborah faced another tough situation: the Canaanites were after her people again. They'd been pestering Israel for twenty years, and God had been urging her that now was the time to act. She had talked with Barak, another Israelite leader, and convinced him to head out for battle. But Barak had expressed some doubts. So Deborah agreed to go with him, then chided him for not trusting in the Lord.

Now, as she thought about the battle ahead, she still felt a confidence that defied human wisdom. The enemy was both powerful and cruel, yet Deborah wouldn't back down. And she wouldn't listen to the voice of fear, either. No, she was a woman who listened to and acted on just one thing: the wisdom of God.

Read the outcome of Deborah and Barak's battle in Judges 4 and 5.

tions, or our hobbies, or our entertainment, do we sort through things and seek out God's best? All too often, I'm afraid, we aren't discerning about the things we take in. Instead, we just let things happen. And we become so busy that we don't even examine whether we're busy with the right or wrong things.

"Dear friends . . . be on your guard so that you may not be carried away by the error of lawless men and fall from your secure position" (2 Peter 3:17). "Examine yourselves to see whether you are in the faith; test yourselves" (2 Cor. 13:5). Those passages remind us to step back and look at our lives with a discerning eye. If we don't discern, we risk giving in to the errors of the world. If we don't test ourselves—our choices, our friends, our motives—we may fall away from our secure position.

And we have a position that we can't afford to lose. We're God's beloveds—cherished by the King of heaven. It breaks God's heart when he sees us carelessly accepting half-truths and bad ideas.

He doesn't want us to give in to evil without a fight. He gave us amazing minds, and he wants us to use them. He wants us to look at life with a critical eye, picking out what's wrong and keeping it away from us.

So as you discern what's best for the wedding, ask discerning questions about the rest of life too. Consider this verse: "The wisdom that comes from heaven is first of all pure; then peace-loving, considerate, submissive, full of mercy and good fruit, impartial and sincere" (James 3:17). And then apply that verse to your life. Ask the tough questions, such as "Is this peace-loving?" "Am I making this decision in submission to God?" "Are these people full of mercy and good fruit?"

Those discerning questions will help you sort out good from bad because they're rooted in God's wisdom. And they'll save you a lot of headaches—because God's wisdom serves a bride well, not only when it comes to seating charts but for all the adventures ahead.

12

· · · · · · · · · · · · · · ·

THE GIFTS

*T*raditionally, couples are showered with gifts throughout their engagement. You'll have fun opening up all those practical and pretty gifts for your home. But as you look forward to the presents, don't forget the details. You'll want to register for items you need and keep careful record of who has given what. Most important, you'll want to say thank you to everyone who opened up their hearts—and their wallets—for your wedding day.

It takes a special bride to keep all this gift excitement in perspective. Amid the store aisles, registry lists, and wrapping paper, greed may tug at your heart. But instead of giving in to the craving for more, find creative ways to share your blessings with others. Now is the perfect opportunity to build gratitude and contentment into your life. And these two virtues are sure to add warmth and welcome to your new home.

Bride of
Contentment

Keep your lives free from the love of money and be content with what you have.—Hebrews 13:5

Give me an eagerness for your decrees; do not inflict me with love for money! Turn my eyes from worthless things.
—Psalm 119:36–37 NLT

Whoever loves money never has money enough; whoever loves wealth is never satisfied with his income.
—Ecclesiastes 5:10

Count Your Blessings

I heard about this guy once. He seemed to be a magnet for trouble.

You see, this man kept having run-ins with the law. The authorities didn't agree with his speeches, and they didn't believe in freedom of speech. So this poor guy got thrown in jail and beaten up—numerous times—all because he said the wrong thing.

As if that weren't enough, he didn't exactly have an easy time even when he was out of jail.

Sometimes he didn't have enough food. Sometimes he didn't have any clothes. Sometimes his travel arrangements fell through—literally—when the ships he sailed on got wrecked. And through it all, he carried the burden of caring for hundreds of people.

Oh yeah—did I mention his name was Paul? He was the greatest apostle in Christian history. Maybe you've heard of him.

Paul understood the word *suffering*. He'd been a victim so many times that he had every reason to spend years in a therapist's office. Just check out his laundry list of sufferings in 2 Corinthians 11:23–28. The guy had barely anything to his name. And he'd been put through it all. Sounds to me like Paul had plenty to complain about.

But you know what Paul had to say about the hardships of his life? "I have learned to be content whatever the circumstances" (Phil. 4:11). What? Content with a life spent in almost constant danger and misery? Content with a job that fills you with worry and sometimes makes you an innocent target? If those words weren't recorded in God's Word, I would doubt their truth. How could anyone be content with a life like Paul's?

I feel this way because I see so much discontent in my own life. It doesn't even take a prison sentence or a shipwreck to get me down. Just show me a new style of winter jacket, and I'll feel discontent with my old coat. Give me a bad day of writing, and I'll probably be grumpy about my job for at least a week.

And I know I'm not alone. Discontentment has reached nearly epidemic proportions in our world. We're constantly told to indulge, to do what it takes to make ourselves happy. To help us in our quest for self-fulfillment, there are endless numbers of gadgets, books, and toys. But for all the wealth and abundance in our culture, so many of us feel discontent. We struggle with this nagging feeling that we deserve more than what we've got.

Discontentment runs deep in our lives. And it can affect our attitudes about anything—jobs, friends, even God. In fact, our discontentment always goes back to God, because when we're discontent with our lives, we're really discontented with what God has given us. We may sing songs of thanks and praise in church, yet in our hearts we're struggling with what God has put (or not put) into our lives. We feel like he's holding out on us, and that makes us confused, even mad.

Have you noticed any discontentment in your own life? Maybe it came after that last bridal shower, when you started noticing how many registry items you haven't received yet. Maybe it came when the house or the car you wanted ended up costing just a little too much for your budget. Maybe discontentment cropped up in your relationship because your fiancé just doesn't seem as attentive as he used to.

If you face any discontentment right now, you're probably wondering the same thing I am: How did Paul do it? How did he stay content during a hard life? And how can I stay content when things don't go my way? I don't have an answer to that question. But thankfully, Paul does. This is what he wrote: "I have learned the secret of being content in any and every situation, whether well fed or hungry . . . I can do everything through him who gives me strength" (Phil. 4:12–13).

Paul found contentment by remembering the source of his strength: God. Somehow, even when he was hungry and cold and naked, Paul had the ability to focus on the things God had given him—things like salvation and peace, which he mentioned so often in his letters. With a firm faith, he trusted God to be his strength—not material possessions or people or power.

"Count your blessings, name them one by one. Count your blessings, see what God has done." When discontentment creeps in, God's brides would do well to remember that old song. Because when it comes to finding contentment, we need to stop thinking about what we don't have and instead think about what is already ours.

What incredible life experiences has God given you? How have you grown in your faith? What do you have that is more valuable than anything here on earth? At a time when many brides get caught up in what they want, you can take a different path, counting those things you already have. And if you do, you'll find out you're richer than you thought—because God has already showered you with priceless gifts.

The Next Best Thing

Beth scanned the pile of opened shower gifts. There were cookie sheets, crystal glasses, bath towels, and more. But no bread maker. She'd registered for one, hoping to receive it at a shower. And though she'd received an abundance of things for her new home, she felt a pang of disappointment. It was silly—but she'd really wanted that bread maker.

Noticing her daughter's frown, Beth's mom walked over and asked why she was looking sad. "Oh, Mom, I'm grateful for all these great things, I really am," Beth replied. "But I was hoping for a bread maker . . ."

I'm grateful . . . but. How often have you said those words—or at least thought them? I know I have. One Christmas as a child, I had my heart set on a particular toy. And despite all the other great gifts I received, I still felt disappointed. I wanted just one more thing.

Now that I'm a little older, I've learned that "just one more thing" is never enough. There will always be something more—the second candlestick to make a pair, the latest cell phone feature,

the shoes to match your new dress. We're living in a culture of "the next best thing." Never mind the fact that we already have everything we really need. There's usually something more that we want.

So what makes us want more? In our world of bigger and better, we're certainly bombarded with advertisements telling us to buy more. But I think there's a deeper problem. The real enemy of contentment is greed—that persistent little voice inside of us that tells us we deserve more than we've got.

Greed is an ugly word. Not exactly the sort of thing you want chiseled on your grave marker some day. But greed in action—that's even uglier. Just imagine a busy shopping mall on Christmas Eve. There are hundreds of hurried shoppers, tired and crabby as they push through the crowds. Few of those people feel the holiday spirit as they grab their last few Christmas items. In fact, some will get downright angry and underhanded to get what they want.

That's exactly what greed does to our lives. It distracts us from what's already good and drives us into a not-so-peaceful quest for more. While we search for more "stuff," we get worn out. We get angry with those around us. And we lose all sense of joy and peace. Our lives turn into that busy shopping mall.

The Bible warns against this kind of lifestyle. Check it out:

But godliness with contentment is great gain. For we brought nothing into the world, and we can take nothing out of it. But if we have food and clothing, we will be content with that. People who want to get rich fall into temptation and a trap and into many foolish and harmful desires that plunge men into ruin and destruction.

1 Timothy 6:6–9

During your engagement days, you're sure to feel the tug of greed at times. It's there in the bridal magazines and the stores where you register. It'll even tempt you at bridal showers, where you're surrounded by new things. So be on the lookout. You don't want to fall into the "foolish and harmful desires that plunge men into ruin." Make a point of pushing greed out of your life and letting contentment settle in.

Throw those advertisements away. Plan a simple date. Make a big sign for your bathroom mirror that says "Today I have all I need. Tomorrow will care for itself." Do whatever it takes to keep your mind off the next best thing filling store shelves. And then smile. Because that feeling of calm and contentment you'll gain— it's *the* best thing. And it's better than anything money can buy.

LOVE STORY FROM GOD

David had every reason to feel frustrated. He'd killed a giant. He'd been anointed a king. And where had it gotten him? Here, in a dark cave, running for his life.

It had been a wild ride. After David killed Goliath, the Israelites had been excited, singing songs about David's triumph. They were ecstatic to have a hero again, especially since King Saul had gone rather soft. Everyone heard the rumors about Saul's moods and paranoia. With such an ineffective king, many were ready for someone new— someone like David.

For his part, David had no intention of hurting Saul. Ever since Samuel had anointed him as God's choice for the next king, David had been confident that he'd someday sit on the throne. But he was content to wait for God's timing—even now, when hope seemed dim.

And right now, hopes were very dim. Saul's paranoia wouldn't be stopped and he'd been hunting David for months, wanting to eliminate his rival. David, along with a few faithful men, had been running from place to place, often huddling in desert caves to hide from the crazy king.

Dealing with this volatile situation on a daily basis, David often wondered about his future. *It could be years before I can walk safely in public again,* he'd muse. *I may be an old man before I finally sit on the throne.* Yet despite the uncertainty of his future, David wrote beautiful songs—songs that cried to God for help, songs that spoke of David's frustration, but also songs of praise. In eloquent poetry, he thanked God for his faithfulness and strength.

And so, even during the darkest days of his life, David didn't give in to greed or try to seize the throne. Instead, he found a reason for contentment, singing of the peace and protection of his God.

Check out the book of Psalms, especially chapters 56, 57, and 63, for many of David's songs written on the run.

Planning for Your Gifts

Setting Up House

While some couples have acquired many household items from years of living on their own, others don't have even a spoon to their name. Depending on your situation, you'll have a unique set of needs and desires for your future home. So before you head off to register for gifts, take time to inventory your current belongings.

For smaller items, such as bathroom linens and dinnerware, inventory your possessions using the gift registry checklist provided later in this chapter. If you already own a listed item, and you don't feel the need to register for a new one, place a check in the column marked "Already Have."

Use the worksheet below to inventory the larger items such as furniture and electronics. For each room, list the items you own and place a check in the "Keep" or "Give Away" column. Then add the items you hope to purchase, along with an estimated cost. Don't forget to inventory home-maintenance items (vacuum cleaner, wheelbarrow, ladder, etc.).

In many cases, bride and groom may have duplicate items or items that simply don't suit each other's tastes. Let a spirit of compromise guide you as you decide which things to keep and which to give away.

PLANNING CHECKLIST

FOUR TO SIX MONTHS BEFORE

☐ Inventory your current household items. Create a list of items to keep, items to throw out, and items needed.

☐ Register for household items at one or more retailers. (You may want to register sooner than six months before your wedding if any showers or special events have been scheduled at an earlier date.)

ONE TO THREE MONTHS BEFORE

☐ Purchase gifts for attendants and plan attendants' party, if having one.

WITHIN TWO WEEKS OF RECEIVING GIFTS

☐ Write thank-you notes to those who attended and gave gifts at your bridal showers.

☐ Send thank-you notes to those who send you wedding gifts before the wedding day.

WITHIN FOUR MONTHS AFTER WEDDING

☐ Write thank-you notes to special wedding participants (musicians, readers, helpful friends, etc.).

☐ Send thank-you notes to each person who gave you a wedding gift.

Home Furnishings/Equipment Inventory

Room	Item	Keep	Give Away	Need to Buy (Est. Cost)
Living Room				
Bedroom				

Room	Item	Keep	Give Away	Need to Buy (Est. Cost)
Kitchen				
Dining Room				
Bathroom				
Office/Study				
Electronics				

Room	Item	Keep	Give Away	Need to Buy (Est. Cost)
Outdoor Furniture				
Maintenance Items				
Other				

When it comes to the big-ticket items—such as bedroom furniture or a television—create a purchase plan that fits your budget. If funds are tight, check out the classified ads of your local newspaper for affordable used items. Or consider adding some of these items to your wedding registry: some guests may want to go in together to give you a larger gift.

You can also request cash gifts to help with the costs of starting a new home. Ask a friend or family member to tactfully spread the word among your guests. But do not express your preference for cash gifts on your invitations—it's considered tacky to do so.

If you're hoping to buy the biggest item of them all—a house—you can now register for a down payment. The Department of Housing and Urban Development offers a Bridal Registry Initiative that allows couples to open an interest-bearing account at approved lenders. Your wedding guests can contribute money to this account and help you build a down payment on your future home. Get more information by calling 1-800-CALLFHA.

Registering for Gifts

While some of your guests may already have the perfect gift in mind, most people appreciate a bridal registry that tells them what the couple wants for their home. Instead of receiving a mismatched hodgepodge of household items, you will receive items in the colors and styles you prefer. Since most stores will take items off your registry as they are purchased, you also have the added benefit of avoiding duplicate gifts that need to be returned.

When and Where

Try to register at least four to six months before your wedding—earlier if you have pre-wedding parties or bridal showers scheduled before then. Waiting until the last minute not only leaves you with more stress, but it is also inconvenient for guests who want to shop early.

Before you register for wedding gifts, think carefully about where you'd like to register. While it's acceptable to register at more than one store, you don't want your guests to run all over town looking for gifts in a dozen different places. Try to limit your registry to three locations. It's easier on your guests, and it makes it simple for you to track and update your registry lists.

If you have several out-of-town guests, register with at least one store with locations around the country. Or use an online gift registry. Many bridal registries are available online, allowing your guests to browse through pictures and purchase items easily from their homes.

Before you register anywhere, ask the store about their policy on returns and exchanges. Do you need a receipt to make an exchange? Will they allow you to return damaged items? If a store can't offer a convenient way to make returns, register elsewhere. Also, ask if they will ship or deliver items that have been purchased by out-

of-town guests, and find out whether those gifts will be insured.

GIFT REGISTRY LOCATIONS

Location #1: _____

Contact information: _____

_____

Web address or toll-free order line: _____

_____

Notes: _____

_____

_____

Location #2: _____

Contact information: _____

_____

Web address or toll-free order line: _____

_____

Notes: _____

_____

_____

Location #3: _____

Contact information: _____

_____

Web address or toll-free order line: _____

_____

Notes: _____

_____

_____

Registry Tips

As you create your personal bridal registry, keep these tips in mind:

Don't register for the same items at different stores, or you may receive duplicate gifts.

Register for gifts in a variety of price ranges.

Be sure the store includes plenty of identifying information (your name, the groom's name, the wedding date, etc.) so that guests will not confuse your registry with someone else's.

Provide the store with a delivery address so all your gifts will arrive at the same location.

Keep track of the items you register for using the Gift Registry Worksheet in this book. Be sure to include the retail price of these items—it will be a helpful record of your belongings for insurance purposes.

As you receive gifts at showers and other special events, double-check with the store to make sure they've been taken off your registry. That way, you'll avoid the hassle of duplicate gifts.

THE NUMBERS GAME

As you plan for the future, be careful to create a lifestyle that you can afford. If you've never followed a budget before, now's the time to start. A simple budget will include one category listing your monthly income and another category listing your monthly expenses (rent/mortgage, utility bills, loan payments, insurance, gas, etc.). You'll also want to include a monthly budget item for things like gifts, entertainment, and home improvements. And if you have a dream vacation or some new furniture you'd like to buy, your budget can help you build up savings for those items as well.

If you're not sure how to get your budget started, purchase a book about budgeting or attend a budgeting workshop. (Keep your eyes open for churches that offer budgeting classes.) There are also several software programs on the market that help you build a budget and track monthly expenses.

Gift Registry Worksheet

	Brand/Style	Quantity	Price	Registry Location	Already Have
Fine China					
Dinner Plates					
Salad Plates					
Bread/Butter Plates					
Cups					

	Brand/Style	Quantity	Price	Registry Location	Already Have
Saucers					
Soup/Cereal Bowls					
Fruit Dishes					
Open Vegetable Dish					
Covered Vegetable Dish					
Small Platter					
Medium Platter					
Large Platter					
Sugar Bowl					
Creamer					
Salt/Pepper Shakers					
Gravy Boat					
Butter Dish					
Teapot					
Coffeepot					
Other					
Other					
Formal Flatware					
5-Piece Setting					
4-Piece Setting					
Teaspoons					
Salad Forks					
Dinner Forks					
Dinner Knives					
Soup Spoons					
Steak Knives					
Butter Knife					
Butter Spreader					
Sugar Spoon					
Gravy Ladle					
Serving Spoon					
Pierced Spoon					
Meat Fork					

	Brand/Style	Quantity	Price	Registry Location	Already Have
Cocktail Forks					
Storage Chest					
Other					
Other					
Crystal					
Goblets					
Wine Glasses					
Champagne Flutes					
Cordials					
Brandy Snifters					
Highballs					
Decanters					
Pitchers					
Other					
Other					
Casual Dinnerware					
5-Piece Setting					
20-Piece Set (includes 4 place settings)					
Dinner Plates					
Salad Plates					
Bread/Butter Plates					
Cups					
Saucers					
Mugs					
Rimmed Soup Bowls					
Cereal Bowls					
Open Vegetable Dish					
Covered Vegetable Dish					
Fruit Dishes					
Small Platter					
Medium Platter					
Large Platter					

	Brand/Style	Quantity	Price	Registry Location	Already Have
Sugar Bowl					
Creamer					
Salt/Pepper Shakers					
Gravy Boat					
Butter Dish					
Teapot					
Coffeepot					
Other					
Other					
Casual Flatware					
5-Piece Setting					
Dinner Forks					
Teaspoons					
Salad Forks					
Dinner Forks					
Dinner Knives					
Soup Spoons					
Steak Knives					
Gravy Ladle					
Serving Spoons					
Other					
Other					
Casual Glassware					
Goblets					
Wine Glasses					
Champagne Glasses					
Water Glasses					
Juice Glasses					
Pilsner Glasses					
Pitcher					
Punch Bowl Set					
Ice Bucket					
Wine Rack					

	Brand/Style	Quantity	Price	Registry Location	Already Have
Martini Set					
Other					
Other					
Serving Accessories					
Coffee Set					
Salt/Pepper Shakers					
Gravy Boat					
Butter Dish					
Covered Casserole					
Salad Bowl					
Salad Tongs					
Chip and Dip Bowl					
Relish Tray					
Cheese Board					
Cheese Slicer					
Cake Plate					
Candlesticks					
Serving Tray					
Other					
Other					
Cookware					
Small Saucepan					
Medium Saucepan					
Large Saucepan					
Small Sauté Pan					
Large Sauté Pan					
Small Frying Pan					
Medium Frying Pan					
Large Frying Pan					
Small Stockpot					
Large Stockpot					
Dutch Oven					
Double Boiler					

	Brand/Style	Quantity	Price	Registry Location	Already Have
Griddle					
Skillet					
Stir-fry Pan					
Steamer					
Colander					
Microwave Cookware					
Other					
Other					
Bakeware					
Casserole Dish Set					
Covered Casserole					
Lasagna Pan					
Quiche Dish					
Rectangular Baking Dish					
Roasting Pan					
Pizza Pan					
Pizza Stone					
Cake Pan					
Cookie Sheet					
Bread Pan					
Muffin Tin					
Bundt Pan					
Springform Cake Pan					
Cooling Rack					
Pie Pans					
Other					
Other					
Kitchen Items					
Utensil Set					
Spice Rack					
Canister Set					
Mixing Bowls					
Measuring Cups					

	Brand/Style	Quantity	Price	Registry Location	Already Have
Rolling Pin					
Storage Containers					
Cutting Board					
Steak Knives					
Cutlery Set					
Carving Set					
Steel Sharpener					
Cookie Jar					
Coffee Mugs					
Oven Timer					
Thermometer					
Teakettle					
Apron					
Dish Towels					
Pot Holders					
Kitchen Shears					
Other					
Other					
Kitchen Linens					
Place Mats					
Napkins					
Napkin Rings					
Tablecloths					
Other					
Small Appliances					
Toaster					
Coffeemaker					
Coffee Grinder					
Espresso Machine					
Can Opener					
Hand Mixer					
Stand Mixer					
Blender					

	Brand/Style	Quantity	Price	Registry Location	Already Have
Food Processor					
Popcorn Popper					
Waffle Maker					
Electric Wok					
Bread Maker					
Pasta Machine					
Juicer					
Toaster Oven					
Convection Oven					
Electric Frying Pan					
Electric Knife					
Sandwich Maker					
Microwave					
Crock-Pot					
Indoor Grill					
Fondue Pot					
Clock					
Iron					
Vacuum Cleaner					
Fan					
Space Heater					
Other					
Other					
Bedroom Linens					
Flat Sheets					
Fitted Sheets					
Pillowcases					
Sheet Sets					
Pillows					
Pillow Protectors					
Pillow Shams					
Down Comforter					
Duvet Cover					

	Brand/Style	Quantity	Price	Registry Location	Already Have
Bedspread					
Dust Ruffle					
Lightweight Blanket					
Wool Blanket					
Electric Blanket					
Window Treatments					
Other					
Other					
Bathroom Items					
Bath Towels					
Hand Towels					
Washcloths					
Fingertip Towels					
Bath Sheets					
Shower Curtain					
Shower Liner					
Bath Mat					
Lid Cover					
Contour Rug					
Tissue Holder					
Soap Dish					
Tumbler					
Toothbrush Holder					
Wastebasket					
Hamper					
Scale					
Other					
Other					
Electronics					
Stereo					
Television					
VCR/DVD Player					
Telephone					

	Brand/Style	Quantity	Price	Registry Location	Already Have
Answering Machine					
Portable Stereo/Radio					
Camera					
Camcorder					
Other					
Laundry					
Laundry Basket					
Ironing Board					
Drying Rack					
Other					
Miscellaneous Items					
Storage Containers					
Cleaning Supplies					
Luggage					
Tool Set					
Games					
Movies					
Picnic Basket					
Lamps					
Picture Frames					
Vases					
Candles					
Candlesticks					
Coasters					
Camping Gear					
Garden Tool Set					
Watering Can					
Outdoor Games					
Beach Towels					
Other					
Other					

Here Come the Gifts

During the months before and after your wedding, you'll receive dozens of gifts for showers, parties, and the wedding itself. Remembering who gave what will be nearly impossible, so careful record-keeping is a must. Ask a friend to jot down notes as you open presents. Then use your guest list box (as described in chapter 5) to create a permanent record of your gifts and thank-you notes. You'll already have a card listing each guest's name and address. Now, use the following example to fill in gift information on the back of each card:

Name of guest(s): _____

Shower gift _____

    Thank-you sent? _____

Shower gift _____

    Thank-you sent? _____

Wedding gift _____

    Thank-you sent? _____

Cash gift _____

    Thank-you sent? _____

Exchanges and Returns

Most couples receive several duplicate gifts, making some exchanges necessary. Before you run off to exchange duplicate shower gifts, though, remember that you'll receive more gifts at the wedding. You don't want to swap that toaster for a new

MEMORIES IN THE MAKING

Have you ever snickered at the avocado and gold dishes that were so popular when your mom got married? Or the ugly carpet that your parents chose for their first home? Home fashions change over the years, and someday you'll have fun looking back at today's trends. Fill out this short worksheet—and then try not to laugh too hard when you look it over in twenty years!

Our wedding year: _____

Kitchen colors and trends: _____

_____

_____

Dinnerware colors and trends: _____

_____

Appliance colors and trends: _____

_____

Furniture colors and trends: _____

_____

Bedding colors and trends: _____

_____

Home decorating trends: _____

_____

_____

Popular home décor stores: _____

_____

_____

Popular home improvement stores: _____

_____

_____

blender, only to find two other blenders among your wedding gifts! Wait until after the wedding before making any exchanges; then you can make exchanges for the things you still need.

When you want to return a gift that doesn't suit your needs or tastes, the situation requires a bit more delicacy. Most people like to see their gift being displayed or used in your home, so it's wise to wait at least a month after the wedding before returning their gift. By that time, things will be put away in your home, and guests will not likely notice if their gift has been returned. If someone does ask about a gift you've returned, be honest and tactfully explain why you needed to return it.

Finally, when it comes to close friends or family members, it's usually best to just keep their gift, even if it's something you'd prefer to return. Unless they've specifically mentioned that you may return their gift, you may offend the people you love the most.

Thank-You Notes

Few people enjoy the taxing process of writing dozens of thank-you notes. But when it comes to wedding gifts, thank-yous are a must.

Many printers offer special cards, called "informals," which are designed for wedding thank-yous. Ask your printer or supplier about various card options when you're shopping for wedding invitations. Of course, special-order stationery is not required. It's perfectly acceptable to purchase thank-you notes from a card shop or to create your own cards using a computer or stamping supplies.

You have a variety of options when it comes to thank-you stationery, but there's one basic rule that applies to all thank-yous: always include a personal message in your note. Even if your thank-you cards came with a printed generic message inside, you should add a personal note thanking the giver for their gift.

As you stretch those fingers and prepare to write those notes, keep these tips in mind:

Always mention the gift and how you plan to use it, even if you did not particularly like the object. For example, you might write a simple message saying, "Dear Aunt Louisa, thank you for the beautiful crystal pitcher you gave us for our wedding. It will look lovely on display in our china cabinet."

When thanking someone for a duplicate or unwanted gift, there's no need to mention that it's been returned or exchanged. Simply thank them for the original gift.

Send thank-you notes promptly. Try to send thank-yous within two weeks of a bridal shower or pre-wedding party, and within four months after the wedding day.

When thanking someone for his or her cash gift, there's no need to mention the amount. Simply thank them for their thoughtful contribution and mention how you plan to spend the money (toward a down payment on a house, for household supplies, furniture, etc.).

Don't forget to thank those who gave a gift of time for your wedding. Musicians, readers, friends who hosted out-of-town guests, family members who stayed late to clean up—anyone who volunteered their time deserves a note of thanks.

The Gifts You Give

Not only will you receive gifts for your wedding, but also, as a thank-you to parents, attendants, and other special wedding participants, you'll probably give a few gifts as well. To keep yourself less frazzled during the final weeks, try to get your gift shopping done at least a month before the wedding. As you shop, keep in mind the unique hobbies and interests of the gift recipient. Each person has given up time and money to be part of your big day, so you want a gift that says thank you in a meaningful way.

Use the Gifts from You checklist to brainstorm gift ideas and track your shopping.

ALL BROKEN UP

With the stress of packaging and transportation, it's not unusual for a wedding gift to arrive broken. Before contacting the gift giver about this problem, call the store where the gift was purchased. If it was insured, you can call the giver so that they can replace the broken items.

However, if the gift was not insured, it's best to just quietly dispose of the gift or pay for a replacement yourself. Thank the gift giver without mentioning the damage. Otherwise, they may feel pressured to pay for a second gift—a burden that shouldn't be placed on any guest.

Gifts from You

Person	Gift Ideas	Gift Bought	Cost
Groom			
Groomsmen			
Bridesmaids			
Best Man			
Maid of Honor			
Flower Girl			
Ring Bearer			
Parents			
Officiant			
Other			
Other			

Favors

Many couples decide to give a small wedding favor to their guests. While favors do provide a nice way to thank guests for their presence at your wedding, they aren't required. They often go unused or get left behind at the reception tables. So you may forgo the giving of wedding favors, especially if your budget is tight.

If you do give wedding favors, offer something that your guests can actually use. Flower bulbs wrapped with colorful fabric, pens with your new name on them, candies tucked into decorative boxes—these are just a few ideas for favors that are both pretty and practical.

Wedding favors can usually be ordered from a wedding supplier or an online store. There are literally hundreds of favors available in the wedding market. But if you'd like to save a little money and have some fun, just purchase some items that you can assemble yourself. Throw a "favor party" and invite some friends or family to help you assemble favors. It's a great way to make aunts, cousins, future in-laws, and others feel like a special part of your wedding plans.

GIVING BACK

As you enjoy the gifts from family and friends, consider ways to share your new blessings with others. Here are a few ideas:

Have a dollar dance at your wedding reception, then donate the money to a local charity.

Instead of throwing out or selling the old items you don't intend to keep, bring them to a Goodwill store or a family in need.

Give a portion of the wedding money you receive to a charity.

Ask your caterer if leftover reception food can be packed up and delivered to a nearby homeless shelter.

Bride of Generosity

But just as you excel in everything—in faith, in speech, in knowledge, in complete earnestness and in your love for us—see that you also excel in this grace of giving.
—2 Corinthians 8:7

Each man should give what he has decided in his heart to give, not reluctantly or under compulsion, for God loves a cheerful giver.
—2 Corinthians 9:7

Cops and Robbers

Did you ever play cops and robbers as a kid? I sure did. Many a summer afternoon, I'd gather with other neighbor kids, ready for the game. Half of us were designated as thieves and ran off to hide; the other half acted like cops, hunting down the robbers and hauling them to "jail"—usually located on the neighbor's front stoop.

Cops and robbers gave us hours of fun in those days. But when a robbery occurs in real life, suddenly the childhood game turns from silly play to a real-life dilemma. Real cops aren't laughing as

they hunt down the thieves. And the view from a real jail cell isn't quite as charming as that from the neighbor's stoop. No, robbery isn't funny business at all. That's probably why God gets so angry when we try to rob him.

Wait a minute, you might be wondering. *We rob God? How in the world does that happen? He doesn't exactly have a house around town that we can break into!*

That's how the Israelites reacted too. When God told them they'd been robbing him, they looked at each other, puzzled. "How did we do that?" they asked. And here's how God responded: "In tithes and offerings. You are under a curse—the whole nation of you—because you are robbing me" (Mal. 3:8–9).

That's some pretty straight talk from God. When it comes to robbery, he doesn't beat around the bush. He's direct. When you don't bring offerings to God, you're robbing him. It's that simple.

In our do-it-yourself kind of world, that truth is hard to swallow. After all, we work hard. We put in the long hours at the office. And conventional wisdom says we should use that money on the things we want. But the conventional wisdom misses something important: it doesn't take into account that "every good and perfect gift is from above" (James 1:17).

Everything we have belongs to God. Everything—from our jobs, to the homes we're saving up to buy, to the investments we've made for the future. Sure, some people will take credit for those things themselves. But we know better. God gives jobs, and he takes them away. He gives us time and health, and he can take them away too. We're living with borrowed belongings—in the graces of God.

Considering that all we have is his, it's not unreasonable that God would ask us to give back. In fact, it makes good sense. When you give a gift to a charity, you expect them to use it wisely, don't you? You expect that your gift will be used to help other people. And God expects the same from us. He wants us to bless others with what we've been given.

All too often, though, instead of giving back to God, we pay for other things we "need." We need to save up for a nicer house. We need to start investments for retirement. We need this, that, and the other thing. And before we know it, we've used up most of our money. If we're fortunate to have a little left, we'll be generous and stick some money in the collection plate.

God doesn't want our leftovers, though. He yearns for us to give him the "firstfruits"—the *first* part of what we earn—and to trust him for the rest (see Prov. 3:9). When we use money to help ourselves first, we're misusing the things God has given us. Actually, it's worse than that. We become robbers—taking what isn't ours and using it selfishly.

"'Bring the whole tithe into the storehouse, that there may be food in my house. Test me in this,' says the LORD Almighty, 'and see if I will not throw open the floodgates of heaven and pour out so much blessing that you will not have room enough for it'" (Mal. 3:10). That's the challenge for all of God's brides—instead of holding so tightly to our money and our financial plans, we need to give back to God first. "Try me," he says. "Give to me and see if I don't take care of all your needs, and then some."

So as you and your fiancé begin your new life together, I hope you'll delight in all those wedding gifts. And I pray you'll receive many other gifts from God—from a warm home to a stable job and good health. But as you take it all in, remember God's warning about robbers. Make a commitment to God and each other that generosity will be your top financial priority.

Once you've done that, you can relax in God's care. Because even though he may not give you everything you want, one thing's for sure: when you give generously to God, he'll always provide what you need.

Gifts of the Heart

Sheila placed the lamp in a storage box and pushed it to the back of the closet. The stained glass was exquisite and the workmanship impressive, but the lamp just didn't fit her and Jake's decorative tastes. Though it had been a wedding gift, Sheila had tried to return it. Unfortunately, the specialty shop where it came from wouldn't accept returns.

Moments after shutting the closet door, Sheila heard the doorbell ring. She caught a glimpse of Aunt Elaine through the window, and her heart thumped faster as she invited her inside. *She's the one who gave me the lamp!* Sheila thought. *I hope she doesn't notice that it's not here.* Moments later, though, Aunt Elaine mentioned the lamp. "I hope you and Jake like it," she said. "I asked the shopkeeper to put lilac blossoms in the pattern because I know how much you loved them as a girl."

Sheila hadn't even noticed the special glass pattern. And she felt sick when she noticed Aunt Elaine scanning the room for her lamp. Feeling bad, Sheila confessed to storing the lamp away. Aunt Elaine nodded politely, but the look of hurt was unmistakable in her eyes.

Maybe it was a birthday or a bridal shower, but somewhere in time you've probably been in Sheila's shoes—stuck with a gift you didn't want to use. Where did it end up? Back at the store. Stuck somewhere in storage. Or maybe you were noble enough to put it on display, in a dark corner of the room. No matter where it ended up, though, you probably share Sheila's fear—hoping your own "Aunt Elaine" won't show up to see what's been done with the gift.

BIBLE BRIDE

She was facing tough times. In fact, some people said she'd lost everything. Her husband was dead, and with few resources of her own, she was in pretty dire condition. She needed every penny she could get.

Considering her circumstances, no one would think her selfish for keeping her money to herself. After all, it was barely enough to get by. Yet even as others felt sorry for her, the woman didn't feel sorry for herself. Yes, she'd suffered great loss. But she still had God—and that was enough. She was grateful for his love; she was content with his provision. And from what little she had, she wanted to give back.

So it wasn't unusual when she showed up at the temple one day and placed her last pennies in the offering plate. But what was unusual were the words of a rabbi named Jesus. He'd seen the woman's selfless generosity and then called his students around. "I tell you the truth," Jesus said, "this poor widow has put more into the treasury than all the others. They all gave out of their wealth; but she, out of her poverty, put in everything—all she had to live on."

Years later, when a couple of Jesus's disciples were writing about their days with the rabbi, the event still stood out in their memory. And even though the woman never knew it, her small act of giving lived in their Gospel accounts.

This amazingly generous woman gets only small mention in the Gospels, but her story is worth remembering. Read it for yourself in Mark 12:41–44 and Luke 21:1–4.

There's a story in the Bible that reminds me of this gift-giving fiasco. Jesus told a parable about a king who travels to a faraway country. As he leaves, he gives gifts to three of his servants—entrusting each of them to care for a portion of his money. When the king returns, he finds that two of his servants have invested his money wisely, earning even greater wealth. As a thank-you for their good work, the king puts each servant in charge of several cities.

But then there's the other servant. He's taken the money and hidden it away under a piece of cloth, afraid to put it to use. And when the king finds out that his gift has been ignored, he's furious. He takes the money away and barks out a stern warning: "I tell you that to everyone who has, more will be given, but as for the one who has nothing, even what he has will be taken away" (Luke 19:26).

As I read about the last servant, I picture Sheila stuffing away that beautiful lamp in a closet and then getting caught in the act. And then I think of something a little closer to home. I think of all the gifts God has given to us. Not just the physical blessings but also the spiritual gifts he's poured out on each of us. And I wonder: how often do we hide them away instead of putting them to good use?

When you think about your own unique personality and talents, what comes to your mind? Are you a gifted singer? Do you have a special knack for encouraging others? Do you have a bold spirit that makes you a great leader? Each special quality is a gift from God. Listen to these words from 1 Corinthians: "Now there are different kinds of spiritual gifts . . . A spiritual gift is given to each of us as a means of helping the entire church (12:4, 7 NLT).

There are a variety of spiritual gifts—a unique combination for each one of Christ's brides. And even though you may not always feel gifted, God's Word is clear: you have been given a spiritual gift. With careful reflection and prayers for God's help, you can discover just what gifts you have.

What comes next is up to you. You may choose to shove that gift in a back closet, promising to use it some other day. Or you can just toss the gift out because it doesn't suit your style. You might spend your time striving instead for the spiritual gifts you see in someone else. Or you can even choose to live in fear, like the servant of Jesus's parable—hiding your gift from others because you're afraid of what might happen if you put it to use.

But those aren't the paths of a generous bride. No, we've been gifted for a reason. And I think our heavenly Groom longs to see our gifts on display—being put to good use as we share them with others. In the coming weeks, as you experience the delightful blessings of bridal showers and wedding gifts, don't forget the gifts of the heart.

And remember, your spiritual gifts don't belong in a closet for "another day." They're the kind of gifts that were designed for everyday use.

A FINAL WORD

*I*t's been an amazing ride, hasn't it? By the time you read this section of the planner, your days as a bride will be drawing to a close. You've gone through all the delights and dramas of the engagement, learning a lot about your character along the way. Soon, you'll be ending this chapter of your life and starting a whole new adventure in married life.

I hope that new chapter will start in a wonderful way—with a wedding that fulfills your girlhood dreams. For each reader who's used this book to plan her special day, I pray that God will bless all your hard work: "May [God] give you the desire of your heart and make all your plans succeed" (Ps. 20:4).

And when the wedding's all over and those precious moments as an earthly bride have passed, may you look back at your engagement with a smile in your heart. Because somewhere along the way—amid the shopping and showers, flowers and phone calls—God did a wondrous thing. He used it all to mold you into his spiritual bride.

And that's a position you'll hold for years and years to come.

ACKNOWLEDGMENTS

No one writes alone. And this book would not have been possible without the love and support of many people. My deepest thanks goes to all of you who've helped me along the way.

To my sister, Jennifer Leep, who helped me believe in myself enough to write this book and then gave me an open door to see it published. Jen, this never would've happened without you—thank you for making it all possible.

To Brian, my husband, who puts up with my grumpy moods on bad writing days and celebrates with me when I've accomplished a goal. Thanks for standing beside me every step of the way.

To my parents, Tim and Bev Leep, who've been praying for me and cultivating my love of words since I was a girl. You've always encouraged me to use my gifts for God—and so much of what I've learned about Christian character has come from watching you.

To the rest of my family—Jeff and Becca Leep, Ben and Judy Tol, Jason and Stephanie Tol—you've offered many well-timed and uplifting words about my writing. In countless little ways, you've given living examples of all the character traits I've written about in this book.

To my wonderful girlfriends—Julie, Katie, Kristi, Lisa, Lora, Megan, Pam, Stacey. You're all such beautiful women—inside and out. Your weddings, your faithful lives, and your wonderful personalities have inspired my ideas about what it means to live as God's bride. Special thanks to Kristi and Lisa for reading parts of this book with your intelligent and critical eyes.

To countless other friends and family members who've given me words of encouragement along the way.

To Lonnie Hull DuPont, Kristin Kornoelje, and all the other Baker staff who used their great editing skills to polish this book.

To Paul Hart, who put his photography skills to work on my behalf and took my publicity photos.

And most of all, to God. You're the reason I've written this book, and I pray that you'll get all the glory in it.

Amy J. Tol is director of youth ministries at her church and works as a freelance writer for Christian websites. She and her groom live in Holland, Michigan.